Mansions of the Moon
FOR THE
Green Witch

ABOUT THE AUTHOR

Born in 1947 and raised in a family tradition of Green Witchcraft learned from her mother and maternal grandmother, Ann Moura wrote down her heritage to preserve it and pass it on to others after her mother passed away. She has regularly conducted open circle Esbats and Sabbats, and teaches about her Craft in workshops and seminars at Pagan gatherings and her own store, Luna Sol Esoterica in Sanford, Florida. She holds both Bachelor of Arts and Master of Arts degrees in History and writes from the perspective of her family training and personal experience. Besides writing, she enjoys painting and creating her own magical arts and crafts.

TO WRITE TO THE AUTHOR

If you wish to contact the author or would like more information about this book, please write to the author in care of Llewellyn Worldwide Ltd. and we will forward your request. Both the author and publisher appreciate hearing from you and learning of your enjoyment of this book and how it has helped you. Llewellyn Worldwide Ltd. cannot guarantee that every letter written to the author can be answered, but all will be forwarded. Please write to:

Ann Moura
℅ Llewellyn Worldwide
2143 Wooddale Drive
Woodbury, MN 55125-2989

Please enclose a self-addressed stamped envelope for reply,
or $1.00 to cover costs. If outside the U.S.A., enclose
an international postal reply coupon.

Many of Llewellyn's authors have websites with additional information and resources. For more information, please visit our website at http://www.llewellyn.com

Mansions of the Moon

FOR THE

Green Witch

A COMPLETE BOOK OF LUNAR MAGIC

Ann Moura

Llewellyn Publications
Woodbury, Minnesota

First Edition
Fifth Printing, 2017

Cover art © PhotoDisc
Cover design by Ellen Lawson

Llewellyn is a registered trademark of Llewellyn Worldwide Ltd.

Library of Congress Cataloging-in-Publication Data (Pending)
Moura, Ann.
  Mansions of the moon for the green witch : a complete book of lunar
magic / Ann Moura. —1st ed.
      p. cm.
  Includes bibliographical references (p.   ) and index.
  ISBN 978-0-7387-2065-4
  1. Magic. 2. Moon—Miscellanea. I. Title.
  BF1623.M66M68 2010
  133.4'4—dc22
                    2010046223 ISBN: 978-0-7387-2065-4

Llewellyn Worldwide Ltd. does not participate in, endorse, or have any authority or responsibility concerning private business transactions between our authors and the public.

All mail addressed to the author is forwarded, but the publisher cannot, unless specifically instructed by the author, give out an address or phone number.

Any Internet references contained in this work are current at publication time, but the publisher cannot guarantee that a specific location will continue to be maintained. Please refer to the publisher's website for links to authors' websites and other sources.

Llewellyn Publications
A Division of Llewellyn Worldwide Ltd.
2143 Wooddale Drive
Woodbury, MN 55125-2989
www.llewellyn.com

Printed in the United States of America

OTHER BOOKS BY THIS AUTHOR

Green Witchcraft: Folk Magic, Fairy Lore, & Herb Craft

Green Witchcraft II: Balancing Light & Shadow

Green Witchcraft III: The Manual

Green Magic: The Sacred Connection to Nature

Grimoire for the Green Witch: A Complete Book of Shadows

Tarot for the Green Witch

CONTENTS

Part One

Part One

LUNAR MAGIC
THROUGH THE ZODIAC

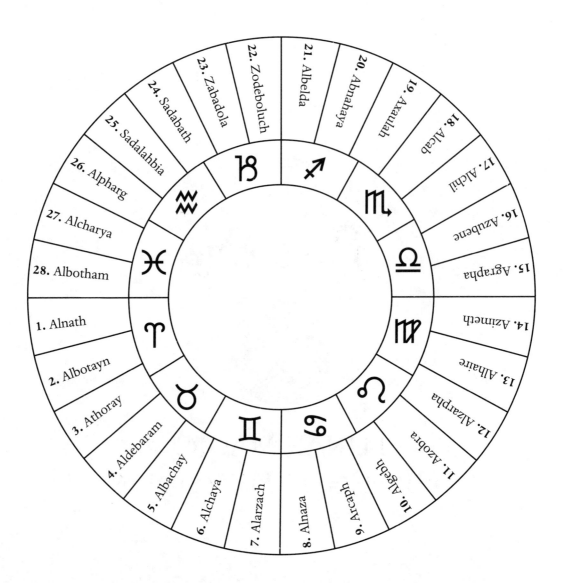

INTRODUCTION

This book is for the more advanced magic worker, so I will not go into such matters as circle casting, and calling the quarters, or presenting Esbat rituals for the various phases of the Moon. These elements may come from your own tradition and practice, or you may adapt to your use the basic rituals I offer in my books *Green Witchcraft: Folk Magic, Fairy Lore, and Herb Craft* and *Grimoire for the Green Witch: A Complete Book of Shadows*. My perspective is obviously that of the Craft, so while magic may be described as a matter of moving energy through the blending and utilizing of available energies to accomplish a goal, it is paramount that the practitioner adhere to an ethical standard such as the Witches' Rede of "Harm none" or my family code of "Do not use the Power to hurt another, for what is sent comes back."

ORIGINS OF THE MANSIONS OF THE MOON

The tradition of the twenty-eight Mansions of the Moon is found in China and in Hellenic Greece in the system of Dorotheus Sidonia (circa 100 CE), and India in 1000 BCE, (using twenty-seven mansions called nakshatras). The mansions are thought to date back to the Sumerians of 3000 BCE, but it is believed that the mansions were unknown in Europe until the Muslims brought the system into Andalusia when they occupied southern Spain. *The Complete Book on the Judgment of the Stars* was written in Tunisia in 1000 CE by the Arab astrologer Abenragel with the Hellenic and Indian perspective on the mansions translated into Old Spanish in 1254 Spain, then into Latin in 1485 in Italy. *The Picatrix: Gayat al-Hakim (The Aim of the Sage)* contains another version of the Mansions of the Moon, written in Arabic in Moorish Spain during the eleventh century CE and translated into Latin two centuries later. Fascination with the occult texts of the East throughout the medieval period of Europe saw the creation of grimoires (instruction manuals) written and published by philosophers and magicians. Most occultists based their magical principles on the Jewish Kabbala augmented with a great amount of Christian terminology, prayers, and invocations, but being associated with this material was still dangerous and some were persecuted as heretics and even burned at the stake.

The mansions spread throughout Europe with publications of *The Picatrix* in Venice in 1503) and more notably in Book II, part 4 of the *Three Books of Occult Philosophy* by Henry Cornelius Agrippa (1531) and *The Magus: A Complete System of Occult Philosophy* by Francis

Barrett (1801). The grimoires included instructions for using the mansions in magic for both beneficial and destructive purposes, mainly through the creation of talismans.

THE MANSIONS OF THE MOON IN WITCHCRAFT

While the mansion meanings from the medieval grimoires form the foundation of the magical works in this book, the works are based in witchcraft and as such, the mansion energies are approached in conjunction with the lunar phase and zodiac energies. Pulling these correlations together and combining them with additional magical correspondences for aromas, colors, magical alphabets, astrological symbolisms, and the plants and stones of nature provides a powerful boost to the working. This is not a book of nineteenth-century ceremonialism, nor one of medieval magic, but one that incorporates elements of each into a uniquely harmonious practice of modern witchcraft.

The grimoires refer to the passage of the Moon through the zodiac and do not differentiate between the phases of the Moon and their energy influences. This is not the case in witchcraft, where the lunar phase matters for specific types of energy. The four major times for magical works that address the appropriate lunar energy are during the waxing New Moon (first sliver of light after the Dark Moon), the Full Moon, the waning New Moon (last sliver of light before the Dark Moon), and the Dark Moon. The phases of the Moon relate to the Goddess in her aspects of Maiden, Mother, Crone, and veiled, and relevant deities, such as Luna, Isis, Cerridwen, and Hecate, may be addressed in ritual and magical work. These lunar phases provide different energies, which may then be applied to the mansions: the waxing to full energies involve commencement, increase, gain, manifestation, and fulfillment, while the waning to dark energies involve decrease, restriction, banishment, introspection, and divination. In this way, the magical works are tailored to the phase of the Moon within a given mansion.

The lunar mansions mostly have both positive and negative elements. I apply the witchcraft perspective of lunar energies to the mansions in their manner of influence by dividing the meanings of each mansion into an appropriate lunar phase of waxing to full for the positive and attracting, and waning to dark for the negative and repelling. If the mansion has only positive elements, these are initiated or brought to culmination with the waxing or full lunar phases. However, these same elements are diminished or afflicted during the waning or dark phases. Through magical work, the negative energies of a mansion can be contravened, warded against, diminished, or transformed to facilitate a positive and ethical result through focus augmented by additional energy correspondences. The Rede and the rule of sent energy returning as much as threefold are incentives to not use negative energies for unethical purposes. Magical works are generally engaged within an Esbat ritual just before the Cakes and Wine portion so that the simple feast assists with returning to a state of normalcy, and the end of the ritual brings the event to a grounded conclusion.

INTERPRETING THE MANSIONS OF THE MOON

Each mansion has traditionally held associations, and the magical work that draws on the energy or wards against it relates to the context of the mansion, the lunar phase, and the energy of the zodiac sign. Some of the mansions overlap signs and provide different energy relationships for the same mansions, depending on the Moon's position at the time of the magical work. Utilizing the sign energy in coordination with the mansion and the lunar phase allows for a coherent magical practice that acknowledges the ancient interpretations and can be updated and applied to modern times and thought.

In the following list of the mansions, I provide their traditional meanings, both positive and negative, separated here as energies of the lunar phases of waxing and waning, with waxing energy culminating with the Full Moon, and waning energy ending with the Dark Moon. Some of the mansion meanings are repetitive, archaic, violent, selfish, and vindictive, which reflects the times in which the various magicians who defined them lived, yet these energies can be understood in modern terms. For example, there are many types of slavery or captivity, such as being bound to something distasteful (low-paying job, unhappy relationship, disability, illness, etc.) for one reason or another. Captivity may be a matter of choice, and release could be sought through personal determination and courage. Negative energies may also be contravened with magical work, so that the lunar mansion energy for holding a slave may be warded and thus freedom from what enslaves one is gained. The names and meanings for the mansions come from Abenragel, *The Picatrix*, Agrippa, and Barrett, and from the examples of seals they describe for using mansion energy. I note the sign energy when it starts, so a mansion beginning in one sign and ending in another can have different nuances from start to finish. I offer suggestions for the medieval viewpoint and modern adaptation in parentheses.

The list shows the MANSION NAME, [zodiac location, *traditional name*], degree in each sign, name of the RULING SPIRIT, sign energy, designated waxing and waning energies, and (*my commentary*).

MANSIONS OF THE MOON

1. ALNATH [Aries; *Horns of Aries*] 0♈ to 12♈51; ruler GENIEL. Aries adds the energy of focus, intensity, and leadership.

   Waxing: safe journey; travel; build energy (*for structures and armies; today this could also be used for enhancing energy in any area, such as with teams and teamwork, initiating new projects, preparing for physical exertion, or increasing enthusiasm*)

   Waning: discord (*creating instability for a rival in business or warfare; today this could be warded against to maintain stability*); destroy a foe (*political, romantic, and territorial rivals were popularly addressed with this; today this could relate to overcoming adversity, addiction, or opposition to plans, or even to a successful battle effort*)

2. ALBOTAYN [Aries; *Belly of Aries*] 12♈51 to 25♈42; ruler ENEDIEL

   Waxing: find treasure; retain captives (*today this can be safeguarding an asset*); reconcile with superiors (*the displeasure of a prince or higher clergy could result in social ostracism, financial ruin, imprisonment, torture, and death; today this could be used to resolve tension in the workplace*)

   Waning: destroy buildings under construction; create arguments (*all tactics for conquest; today these hostile energies could be warded against*)

3. ATHORAY [Taurus; *Showering of Pleiades*] 25♈42 to 8♉34; ruler AMIXIEL. Taurus adds the energy of stability, reliability, stubbornness, and productivity.

   Waxing: good fortune; safety for sailors; favorable hunts; helpful alchemy (*early chemistry for making gold and finding the elixir of life; today this could relate to helpful connections and health, bringing these into secure manifestation*); every good thing

   Waning: overindulgence (*derived from the waning lunar energy as a negative excess of every good thing coupled with the stubborn energy of the sign*)

4. ALDEBARAN [Taurus; *Eye of Taurus*] 8 ♉ 34 to 21 ♉ 25; ruler AZARIEL

   Waxing: favorable outcome in important things; seek substantial items (*boons from the rulers; today it could be loans, mortgages, and grants*)

   Waning: discord, hindrance, revenge, enmity, separation (*originally referring to separating lovers; it can also be seen as being apart due to military service, distance, disaffection between people, or a winnowing process of wheat from chaff, good from bad, new from old, or functional from worthless*)

5. ALBACHAY [Taurus to Gemini; *Head of Orion*] 21 ♉ 25 to 4 ♊ 17; ruler GABRIEL. Gemini adds the energy of wit, versatility, perception, and rationality.

   Waxing: gain favors; fun; health; scholarship; strong buildings; safe trips

   Waning: destroy alliances or friendships (*once mainly a political tactic to gain power; today this energy can be warded against to preserve friendships*)

6. ALCHAYA [Gemini; *Little Star of Great Light*] 4 ♊ 17 to 17 ♊ 8; ruler DIRACHIEL

   Waxing: love between two people; links; friendships; hunting (*literally; today this could also be hunting for a job, partner, etc.*); gain power (*aspiration to tyranny in the past; today this could be for promotion or other advancement*)

   Waning: destroy business empires or cities or crops or health (*a scorched earth approach to conquest, but today this energy can be channeled away or warded against*); revenge (*unethical due to karma and the energy returning*)

7. ALARZACH [Gemini to Cancer; *Arm of Gemini*] 17 ♊ 8 to 0 ♋ 0; ruler SELHIEL

   Waxing: acquisition; gains and favors; good travel; love; contacts

   Waning: destruction of high offices; cooperation of flies (*insects associated with plague, disease, death, and the devil, hence demonology in the past; today this could relate to a peaceful picnic or insect control*)

8. ALNAZA [Cancer; *Misty Clouds*] 0 ♋ 0 to 12 ♋ 51; ruler AMNEDIEL. Cancer adds the energy of intuition, psychic awareness, introspection, and nurturing.

   Waxing: love/friendship; companions; safe travel; battle victory

   Waning: maltreatment of captives (*reflecting vengeance; unethical today and could be warded against, especially in legal cases*); control of mice (*problem for the spread of disease, ruined harvests, and contaminated stored food; today this is still a problem*)

9. ARCAPH [Cancer; *Eye of the Lion*] 12♋51 to 25♋42; ruler RAUBIEL

   Waxing: self-defense; help others; empathy (*meaning compassion*), and abilities (*being capable*)

   Waning: destroy harvest (*scorched earth in warfare; today this could be warded against to protect a harvest of any kind, from crops to success*); hinder travel (*related to obstructing news, aid, or material success for a foe; today this energy could be warded against for smooth travel*); create discord or infirmities (*a war or vengeance tactic; today this could be warded against to maintain peace and health*)

10. ALGEBH [Leo; *Forehead of the Lion*] 25♋42 to 8♌34; ruler ARDESIEL. Leo adds the energy of power, optimism, and vitality.

    Waxing: love/benevolence; goodwill of allies; strengthen buildings (*to withstanding assaults by siege engines; today this could relate to protecting against natural disasters*)

    Waning: destroy enemies (*battlefield or political rivals; today this would be unethical even in warfare*); ease childbirth; banish illness (*the latter two are diminishing energies that yield positive results*)

11. AZOBRA [Leo; *Mane of the Lion*] 8♌34 to 21♌25; ruler NECIEL

    Waxing: voyages; retail gains (*Italian princes were basically wealthy merchants; today this could be used to enhance sales for stores, shops, and corporations*); release of captives (*indicating a settlement or peace; today this could be used to gain freedom in any area of life*); reverence (*many of the higher clergy were sons of the nobility who retained the power of their class; today this could be used for personal spiritual development*)

    Waxing: attack; aggression; inspire fear (*tactics used by the autocratic prince or cleric; today aggression could be applied to gaining ethical goals, while attack and fear could be warded against to maintain peace*)

12. ALZARPHA [Leo; *Tail of the Lion*] 21♌25 to 4♍17; ruler ABDIZUEL. Virgo adds the energy of analysis, attention to detail, perfectionism, and service.

Waxing: prosperous harvest; start a building; improvements for those in service or labor (*faithful duty to a more powerful person could lead to a better station in life; today this could be used for career promotion or pay increase*)

Waning: hinder sailing (*of rival merchant ships or enemy warships; today this could be warded against to ensure smooth sailing*); loss of investment (*for a social rival or business competitor, which would bring ruination; today this could be warded against to maintain finances or employment, or to not waste time and energy*); separation (*intended to break up couples; today this could be used to separate in relation to a winnowing process*)

13. ALHAIRE [Virgo; *Wings of Virgo*] 4♍17 to 17♍8; ruler JAZERIEL.

Waxing: increase trade/harvests; liberate captives (*indicating a successful venture, whether diplomatic or paying a ransom; today this could be applied to other types of liberation, such as from an unpleasant situation*); agreement in marriage (*rare, when most were arranged for financial gain or family connections; today could be used for a peaceful home life*); restore potency (*high infant mortality rates required producing many children to have an heir; today this could be a return of health, influence, or career strength*); gain, clever financial dealings (*implying wise, not sly*), and voyages

Waning: diminishing gains or status quo (*derived from lunar and sign energy so that what has been gained could be lost or held in stasis due to a lack of attention to detail; today this could be warded against to preserve gains*); clever financial dealings (*lunar and sign energy imply sly, not wise; this could be restricted to avoid unethical and unstable financial gains, such as pyramid schemes*)

14. AZIMETH [Virgo; *Flying Spike*] 17♍8 to 0♎0; ruler ERGEDIEL

Waxing: marital love; cure the sick; profitable sailing

Waning: destroy harvests; destroy desires (*remove ambition from a political or financial rival, or prevent heirs to a rival political, merchant, or prominent family; today this could be warded against to maintain success and affection*); hinder land journeys (*mainly to obstruct news, inconvenience or ruin a rival; today this could be warded against to ensure travels go smoothly*); divorce (*used for political or personal gain; today this could be warded against to protect a marriage or used to help bring an unsatisfactory one to an agreeable end*); separation

15. AGRAPHA [Libra: *Covered* or *Covered Flying*] 0♎0 to 12♎51; ruler ACHALIEL. Libra adds the energy of balance, harmony, affection, and indecision.

    Waxing: extracting treasure (*through trade, mining, or discovery even today*); use or promote new opportunities through goodwill or friendship (*alliances with powerful people were needed for self-advancement; today this could be used for networking and making influential contacts*)

    Waning: hinder travelers; promote divorce; promote discord; destroy houses (*meaning entire families or heritages; today this could be warded against to keep families intact*); destroy enemies

16. AZUBENE [Libra: *Horns of Scorpio*] 12♎51 to 25♎42; ruler AZERUEL

    Waxing: liberation; universal friendship; opportunities; increase possessions

    Waning: hinder journeys, trips, or wedlock (*prevent a marriage that would give a rival a superior social/political position; today that energy can be warded against to ensure a hassle-free wedding day*); hinder harvests or merchandise (*of rivals or competitors; today this could be warded against to preserve efforts in business or other areas where rewards are reaped*)

17. ALCHIL [Scorpio: *Crown of Scorpio*] 25♎42 to 8♏34; ruler ADRIEL. Scorpio adds the energy of order, transformation, passion, and suspicion.

    Waxing: strengthen love; strengthen buildings; improve fortune; help sailors

    Waning: drive away thieves/robbers (*banishing energy with a positive result*); seek redress (*reduces the power one person has over another; this could be used for legal issues and court cases, or matters of reputation for a positive result for the petitioner*)

18. ALCAB [Scorpio: *Heart of Scorpio*] 8♏34 to 21♏25; ruler EGRIBIEL

    Waxing: victory over enemies; strengthen buildings; freedom; heal fevers and stomach pain (*serious debilitating problems in medieval Europe; today this could be used for general good health*)

    Waning: discord; sedition; conspiracy (*plots against influential people, lords, or lands; today these could be warded against to ensure safety and open communications or expose duplicity*); destroy friendships (*breaking of alliances; today this could be warded against to maintain friendships*)

19. AXAULAH [Sagittarius: *Tail of Scorpio*] 21♏25 to 4♐17; ruler ANUCIEL. Sagittarius adds the energy of idealism, independence, education, and cheerfulness.

   Waxing: military gains; capture fugitives (*usually relating to adversaries; today this could be used to recapture escaped criminals*); ease birth; start menses (*this may have implied ending an inopportune pregnancy, perhaps with a potion; today this could be used for health issues*)

   Waning: destroy ships; ruination of captives (*meaning no ransom, prisoner exchange, or release for those captured in battle, and possibly slavery, torture, or execution; today this could be warded against to preserve something that is not liked but necessary, such as a low-paying job*)

20. ABNAHAYA [Sagittarius: *Beam*] 4♐17 to 17♐8; ruler KYHIEL

   Waxing: tame animals; hunting; compel one to a place (*having the authority to control people; today this could be unethical, unless the purpose is to protect someone from danger or disaster*); fortify bondages (*keep peasants tied to the land of their overlord; today this would be unethical, unless used to strengthen existing alliances or associations*)

   Waning: destroy social wealth (*of a rival; today this could be warded against to preserve prosperity for a person, group, or nation*); create arguments among friends (*a tactic of divide and conquer; today this could be warded against to preserve friendships*)

21. ALBELDA [Capricorn: *Defeat*] 17♐8 to 0♑0; ruler BETHNAEL

   Waxing: strengthen buildings; good harvests, good travel, gains

   Waning: cause divorce; destroy a person (*reputation was easily lost with little more than an accusation of heresy or treason sending a person to prison or worse; today this could be warded against for self-preservation*)

22. ZODEBOLUCH [Capricorn: *A Pastor*] 0♑0 to 12♑51; ruler GELIEL. Capricorn adds the energy of industry, discipline, materialism, and solitude.

   Waxing: cure illness; useful and profitable partnership; putting on new clothes/jewelry (*new attire and jewelry shows a rise in social status and gaining the favor with those in power; today this could be used for a change in life-style*); escape captivity (*such as with a knight getting free to rejoin his lord; today this could be used to combat unjustified or illegal imprisonment, or to find freedom from something distasteful*)

Waning: discord between two people; broken engagement or enduring constant marital conflicts (*used for political gain, vengeance, or personal gains; today this can be warded against to prevent upsets or bickering in relationships*)

23. ZABADOLA [Capricorn; *Swallowing*] 12♑51 to 25♑42; ruler ZEQUIEL
    Waxing: cure the ill; marriage; reveal secrets (*expose plots or gain occult knowledge; today this could be used to make discoveries in various fields of science and technology or to expose deceptions*); liberate captives (*implies a successful military campaign; today this could be used to gain freedoms for individuals or groups*)
    Waning: destruction; laying waste (*warfare tactic to force surrender in a siege; today this could be warded against to preserve property and finances*); divorce

24. SADABATH [Aquarius; *Star of Fortune*] 25♑42 to 8♒34; ruler ABRINIEL. Aquarius adds the energy of individuality, inventiveness, eccentricity, and idealism.
    Waxing: peace between couples; win war; increase trade/herds
    Waning: gain power over enemies (*this implies the negative energy of subterfuge or ruthlessness used against political or economic rivals; today this could be warded against to ensure fair play, or it could be used to end conflicts or enforce peace to bring about a positive outcome*); hinder governance or rule (*to destabilize a rival power or country; today this could be warded against to preserve a nation against its enemies, or used against tyranny*)

25. SADALAHBIA [Aquarius; *A Butterfly*] 8♒34 to 21♒25; ruler AZIEL
    Waxing: repair structures; protect trees/crops; destroy enemies; fast news (*news was extremely slow and unreliable; today this could be used to hear from distant loved ones or to learn about events quickly*)
    Waning: divorce; revenge; besiege (*a place or a person, as with relentless harassment with the intention of harm; today this could be warded against to maintain peace in any area of life*); bind someone against their duty (*blackmail or extortion; today this could be warded against to be unhindered in work or other responsibilities*)

26. ALPHARG [Pisces; *Spout of the Urn*] 21♒25 to 4♓17; ruler TAGRIEL. Pisces adds the energy of mysticism, sensitivity, imagination, and intuition.
    Waxing: unity and goodwill of men; instigate love and favor
    Waning: break barriers (*forcing through enemy fortifications; today this could be used to destroy the barriers to achieving a goal, yielding positive results*); destroy

buildings and prisons (*warfare and creating chaos with the escape of prisoners; today these can be warded against to protect structures*)

27. ALCHARYA [Pisces; *Lip of the Urn*] 4♓17 to 17♓8; ruler ABLEMIEL

    Waxing: increase harvest; increase income; increase gain; heal sick; psychic power (*predictions were sought by leaders on matters of state; today this could be used to enhance personal psychic ability*)

    Waning: obstruct construction of buildings; endanger sailors; destroy springs, wells, baths, and medicinal waters (*military tactic to poison an enemy's water supply; today this could be warded against to maintain fresh waters*); send mischief as desired (*malicious harm to others for personal gain and power; today this could be warded against to maintain general well-being and good fortune*)

28. ALBOTHAM [Aries: *Belly of the Fish*] 17♓8 to 0♈0; ruler ANUXIEL

    Waxing: increase harvest; increase trade; safe travel; marital joy; gather in fish (*a harvest of the sea; today this could be used for fishing success or for collecting support in a matter*)

    Waning: strengthen captivity (*obstructing liberation; today this could warded against to let justice prevail*); instigate loss of wealth or treasures (*of political or economic rivals; today this could be warded to preserve finances, art, or property*)

DETERMINING THE MANSION OF THE MOON

The energy of the Moon is influenced by the zodiac sign in which it resides, and additionally by the degree within that sign. Since the Moon travels through the zodiac in an approximate lunar month of 27.32 days, the mansions of the Arabic and European system are divided into twenty-eight segments of 12 degrees, 51 minutes, 25.7 seconds, usually rounded to 12'52". The mansions are overlaid on the zodiac of twelve signs in a 360-degree cycle, with 0 Aries as the usual starting point (Vernal Equinox), and with eight of the mansions spanning two signs of the zodiac.

Since my perspective is that of the Craft, my use of the Mansions of the Moon for magic is in conjunction with the Esbats on the days of their lunar events. When having a ritual and magical work on the appropriate date and time, the mansion may be identified by checking the specific Moon phases in an ephemeris. I use *The American Ephemeris for the 21st Century: 2000 to 2050 at Midnight,* by Neil F. Michelsen, because it contains a monthly list of Moon phases, including waxing and waning, as well as all eclipses; and it gives the time of day and the zodiac position. It also contains a monthly list of ingress dates and times for the Moon, showing when it enters a sign. This makes identifying the mansion an easier matter.

For example, if the ephemeris shows a Full Moon on September 4, 2009, at 16:04 (4:04 PM) ET (Ephemeris Time—same as GMT, Greenwich Mean Time) in 12♓15, the Moon is in the mansion Alcharya, with the energy of increase in harvest, income, and gains, healing the sick; and enhancing psychic awareness, when magical works for investments, good health, or opening psychic channels is favored. To know the Eastern Standard Time (EST), subtract four hours from the ET/GMT during standard time (12:04 PM). During Daylight Saving Time, five hours are subtracted from the ET/GMT for the EST. The Dark Moon is listed on September 18, 2009, at 18:45 (6:45 PM) ET in 25♍59, which is in the mansion Azimeth, with the energy for destroying harvests, destroying desires, hindering land journeys, and instigating divorce. At 2:45 PM EST, this energy could be used in a positive manner as a magical aid for dieting (destroy desire for sweets!), or it could be contravened with magic to ensure stability of a marriage or protection of a harvest of any sort. I consider this ephemeris to be a good investment, as it lasts for decades. It has to be ordered, which most major bookstores will do for you, or purchased online.

There are ephemerides websites that offer accurate information, such as with http://www.astrology.com/aboutastrology/resources/ephemeris/9.html. As with most ephemeris (unless otherwise noted), however, remember to add or subtract hours according to your time zone. Using the 24-hour day, the planet is divided into longitudes of 15 degrees each for a total of 360 degrees. These are the time zones, with each zone representing one hour. The difference between your local time and GMT or ET is found by adding one hour for each zone east of Greenwich, England, or subtracting one hour for each zone west of Greenwich. For example, you would subtract four hours from GMT for Eastern Standard Time (EST), five for Central (CST), six for Mountain (MST), and seven for Pacific (PST). Subtract another hour when in Daylight Saving Time. If the Moon is in 0♌0 at midnight (2400 GMT or 0 ET), it will be in 0♌0 at 8 PM (2000 EST) in Boston, Massachusetts, during standard time, or 7 PM (1900) during Daylight Saving Time.

If the ritual and magic is pre-scheduled for a particular date and time, then you will be looking for the mansion being occupied by the Moon at that time in order to correlate magical work with the mansion energy. If the ephemeris is not sufficiently helpful, you can find the lunar mansion by checking the location of the Moon at the scheduled date and time, using an online free astrological chart site. Simply enter your local latitude and longi-

Part Two

ADDITIONAL COMPONENTS
FOR LUNAR MAGIC

BLENDING ENERGIES

My magical works show how I draw together and balance a variety of energies addressed since ancient times, but applied in a modern context. The magical works portion of this book demonstrates how correlating energies can be blended to achieve a goal. The practitioner may combine as many or as few of the available energies as desired, with the components forming a buffet of magical options, including Moon phase, zodiac sign, lunar mansion, planetary energies, sigils, seals, and squares; fixed-star energy, colors, runes, herbs, stones, incense, and essential oils. The day of the week and hour of the day are additional choices that could be addressed to play a role in selecting the timing of Esbat and magical work within a lunar mansion. All the energies are selected by the influence that can be called upon in relation to the work. The lunar phase itself embraces three days: the day before, the day of, and the day after. Beyond this, on either side of the lunar event, the energy changes. How you creatively pull together some or all of these influences is what defines your personal Craft.

LUNAR ENERGY

The first sliver of light of the waxing New Moon is appropriate for beginnings and initiation, a time to start new projects or move in a new direction; the Full Moon, for fulfillment and gains, a time to push the desired result into culmination or manifestation by envisioning the goal as attained; the waning New Moon, for decreasing, restricting, containing, binding, banishing, and ending, a time for releasing what is unwanted, reducing difficulties, and removing obstacles; and the Dark Moon, for quiet, a time for cleansings, magical studies, divinations, journey or shadow work, meditations, communion with spirits and the entities of other worlds, and nature magic. If the need is urgent and you do not want to wait for the most auspicious lunar phase, it is always possible to work around the existing phase by altering the focus of the spell. For example, during the waning phase, a spell for finding a job can be envisioned and worked to remove unemployment, while during a waxing phase, a spell for ending a creative block can be visualized as opening creativity.

THE SIGNS OF THE ZODIAC

The twelve signs of the zodiac are based on the passage of the Sun and provide energy alignments that can be used in lunar magic. Some systems utilize the thirteenth sign of

Ophiuchus (O-foo' kus), the Serpent Bearer, which is a sign normally ignored, although it was used by Nostradamus and others in astrology and is said to date back to Sumerian usage. Called the thirteenth sign of the zodiac, it actually falls between Scorpio and Sagittarius, but even this fluctuates according to the ecliptic (path) of the Sun. Because the Sun only passes through the foot of the Serpent Bearer, most astrologers dismiss it as unimportant. It regained significance with the approach of the year 2012, when the Mayan calendar ends with the Winter Solstice alignment of the earth and the Dark Rift (or black hole) of the Galactic Center through Ophiuchus.

In the following list, the symbol and name of the ruling sun sign is followed by that of the ruling planet of the sign, the sign's starting degree in the twelve-sign zodiac by Tropical dates based on the equinoxes and solstices on the earth, and in parentheses the Sidereal dates based on the constellations. Use this list to determine your zodiac (Sun) sign and ruling planet for magical works in the next two parts of the book.

LISTING ZODIAC SIGNS AND THEIR RULERS

♈ **Aries**, the Ram; ♂ **Mars:** 0°; 3/21–4/20 (4/14–5/14)

♉ **Taurus**, the Bull; ♀ **Venus:** 30°; 4/21–5/21 (5/15–6/14)

♊ **Gemini**, the Twins; ☿ **Mercury:** 60°; 5/22–6/23 (6/15–7/16)

♋ **Cancer**, the Crab; ☽ **Moon:** 90°; 6/23–7/22 (7/17–8/16)

♌ **Leo**, the Lion; ☉ **Sun:** 120°; 7/23–8/23 (8/17–9/16)

♍ **Virgo**, the Virgin; ☿ **Mercury:** 150°; 8/24–9/22 (9/17–10/17)

♎ **Libra**, the Scale; ♀ **Venus:** 180°; 9/23–10/23 (10/18–11/16)

♏ **Scorpio**, the Scorpion; ♇ **Pluto:** 210°; 10/24–11/22 (11/17–12/15)

♐ **Sagittarius**, the Centaur; ♃ **Jupiter:** 240°; 11/23–12/21 (12/16–1/14)

♑ **Capricorn**, the Sea/Horned Goat; ♄ **Saturn:** 270°; 12/22–1/19 (1/15–2/12)

♒ **Aquarius**, the Water Bearer; ♅ **Uranus:** 300°; 1/20–2/18 (2/13–3/14)

♓ **Pisces**, the Fishes; ♆ **Neptune:** 330°; 2/19–3/20 (3/15–4/13)

PLANETARY ENERGIES

The energies of planets can be invoked into magical work for the properties related to it by using planetary symbols, sigils, and seals, which may be incised on a candle, drawn on a paper or stone, and so on. Since each planet has several energy themes, the relevant ones need to be specified (called upon) during the magical procedure.

⊙ **Sun:** individuality, success, happiness, pride, honors, energy, display, power

☽ **Moon:** sensitivity, nurture, cycles, home, psychic awareness

☿ **Mercury:** communication, skills, agility, intellect, commerce, trade

♀ **Venus:** friendships, sociability, artistry, luxuries, love, camaraderie

♂ **Mars:** dynamic energy, aggressiveness, will power, sex drive

♄ **Saturn:** ambition, structure, realism, self-preservation, business, restrictions

♃ **Jupiter:** opportunity, optimism, finance, growth, health, justice, legal matters

♆ **Neptune:** occult, psychic, subconscious, spirits, idealism, creativity, illusion

♅ **Uranus:** sudden change, tensions, originality, news, knowledge, divination

♇ **Pluto:** transformation, sex, death, spirituality, evolution, rebirth, extremes

OLYMPIC PLANETARY SPIRITS

The following names and symbols are from the Greek view of the primal forces of nature and represent the ancient solar system energies and powers along with their metal and zodiac associations. Popular in medieval grimoires, today I use these on candles, mandalas (double- or triple-ringed circle), talismans, and paper or parchment to give an energy boost to magical work:

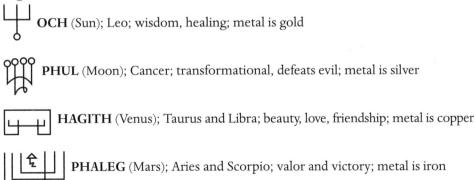

OCH (Sun); Leo; wisdom, healing; metal is gold

PHUL (Moon); Cancer; transformational, defeats evil; metal is silver

HAGITH (Venus); Taurus and Libra; beauty, love, friendship; metal is copper

PHALEG (Mars); Aries and Scorpio; valor and victory; metal is iron

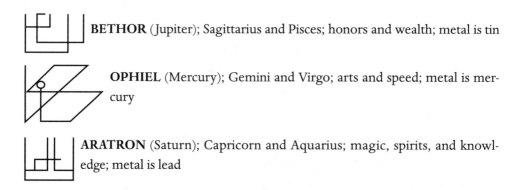

BETHOR (Jupiter); Sagittarius and Pisces; honors and wealth; metal is tin

OPHIEL (Mercury); Gemini and Virgo; arts and speed; metal is mercury

ARATRON (Saturn); Capricorn and Aquarius; magic, spirits, and knowledge; metal is lead

PLANETARY SIGILS AND SEALS

These symbols and names, based on the Kabbala, are found in the medieval grimoires. Today they are typically associated with ceremonial magic, which considers the spirit of the planet to be malevolent and therefore not used. I show those sigils here for information, but I use the Olympic planetary spirits with the seals and intelligences for their primal energies, which I do not associate with the ceremonial. While most of the planets have three sigils associated with them, Venus and the Moon have four. The sigils may be used in a mandala by placing the seal of the planet in the center-top portion, the sigil of the planet intelligence at the bottom portion, and the planet astrological symbol to one side, between or below, however, gives a balanced appearance.

The Sun

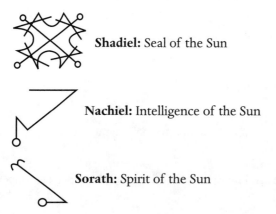

Shadiel: Seal of the Sun

Nachiel: Intelligence of the Sun

Sorath: Spirit of the Sun

The Moon

 Azarel: Seal of the Moon

 Hasmodai: Spirit of the Moon

 Ichadeil: Spirit of the Spirits of the Moon

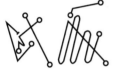 **Yashiel:** Intelligence of the Intelligences of the Moon

Mercury

 Vehiel: Seal of Mercury

 Tiriel: Intelligence of Mercury

 Cassiel: Spirit of Mercury

Venus

 Habondia: Seal of Venus

Hagiel: Intelligence of Venus

 Kedemel: Spirit of Venus

 Aeliel: Intelligences of Venus

Mars

 Ithuriel: Seal of Mars

 Graphiel: Intelligence of Mars

 Barzabel: Spirit of Mars

Jupiter

 Netoniel: Seal of Jupiter

 Johphiel: Intelligence of Jupiter

 Hismael: Spirit of Jupiter

Saturn

 Omeliel: Seal of Saturn

 Agiel: Intelligence of Saturn

 Zazel: Spirit of Saturn

PLANETARY SQUARES

The planetary square and the number are another ceremonial magic adaptation from the Kabbala. These may be placed within a double circle on the back of the mandala or talisman that has the planetary seal on the front. With the columns, rows, and diagonals adding up to the number of the square, they contain the mathematical energy resonating with the planet for a completed seal.

6	32	3	34	35	1
7	11	27	28	8	30
19	14	16	15	23	24
18	20	22	21	17	13
25	29	10	9	26	12
36	5	33	4	2	31

Square of the Sun

111

37	78	29	70	21	62	13	54	5
6	38	79	30	71	22	63	14	46
47	7	39	80	31	72	23	55	15
16	48	8	40	81	32	64	24	56
57	17	49	9	41	73	33	65	25
26	58	18	50	1	42	74	34	66
67	27	59	10	51	2	43	75	35
36	68	19	60	11	52	3	44	76
77	28	69	20	61	12	53	4	45

Square of the Moon

369

8	58	59	5	4	62	63	1
49	15	14	52	53	11	10	56
41	23	22	44	45	19	18	48
32	34	35	29	28	38	39	25
40	26	27	37	36	30	31	33
17	47	46	20	21	43	42	24
9	55	54	12	13	51	50	16
64	2	3	61	60	6	7	57

Square of Mercury

260

22	47	16	41	10	35	4
5	23	48	17	42	11	29
30	6	24	49	18	36	12
13	31	7	25	43	19	37
38	14	32	1	26	44	20
21	39	8	33	2	27	45
46	15	40	9	34	3	28

Square of Venus

175

11	24	7	20	3
4	12	25	8	16
17	5	13	21	9
10	18	1	14	22
23	6	19	2	15

Square of Mars

65

4	14	15	1
9	7	6	12
5	11	10	8
16	2	3	13

Square of Jupiter

34

4	9	2
3	5	7
8	1	6

Square of Saturn

15

ENERGIES OF THE FIXED STARS

The sigils I use here for the fixed stars appear in an untitled fourteenth-century manuscript housed in the British Museum, as well as in a French translation in Trinity College at Cambridge, and the *Book of Enoch*, a fifteenth-century manuscript now located in the Bodleian Library at Oxford. Agrippa, in writing about the fifteen fixed stars in his *Occult Philosophy*, varied some of the sigils, called them the "Behenian Fixed Stars" (possibly from the Arabic word meaning "root"), and attributed the list to Hermes Trismegistus in *The Book of Hermes on the 15 Fixed Stars*. This latter source is considered to date from antiquity, although the personage is allegedly the God Hermes, the God Thoth, or a combination of both. Hemeticism and Gnosticism both draw upon this occult tradition which may actually have been a merging of Greek and Egyptian religious traditions during the rule of the Ptolemy pharaohs of Egypt. Emerald tablets with his writings engraved upon them were said to have been found in Hebron.

The star energies are associated with planets, signs, stones, and herbs, and their powers in the grimoires were drawn into talismans. However, these do not always agree with the stars associated with the zodiac signs noted in Part One. I use the Behenian list for magical work because these are traditional energy alignments. For example, the star Cor Scorpii in astronomy is the main star of Scorpio, but astrologically in the Behenian list, it is associated with Sagittarius, while Scorpio is associated with Alphecca (Elpheia). Magic uses the practitioner's focus on correlations for moving energy, so you have your choice as to what correspondences work best for you. Since the Behenian stars with their magical symbols have been used for centuries, and perhaps for thousands of years, the energies may be drawn upon in that context. Modern astronomy uses a mixture of Arabic and Latin names for the stars, which is reflected in the list. I show both the astrological and Latin names associated with the fixed stars, and choose the one I use in magical works by the sound and rhythm that appeals to me.

The magical symbols ascribed to the stars are used to invoke their power, and while these images have evolved over the centuries with slight variations between sources, they may be added to magical work along with the other components. The star character may be used in spells, inscribed on a candle, drawn on paper or parchment, added to a charm, inscribed on a ring to wear as a talisman, or used in whatever magical application is desired. The specific energy of the star being invoked is addressed as the design is drawn, but artistic precision is not paramount as long as you know what you are addressing and pulling into the representation. The following list shows the star symbol, name(s), influence, planetary and zodiac correlations, and associated stone and herb. When two planets are listed, it is best to work with both in the order shown for complementary energies. *Use care with herbs and be aware that some may be toxic, such as hellebore and snakeroot.*

LIST OF FIXED STARS AND THEIR SIGILS

Algol (Caput Algo): Head of Algol; audacity, victory, protection; planets Saturn and Jupiter; sign Taurus; stone diamond; herb hellebore (poisonous)

Pleiades: Seven Sisters; secrets, talk to spirits; planets Moon and Mars; sign Taurus; stone crystal; herb fennel

Aldebaran (Aldaboram): The Bull's Eye; good fortune, create discord; planets Mars and Venus; sign Taurus; stone ruby/garnet; herb milk thistle

Capella (Alhayhoch): Goat Star; honors, favor of superiors; planets Jupiter and Saturn; sign Gemini; stone sapphire; herb thyme

Sirius (Canis Major): Greater Dog Star; communication, favor of earth and air spirits, marital peace; planet Venus; sign Cancer; stone beryl; herb juniper

Procyon (Canis Minor): Lesser Dog Star; magic, power, good health; planets Mercury and Mars; sign Cancer; stone agate; herb buttercup

Regulus (Cor Leonis): Heart of the Lion; strength, nobility; planets Jupiter and Mars; sign Leo; stone granite; herb mugwort

Polaris (Cauda Ursa): Tail of the Bear; protection from personal violence and thieves; planets Venus and the Moon; sign Gemini; stone lodestone (magnet); herb chicory (or endive)

Gienah (Ala Corvi): Wing of the Crow; strength of will, induce sleep, create hostility, bind another's magic; planets Saturn and Mars; sign Libra; stone onyx; herb burdock

Spica: Ear of Grain; resolve disputes, bind enemies, protect from danger, enhance telepathy, reap abundance; planets Venus and Mercury; sign Libra; stone emerald; herb sage

Arcturus (Alchameth): Guardian of the Bear; good health, heal wounds and fever; planets Mars and Jupiter; sign Libra; stone jasper; herb snakeweed (common plantain)

Alphecca (Elpheia): Bright Star of the Radiant Circle; love and honor, restoration of purity; planets Venus and Mars; sign Scorpio; stone topaz; herb rosemary

Antares (Cor Scorpii): Heart of the Scorpion; aid memory, restore good health, defense, protection; planets Venus and Jupiter; sign Sagittarius; herb birthwort (snakeroot or aristolochia)

Vega (Vultur Cadens): Vulture Falling; avert fears, talk with animals, avert or end nightmares; planets Mercury and Venus; sign Capricorn; stone chrysolite (golden peridot); herb winter savory

 Deneb Algedi (Cauda Capricorni): Tail of the Sea-Goat; aid a just cause, bring peace, protect from harm; planets Saturn and Mercury; sign Pisces; stone chalcedony; herb marjoram

Some of the stones listed for the stars have varieties. Chalcedony may be a bloodstone, agate, carnelian, and so on, while jaspers may be ocean, moss, moochite, picture, red, brown, etc. Agates come in many styles and colors, as do beryls, so a book on stones may be of help.

ENERGIES FOR THE DAYS OF THE WEEK

The day of the week in which the Moon phase takes place has its own planetary energy, which can be utilized or neutralized as needed.

Monday (Moon energy): dreams, emotions, home, family, medicine, peace, hearth and healing, psychic awareness, personality, merchandising, and theft

Tuesday (Mars energy): dynamic energy, aggression, war, enemies, politics, contests, courage, protection, passion, sex, matrimony, surgery, prison

Wednesday (Mercury energy): communication, skill, teaching, reason, wisdom, divination, intellect, self-improvement, studies, travel, loss, debt, and fear

Thursday (Jupiter energy): health, luck, honor, legal matters, desires, prosperity, money, generosity, and attire

Friday (Venus energy): love, friendship, social activities, pleasure, art, music, incense, perfumes, beauty, good taste, reconciliations, and strangers

Saturday (Saturn energy): self-discipline, life, boundaries, protection, freedom, doctrine, protection, endings, longevity, destruction of disease/pests, house, exorcism

Sunday (Sun energy): individuality, success, strength, protection, spirituality, hope, fortune, money, work, power, healing, and promotions

PLANETARY ENERGIES OF THE HOURS

You can also work with the planetary energy for the hour of day or night that best aligns with your work. The following charts show the hours from sunrise to sunset and from sunset to sunrise. The day is divided into two sets of twelve-hour blocks of day and night, and to adjust for actual daylight and nighttime hours, the minutes of each hour are changed to fit into twelve settings for day and for night based on the time of sunrise and sunset on any particular day.

To calculate the length of the hours, change the sunrise and sunset time to military time (a twenty-four-hour clock), convert these into minutes, subtract sunrise from sunset to get the total daytime minutes, and divide by twelve for the length of each hour. For the length of nighttime hours, subtract the total daytime minutes of the prior calculation from 144,000 (2400 hours X 60 minutes), divide the remainder by twelve and you have the number of minutes in the sunset hours.

Sunrise Hours							
	SUN	**MON**	**TUE**	**WED**	**THURS**	**FRI**	**SAT**
Hour 1	Sun	Moon	Mars	Mercury	Jupiter	Venus	Saturn
Hour 2	Venus	Saturn	Sun	Moon	Mars	Mercury	Jupiter
Hour 3	Mercury	Jupiter	Venus	Saturn	Sun	Moon	Mars
Hour 4	Moon	Mars	Mercury	Jupiter	Venus	Saturn	Sun
Hour 5	Saturn	Sun	Moon	Mars	Mercury	Jupiter	Venus
Hour 6	Jupiter	Venus	Saturn	Sun	Moon	Mars	Mercury
Hour 7	Mars	Mercury	Jupiter	Venus	Saturn	Sun	Moon
Hour 8	Sun	Moon	Mars	Mercury	Jupiter	Venus	Saturn
Hour 9	Venus	Sun	Saturn	Moon	Mars	Mercury	Jupiter
Hour 10	Mercury	Jupiter	Venus	Saturn	Sun	Moon	Mars
Hour 11	Moon	Mars	Mercury	Jupiter	Venus	Saturn	Sun
Hour 12	Saturn	Sun	Moon	Mars	Mercury	Jupiter	Venus

	SUN	MON	TUE	WED	THURS	FRI	SAT
Sunset Hours							
Hour 1	Jupiter	Venus	Saturn	Sun	Moon	Mars	Mercury
Hour 2	Mars	Mercury	Jupiter	Venus	Saturn	Sun	Moon
Hour 3	Sun	Moon	Mars	Mercury	Jupiter	Venus	Saturn
Hour 4	Venus	Saturn	Sun	Moon	Mars	Mercury	Jupiter
Hour 5	Mercury	Jupiter	Venus	Saturn	Sun	Moon	Mars
Hour 6	Moon	Mars	Mercury	Jupiter	Venus	Saturn	Sun
Hour 7	Saturn	Sun	Moon	Mars	Mercury	Jupiter	Venus
Hour 8	Jupiter	Venus	Saturn	Sun	Moon	Mars	Mercury
Hour 9	Mars	Mercury	Jupiter	Venus	Saturn	Sun	Moon
Hour 10	Sun	Moon	Mars	Mercury	Jupiter	Venus	Saturn
Hour 11	Venus	Saturn	Sun	Moon	Mars	Mercury	Jupiter
Hour 12	Mercury	Jupiter	Venus	Saturn	Sun	Moon	Mars

The Planetary Energies list and the Days of the Week list are used to help determine which planetary hour you want to work within. If you want success in a legal matter, for example, you could perform your magical work on a Sunday during one of the Jupiter hours, or on a Thursday during a Jupiter or a Sun hour.

OTHER ENERGY INGREDIENTS FOR MAGICAL WORKS

As with all magic, it can be as simple or as complex as you, the practitioner, desires. You decide what factors you want to incorporate into your magical work. Besides the astrological possibilities, there are many other correspondences that can be used to augment the focus and energy of your magical work. I use the Germanic Elder Futhark, Anglo-Saxon, and Northumbrian runes as both magical alphabets and as representations of specific energies, such as victory, harvest, protection, and prosperity. These energy symbols are easily added to candles, charms, talismans, and other magical works, as well as to magical tools such as wands and athames. Color correspondences are used in selecting candles, fabrics, Elemental associations, and energy vibration for magic.

Herbs, plants, and resins are used in candles, talismans, charms, and other magical works. Some of the herbs and plants are familiar to the spice rack and cooking and may be used in teas, but others are not meant for consumption. Use common sense and avoid potions or incense that include unusual or unfamiliar plants that can provoke illness or other toxic reactions. Essential oils are selected individually or blended for desired energy properties and aromas. These are used to anoint candles or added to a bit of cotton in charm bags; they are dabbed on objects or worn to enhance an aspect of the aura. Again, use common sense—cinnamon oil may smell terrific, but it burns the skin. Oils may also be created by placing chopped or crushed herbs in a jar and adding a basic carrier oil, such as grapeseed, safflower, or olive oil. Stir or shake, and let soak until the desired scent is achieved, then strain out the herbs and bottle the oil.

Stones are another favorite addition of mine to magical works, as they radiate their vibrations and add to the energy being raised. They are placed in charm bags, herbal pouches, or dream pillows; set in a desired location such as a doorway, windowsill, car glove compartment, briefcase, or purse; carried loose in a pocket or worn in jewelry; dropped into a candle spell or made into an elixir by soaking in spring water in the moonlight for an hour, then removing. The elixir is consecrated and the transferred energies held with a drop of vodka, whiskey, or brandy. Just be sure a stone that dissolves in water (such as covellite, a stone for psychic ability) is not used.

PUTTING TOGETHER THE ENERGY CORRESPONDENCES

Because there are overlapping associations with many herbs and stones, knowing the correlations allows for substitutions in magical works when the recommended ingredients are not available. By using a number of energy correspondences, you align them to work harmoniously with you in attaining your goals. You do not need to use everything with matching energy, but you have the option of picking and choosing which ones are practical and useful to you, and even drawing upon numerological significances to decide how many of each type of item you want to include. Creating a double-circle mandala with inscriptions in between the rims; including symbols and sigils in the center; setting an inscribed and anointed candle on top of the center; lighting the candle—adding herbs and stones to the flame—all with the your words of intention and blessings given and received from the Divine, the Elementals, and the spirits and entities of nature—can provide a very powerful and rewarding magical experience. Your magical work may be as complex or as simple as you desire or have the time and means to accomplish. It is possible that simply the spoken word when combined with focus and directed energy may be sufficient to achieve the desired result. But magical work that draws upon a variety of sources is a powerful aid that adds visual and tactile reinforcement to the spoken words. Use those energy descriptions that resonate with you or otherwise draw from your personal preferences, but in all magical work, the rule of harming none, which includes yourself, is the overriding principle.

CLEANSING CANDLES FOR RITUAL AND MAGIC

I use three altar candles, a working candle, and sometimes a spell candle for magical work. Altar candles represent the deities as both the Goddess and the God, bringing spiritual influence to the ritual and the magic. The working candle is used as a focus for energy relating to the magical work, and it is only lit at the start of that work. Usually it is red for strength and power, but the working candle may be another color as desired. The spell candle is only used for candle magic, and the color relates to the goal. All of these candles need to be cleaned with spring water or blessed water, trimmed of excess wax, blemishes, and if needed, wiped with rubbing alcohol to remove dust or dirt. For jar candles, remove labels, price tags, glue remains, and any other debris. The wick should be trimmed to about a quarter of an inch to half an inch in length, although specialty candles will have bits of colorful charges in the wick, so you could leave those untrimmed for the full effect. Using an essential, olive, saffron, grapeseed, or almond oil as desired, anoint the bottom of the altar candles with the symbol of the solar cross $\oplus$ with the + drawn first and the circle around it drawn deosil.

The working candle and spell candle (if used) should be anointed with the solar cross with the circle made deosil if doing a drawing or blessing work, or widdershins if doing a banishing or repelling work. During the actual magical work, the working candle and spell candle will be dressed with a relevant essential oil. The working candle represents Elemental Fire for the charging of spell work and should be placed to the between the middle altar candle and the pentacle or in the God portion of the altar. At the appropriate time, and using a thin beeswax taper, the working candle is lit from the central altar candle. A spell candle is lit from the working candle. When I dress working and spell candles, I see the entire candle as the current situation and rub the oil from top to bottom to draw in energy or from bottom to top to remove energy, but you may use whatever method is your custom. I also light incense from the center altar candle or with the taper to bring the ritual and magical energy together.

TOOLS USED FOR THE MAGICAL WORKS

The magical works use basic altar tools, such as wand, athame, incense, pentacle, cauldron, and candles. It does not matter if the incense is stick, cone, resin, or herbal blends, as long as the aroma and derivation correlates with your intention. The pentacle is placed at the center of the working space or altar to represent Elemental Earth and manifestation. It is usually made of wood, metal, or tile to withstand the heat of a candle or cauldron set upon it. Always have something to snuff the candle flame readily at hand.

CONSECRATING SPELL MATERIALS

Some items used in the magical works in this book are consecrated during the activity. These could be stones, candles, or tools. When instructed to consecrate an item, use your own method or hold the item over the pentacle and say:

I call upon the Goddess and the God to aid me in my work.

Pass the item through the symbols of the Elementals, asking for their aid in your work: **This** (say the item) **is consecrated by Elemental Earth.** Sprinkle the item with salt or powdered burdock root, then brush off and continue: **by Elemental Air.** Pass it through the incense smoke and continue: **by Elemental Fire.** Pass it quickly through the flame of the working candle and continue: **and by Elemental Water.** Sprinkle the item with spring water or blessed water and pat it dry.

CHARGING THE MAGICAL WORK

The magical works are charged (personally energized) and empowered (endorsed through the greater powers of the Divine and the Elementals) and I will state when to do this. Use your own method of charging an item, or use the following:

Raise the magical work, object, or tool over the pentacle, then place it on the pentacle and cup your hands over it, envisioning energy passing from the palms of your hands into the item:

I charge and empower you to work my will; I call upon Earth to bring my work into manifestation; I call upon Air to carry my work to fruition; I call upon Fire to energize my work; I call upon Water to bring satisfaction from my work. Through the power of the Lady and Lord this work is blessed that as I will, So Mote It Be!

MAGIC DURING RITUAL

Incorporating magic in a ritual setting adds to the energy and focus, so it is important to have all the materials at hand during an Esbat so that the flow is not interrupted. Review your ritual, set up your altar space, cast your circle, and interject your working where it seems best to you, but normally just prior to the simple feast portion of the ritual. If doing a magical work with a group, have them sit or otherwise relax within the Circle for either a group participation project or for individually accomplished projects. The working portion of the Esbat could be prefaced with an introduction such as the following:

The Moon passes through the signs of the zodiac, daily taking up temporary residence in a different Mansion of the Moon, which affords special energies that can be utilized in magical work.

From there, select the appropriate work from the lunar phase and mansion in Part Three, which contains works for the Waxing Moon and the Full Moon, or Part Four, which has works for the Waning Moon and the Dark Moon. Using the energies, symbols, and correspondences, you may create your own work, tailored to your needs within the mansion. For group work, be sure to have enough materials for everyone, and guide them through the steps of the activity.

Part Three

WAXING MOON TO
FULL MOON

TABLE OF CONTENTS FOR MAGICAL WORKS

GEMINI . . . 61

ALBACHAY, the Head of Orion (21♉25 to 4♊17) ruled by GABIEL for gaining favors, having fun, health, scholarship, strong buildings, and safe trips
> *New Moon Waxing:* charm for beginning successful studies
> *Full Moon:* tea for good health

ALCHAYA, the Little Star of Great Light (4♊17 to 17♊8) ruled by DIRACHIEL for love between two people, friendships, hunting, links, and gaining power
> *New Moon Waxing:* tea for initiating friendships
> *Full Moon:* amulet for gaining power

ALARZACH, the Arm of Gemini (17♊8 to 0♋0) ruled by SELHIEL for acquisitions, gains and favors, good travel, love, and contacts
> *New Moon Waxing:* Amulet for acquisitions and favors
> *Full Moon:* candle spell for acquiring what is desired

CANCER . . . 67

ALNAZA, Misty Clouds (0♋0 to 12♋51) ruled by AMNEDIEL for love and friendship, companions, safe travel, and battle victory
> *New Moon Waxing:* bath salts for initiating love energy
> *Full Moon:* oil for family love and friendship

ARCAPH, the Eye of the Lion (12♋51 to 25♋42) ruled by RAUBIEL for self-defense, helping others, empathy, and abilities
> *New Moon Waxing:* powder for boosting psychic self-defense
> *Full Moon:* talisman for enhancing empathy

ALGEBH, the Forehead of the Lion (25♋42 to 8♌34) ruled by ARDESIEL for love and benevolence, the goodwill of allies, and strengthening buildings
> *New Moon Waxing:* candle for initiating goodwill
> *Full Moon:* herbal incense for goodwill of allies

LEO . . . 73

ALGEBH, the Forehead of the Lion (25♋42 to 8♌34) ruled by ARDESIEL for love and benevolence, the goodwill of allies, and to strengthen buildings
   New Moon Waxing: amulet for attracting love and benevolence
   Full Moon: charm for protective solar cross

AZOBRA, the Mane of the Lion (8♌34 to 21♌25) ruled by NECIEL for voyages, retail gains, the release of captives, and reverence
   New Moon Waxing: charm for generating money
   Full Moon: tea for spiritual reverence

ALZARPHA, the Tail of the Lion (21♌25 to 4♍17) ruled by ABDIZUEL for a prosperous harvest, starting a building, and improvements for those in service or labor
   New Moon Waxing: charm for improvement in work situation
   Full Moon: charm for a prosperous harvest

VIRGO . . . 79

ALZARPHA, the Tail of the Lion (21♌25 to 4♍17) ruled by ABDIZUEL for a prosperous harvest, starting a building, and improvements for those in service or labor
   New Moon Waxing: talisman for improvements for service or labor
   Full Moon: candle for rewarding service or labor

ALHAIRE, the Wings of Virgo (4♍17 to 17♍8) ruled by JAZERIEL for increase in trade and harvests, liberation of captives, agreement in marriage, restoration of potency, gain, clever financial dealings, voyages
   New Moon Waxing: incense for agreement in marriage
   Full Moon: powder for increasing in trade and harvest

AZIMETH, the Flying Spike (17♍8 to 0♎0) ruled by ERGEDIEL for marital love, curing the sick, and profitable sailing
   New Moon Waxing: candle for healing energies
   Full Moon: oil for marital love

LIBRA . . . 85

AGRAPHA, Covered or Covered Flying (0♎0 to 12♎51) ruled by ACHALIEL for extracting treasure, using or promoting new opportunities through goodwill or friendship
  New Moon Waxing: oil for promoting new opportunities through goodwill
  Full Moon: amulet for using new opportunities

AZUBENE, the Horns of Scorpio (12♎51 to 25♎42) ruled by AZERUEL for liberation, universal friendship, opportunities, and increasing possessions
  New Moon Waxing: talisman to initiate opportunities
  Full Moon: charm for universal friendship

ALCHIL, the Crown of Scorpio (25♎42 to 8♏34) ruled by ADRIEL for strengthening love, strengthening buildings, improving fortune, and helping sailors
  New Moon Waxing: charm for improving fortune
  Full Moon: incense for love and harmony

SCORPIO . . . 91

ALCHIL, the Crown of Scorpio (25♎42 to 8♏34) ruled by ADRIEL for strengthening love, strengthening buildings, improving fortune, and helping sailors
  New Moon Waxing: candle for strengthening love
  Full Moon: candle to improve fortune

ALCAB, the Heart of Scorpio (8♏34 to 21♏25) ruled by EGRIBIEL for victory over enemies, strengthening buildings, freedom, and healing fevers and stomach pain
  New Moon Waxing: water for strengthening a building and protecting it from damage
  Full Moon: bath salt for good health and healing energy

AXAULAH, the Tail of Scorpio (21♏25 to 4♐17) ruled by ANUCIEL for military gains, capturing fugitives, easing birth, and starting the menses
  New Moon Waxing: talisman for initiating military gains
  Full Moon: candle spell for capturing a criminal

SAGITTARIUS . . . 97

AXAULAH, the Tail of Scorpio (21♏25 to 4♐17) ruled by ANUCIEL for military gains, capturing fugitives, easing birth, and starting the menses

New Moon Waxing: amulet for easing birth

Full Moon: candle for starting the menses

ABNAHAYA, the Beam (4♐17 to 17♐8) ruled by KYHIEL for taming animals, hunting, compelling one to a place, and fortifying bondages

New Moon Waxing: charm for communicating with animals

Full Moon: charm for a good hunt

ALBELDA, Defeat (17♐8 to 0♑) ruled by BETHNAEL for strengthening buildings, good harvests, good travel, and gains

New Moon Waxing: tea for good travel and gains

Full Moon: powder for a good harvest

CAPRICORN . . . 103

ZODEBOLUCH, a Pastor (0♑0 to 12♑51) ruled by GELIEL for curing illness, useful and profitable partnership, putting on new clothes/jewelry, and escaping captivity

New Moon Waxing: talisman for useful and profitable partnership

Full Moon: talisman for social advancement

ZABADOLA, Swallowing (12♑51 to 25♑42) ruled by ZEQUIEL for curing the ill, marriage, revealing secrets, and liberating captives

New Moon Waxing: oil for healing illness

Full Moon: amulet for good health

SADABATH, the Star of Fortune (25♑42 to 8♒34) ruled by ABRINIEL for peace between couples, winning a war, and increasing trade/herds

New Moon Waxing: bath salts for peaceful relations

Full Moon: charm for increasing trade

AQUARIUS . . . 109

SADABATH, the Star of Fortune (25 ♑ 42 to 8 ♒ 34) ruled by ABRINIEL for peace between couples, winning a war, and increasing trade / herds
New Moon Waxing: candle for increasing trade
Full Moon: tea for peaceful relations

SADALAHBIA, a Butterfly (8 ♒ 34 to 21 ♒ 25) ruled by AZIEL for repairing structures, protecting trees / crops, destroying enemies, and getting fast news
New Moon Waxing: incense for urging news to come quickly
Full Moon: oil for protecting crops and trees

ALPHARG, the Spout of the Urn (21 ♒ 25 to 4 ♓ 17) ruled by TAGRIEL for unity and goodwill, and instigating love and favor
New Moon Waxing: amulet to initiate unity, goodwill, love, and favor
Full Moon: charm for unity and goodwill

PISCES . . . 115

ALPHARG, the Spout of the Urn (21 ♒ 25 to 4 ♓ 17) ruled by TAGRIEL for unity and goodwill, and instigating love and favor
New Moon Waxing: candle for instigating love and favor
Full Moon: candle spell for unity and goodwill

ALCHARYA, the Lip of the Urn (4 ♓ 17 to 17 ♓ 8) ruled by ABLEMIEL for increasing the harvest, increasing income, increasing gain, healing the sick, and psychic power
New Moon Waxing: charm for increasing income
Full Moon: incense for psychic power

ALBOTHAM, the Belly of the Fish (17 ♓ 8 to 0 ♈ 0) ruled by ANUXIEL for increase of harvest, increase of trade, safe travel, marital joy, and gathering in fish
New Moon Waxing: amulet for increasing harvest or trade
Full Moon: charm for safe travel in a car

INTRODUCTION

This section contains the activities for magical works that may be performed during the Maiden Moon and Mother Moon Esbats. These works involve magic for emerging new ideas, fresh beginnings, starting new projects, moving in new directions, opening new doors, initiating changes, creating opportunities, abundance, fruition, accomplishment, fulfillment, and spiritual enrichment. By reinterpreting the older meanings of the mansions in a modern light, the energies of the mansions can be drawn upon in a new way. Service can become employment; building can relate to anything from construction of a new home to creating a new business or expanding contacts; and liberating captives can mean exactly that in a time when hostages are taken by bank robbers or terrorists, or it could simply mean freeing oneself from something that is personally restricting, such as an unrewarding job. My magical works show how I draw together and balance the ancient energies to work in a modern context, but of course you are free to modify or invent your own works. Witchcraft is an art, and as such, imagination and creative approaches keep it lively and personal.

While the energies of the Waxing to Full Moon mansions are generally positive, those that involve violent activities such as retaining captives or gaining power may be viewed in the light of current events, such as preventing gangsters from breaking out of prison or increasing support for a favorite cause or charity. In this way these energies may be turned to a positive result, but they can also be counteracted or warded against in magical works for the protection of oneself, family, property, or job security. The mansions offer a time for evaluating how those energies can be successfully applied to address your needs.

The symbols and items I use within the magical works are drawn from the correspondences that are part of my practice, but you may substitute from your own customary correlations as long as you understand the energy being moved in the working. To better facilitate this, each work has an introductory statement about the purpose or function. There are some mansions that overlap zodiac signs, so these mansions will be have magical works relevant to the influence of both signs. The energies of the signs, lunar phase, and mansion are combined so that while some works are similar in theme, they are not exact, as with initiating energy and fulfillment energy. Star energy may be engaged with their related correlations added into the work.

NOTES FOR THE MAGICAL WORKS

Refer to Part Two for cleansing candles, consecrations, charging, and finding your sun sign and the ruling planet. The working candle may be a votive, small pillar, or taper candle. I do not recommend tapers or bottle candles for spell candles, but if bottle candles are used for working or spell candles, draw the images on the glass with a marker. When drawing a mandala (a double ring circle), leave space in the center of the circle for symbols and space between the rings for writing or symbols. For carving symbols on candles, mandalas, etc., **the bold print** in the text shows the **words that are spoken** as the images are drawn. A votive spell candle should have an appropriate container (such as a cauldron) that can hold melted wax and burning herbs without breaking or damaging the pentacle. Have a cover to smother the flame. A candle snuffer should be used to extinguish the working candle and altar candles, but if blown out, say: **With the breath of life**. For activities making an incense or powder, the herbs may be ground prior to the ritual, but blended during the activity. Use glass, china, or pottery bowls and bottles to prepare and store herbal blends, tea blends, and oil blends. Label the stored bottles. Loose black tea leaves normally form the base of herbal tea blends. Green tea leaves have a cleansing energy whereas black is associated with strength and power.

THE MANSIONS OF THE MOON

ARIES

The Moon in ♈ Aries, the Ram, ruled by ♂ Mars with the aggressive energy for leadership, vitality, focus, and exactitude

In the Mansion of the Moon called:

New Moon Waxing

- **ALNATH, the Horns of Aries** (0♈to 12♈51) **ruled by GENIEL for safe journey, travel, and building energy**

This directs energy into building success energy in any area desired, be it work, career, studies, construction, or personal achievement.

Magical work: candle spell for building success. Dress a red working candle with dragon's blood oil: **Red for energy; dragon's blood for power and strength.** Light the working candle from the center altar candle: **This flame burns to build my success!** Consecrate an orange votive spell candle and dress with bergamot oil: **Orange for business and work success; bergamot for success and money**. In the wax, carve around it: **ᛏ Tyr for victory in my endeavors! ᚠ Feoh for prosperity in my endeavors! ᚲ Ken for opening energy in my endeavors! Phaleg for victory! Bethor for honors and wealth! ♂ Mars for dynamic energy! ♃ Jupiter for expansion! ☉ the Sun for success and energy! With this candle is business and work success brought to me!** Set the spell candle in a cauldron on top of the pentacle. Light a taper from the working candle and use it to light the spell candle. One at a time, hold up a pinch of each herb over the pentacle, state the intention, and drop into the candle flame: **I call upon you allspice to bring me prosperity, energy, money, and luck! I call upon you mint to bring me prosperity and business growth! I call upon you cinnamon to bring me business success!** Charge the candle. With the wand or athame, gather energy deosil: **Through the Goddess and the God, through the Sun and the Moon; through the Elementals, planets, herbs and runes; through Phaleg and Bethor; with the energy of Geniel in Alnath; this candle brings work success to me!** Direct and release the energy into the candle: **WORK SUCCESS! So Mote It Be!** Let the candle burn for thirty minutes to an hour, then snuff and look at the wax for images indicating the time frame for the results to manifest. Dispose of candle remains.

Full Moon

• **ALNATH, the Horns of Aries** (0♈0 to 12♈51) **ruled by GENIEL for safe journey, travel, and building energy**

This is good for safety on a business trip by car, train, plane, or ship, and the charm may be re-energized after each use.

Magical work: charm for safe business travels. Dress a red working candle with rosemary oil: **Red for energy; rosemary for protection.** In the wax, carve around it: ᚦ **Thorn for protection;** ᛗ **Eh for safety.** Light the working candle from the center altar candle: **This flame burns for protection from accident or danger!** Lay out a six-inch square of black cloth: **Black to ward against negative energies!** Set out a six-inch-long narrow red ribbon to tie the charm bundle (or thread if sewing it): **Red for power!** and/ or a black ribbon: **Black for protection!** One at a time, hold up over the pentacle some of each of the following herbs, state the intention, then place on the cloth: **I call upon you anise for protection! I call upon you comfrey for safety! I call upon you mullein for protection! I call upon you heather for protection!** Hold up over the pentacle two lodestones (magnets): **I call upon you lodestones; one to draw favorable energies to me and one to repel unfavorable energies from me!** Put them on the cloth. Add three small drops of frankincense oil to a cotton ball: **With the power of frankincense do I draw these energies together for safe business travel!** Set this on top of the bundle. Tie the bundle with the ribbon(s) (or sew shut) and set it on the pentacle. Charge the charm. With the wand or athame, raise energy moving deosil: **Through the Goddess and the God, through the Moon and the Sun, through the Elementals, herbs, stones, and runes; with the energy of Geniel in Alnath; this charm keeps business travel safe!** Direct and release the energy into the charm: **PROTECTION! So Mote It Be!** Leave the charm on the pentacle for thirty minutes to an hour. Snuff the candle and dispose of the remains. Carry or place the charm where desired.

New Moon Waxing

• **ALBOTAYN, the Belly of Aries** (12♈51 to 25♈42) **ruled by ENEDIEL for finding treasure, retaining captives, and reconciling with superiors**

The oil can be worn or dabbed in a personal work area to favorably enhance your aura to superiors in business and career where relations are uncertain or strained.

Magical work: oil for gaining the favor of superiors. Dress a red working candle with vetiver oil: **Red for energy; vetiver to align and unify the energies.** In the wax, carve around it: ᛉ **Osa for a favorable outcome;** ᛗ **Mannaz for cooperation; and** ᚠ **Feoh for fulfillment and ambition satisfied.** Carve by the wick: ♈ **With the strength of the Ram;** ♂ **and the energy of Mars, are my goals are quickly initiated.** Light the working candle from the center altar candle: **This flame burns for bringing the favor of my superiors to me!** In a small glass bottle with lid, blend the following essential oils: 4 parts bay: **I call upon you bay to bring success to me that I attain my desires as I work with my superiors!** 1 part peppermint: **I call upon you peppermint to keep me alert and aid me with mental clarity as I work with my superiors!** 3 parts bergamot: **I call upon you bergamot to bring me success and wealth as I work with my superiors!** ½ part pine: **I call upon you pine to clear away any barrier to my working harmoniously with my superiors!** Add 4 parts grapeseed, saffron, or canola oil. Put the lid on the bottle, shake: **All are blended to work together for my purpose!** With a red marker or ink, draw on the bottle: **Red for energy and** ⊞ **Phaleg for the power of Mars to bring me success and overcome obstacles at work!** On the opposite side of the bottle, draw the symbols of your Sun sign and ruling planet: **With** (sun sign) **and** (planetary ruler) **is success brought to me!** Place the bottle on the pentacle. Charge the oil. With the wand or athame, gather energy deosil: **Through the Goddess and the God; the Moon and the Sun; through the Elementals, planets, and stars; through runes and herbal oils; with the power of Phaleg and the energy of Enediel in Albotayn; this oil initiates my entering into good standing with my superiors!** Direct and release the energy into the bottle: **ENHANCE ME! So Mote It Be!** Leave the oil on the pentacle for thirty minutes to an hour. Snuff the candle and dispose of the remains. Use a dab of oil as needed.

Full Moon

• **ALBOTAYN, the Belly of Aries** (12♈51 to 25♈42) **ruled by ENEDIEL for finding treasure, retaining captives, and reconciling with superiors**

This talisman directs the energies to manifest improvement in your relationship with superiors who are in a position to make a difference in your career, business, studies, or personal advancement.

Magical work: talisman for good relations with superiors. Dress a red working candle with dragon's blood oil: **Red for energy; dragon's blood for power and strength.** In the wax, carve around it: ᛉ **Eolh to gain my aspirations;** ↑ **Tyr for a favorable outcome to my endeavors;** ᚲ **Ken for opening energy to receive well-being; and** ᛞ **Daeg to commence a fresh start in good relations with my superiors.** Light the working candle from the center altar candle: **This flame burns for good relations with my superiors!** On a piece of parchment or paper no more than three inches square, draw in red ink a double ring circle to fill the space: **I draw this mandala in red for energy.** In the center of the circle, draw: ⬚ **With the Seal of Shadiel for vitality, honors, and success!** Under or through the Seal of Shadiel, draw: ⬚ **With the Seal of Nachiel to enhance my leadership!** In the ring around the circle, write: **SHADIEL · NACHIEL · ENEDIEL ·** (the symbol of your sun sign) **·** (the symbol of your ruling planet)**.** On the back of the paper draw:

6	32	3	34	35	1
7	11	27	28	8	30
19	14	16	15	23	24
18	20	22	21	17	13
25	29	10	9	26	12
36	5	33	4	2	31

111

With the Square of the Sun do I gain success, leadership, vitality, and honors to me! Turn the talisman over so the mandala is face up. Charge the talisman. With wand or athame, gather energy deosil: **Through the Goddess and the God; the Moon and the Sun; through the Elementals and the runes; through the power of Shadiel and Nachiel; with the energy of Enediel in Albotayn; this talisman brings me leadership and vitality for good relations with superiors!** Direct and release the energy into the talisman: **SUPERIORS HONOR ME! So Mote It Be!** Leave the talisman on the pentacle for thirty minutes to an hour. Snuff the candle and dispose of the remains. Place, carry, or wear the talisman as desired.

New Moon Waxing

• **ATHORAY, the Showering of Pleiades** (25 ♈ 42 to 8 ♉ 34) **ruled by AMIXIEL for good fortune, safety for sailors, favorable hunts, helpful alchemy, and every good thing**

Use this talisman to invite general success and good luck to come your way.

Magical work: talisman for initiating good fortune. Dress a red working candle with orange or neroli oil: **Red for energy; orange for good fortune.** In the wax, carve around it: ↑ **Tyr for victory and success;** ᚺ **Uruz for good health and strength;** ᚠ **Feoh for fulfillment and material wealth;** ᛇ **Gera for reaping good rewards.** Light the working candle from the center altar candle: **This flame burns to bring good fortune to me!** Consecrate an aventurine stone that is large enough to draw on. With permanent gold marker or acrylic paint, draw on one side of the stone: ⊞ **Bethor, for honors and wealth!** Draw on the reverse side of the stone:

4	14	15	1
9	7	6	12
5	11	10	8
16	2	3	13

34

The Square of Jupiter for good fortune and success! Draw ⊠ over the square: **And Netoniel, the Seal of Jupiter to hold the good fortune!** Set the talisman on the pentacle and charge. With wand or athame, gather energy deosil: **Through the Goddess and the God; through the Moon and the Sun; through the Elementals, runes, and stone; through the power of Bethor and Netoniel; with the energy of Amixiel in Athoray; this stone brings all good fortune to me!** Direct and release the energy into the talisman: **GOOD FORTUNE BEGINS! So Mote It Be!** Leave the talisman on the pentacle for thirty minutes to an hour. Snuff the candle and dispose of the remains. Place, carry, or wear the talisman as desired.

Full Moon

• **ATHORAY, the Showering of Pleiades** (25 ♈ 42 to 8 ♉ 34) **ruled by AMIXIEL for good fortune, safety for sailors, favorable hunts, helpful alchemy, and every good thing**

Light this candle to bring your good luck into a material or practical fulfillment.

Magical work: candle for fulfillment of good fortune. Dress a red working candle with orange or neroli oil: **Red for energy; orange for good fortune.** In the wax, carve around it: ᛗ **Osa for a favorable outcome;** ᛗ **Daeg for transformation;** ᛩ **Gera for reaping good rewards.** Light the working candle from the center altar candle: **This flame burns to bring the fulfillment I desire to me!** Consecrate an orange votive spell candle and dress with bay oil: **Orange for fulfillment; bay to attain my desires.** In the wax, carve around it: **With the energies of** (your sun sign symbol) **and** (the ruling planet) **to represent me!** ᚠ **Feoh for fulfillment and ambition satisfied!** ᚹ **Wyn for success and well-being!** ᚦ **Thorn for luck!** ᛚ **and Lagu to gather the energies to fulfill my wishes!** Set the spell candle in a cauldron on top of the pentacle. Light a taper from the working candle and use it to light the spell candle. Charge a piece of jade, then drop it into the candle flame: **With Jade to bring me good luck!** Charge the candle. With the wand or athame, gather energy deosil: **Through the Goddess and the God; through the Moon and the Sun; through the Elementals, rune, oil, and stone; with the energy of Amixiel in Athoray; this candle brings fulfillment of good fortune to me!** Direct and release the energy into the candle: **FORTUNATE ME! So Mote It Be!** Let the candle burn for thirty minutes to an hour, then snuff it and look at the wax for images indicating the time frame for the results to manifest. Remove the jade and clean it to place, carry, or wear as desired. Dispose of candle remains.

TAURUS

The Moon in ♉ Taurus, the Bull, ruled by ♀ Venus with energies for the values of stability, productivity, and practicality, and the available energy of three fixed stars:

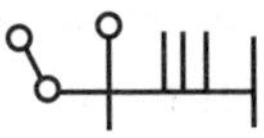
Algol, the Head of Algol: Audacity, victory, protection; Saturn and Jupiter; Taurus; diamond; hellebore

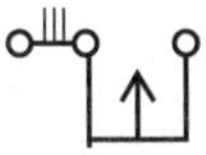
Pleiades: Secrets, talk to spirits; Moon and Mars; Taurus; crystal; fennel

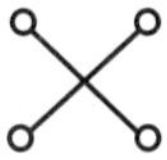
Aldebaran: Good fortune, create discord; Mars and Venus; Gemini; ruby or garnet; milk thistle

In the Mansion of the Moon called:

New Moon Waxing

- **ATHORAY, the Showering of Pleiades** (25♈42 to 8♉34) **ruled by AMIXIEL for good fortune, safety for sailors, favorable hunts, helpful alchemy, and every good thing**

  This candle spell is helpful for entering a period of successful productivity.

Magical work: candle spell for initiating good fortune. Dress a red working candle with peppermint oil or extract: **Red for power; peppermint for action.** Light the working candle from the center altar candle. **This flame burns for long-term good fortune, stability, and productivity!** Consecrate an orange votive spell candle and dress with pine oil: **Orange for success and attaining goals; pine for energy, strength, and action.** In the wax, carve around it: **Algol for the courage to initiate action for victory! Aldebaran for good fortune! ♉ Taurus for enduring strength and productive work! ♀ Venus for amiability! ᚦ Thorn for protection! ᛖ Eh for steady progress! This candle initiates the long-term good fortune, stability and productivity that will bring me solid successful results!** Charge the candle and set it in a cauldron on top of the pentacle. Light a taper from the working candle and use it to light the spell candle. Let the candle burn for a short time while focusing on the desired goals. One at a time, hold up a pinch of each herb over the pentacle, state the intention, and drop into the candle flame: **I call upon you bay to bring me success in attaining my desire! I call upon you clove to make my endeavors prosper! I call upon you bergamot to**

bring me the benefits of success! I call upon you rose to ensure my success comes with joy and harmony! Charge the candle. With the wand or athame, gather energy deosil: **Through the Goddess and the God; through the Moon and the Sun; through the Elementals, planets, stars and runes; with the energy Amixiel in Athoray; this candle burns to initiate long-term good fortune, stability and productivity for me!** Direct and release the energy into the candle: **PRODUCTIVE! So Mote It Be!** Let the candle burn for thirty minutes to an hour, then snuff it and look at the wax for images indicating the time frame for the results to manifest. Dispose of candle remains.

Full Moon

- **ATHORAY, the Showering of Pleiades** (25♈42 to 8♉34) **ruled by AMIXIEL for good fortune, safety for sailors, favorable hunts, helpful alchemy, and every good thing**

This offers protective energies for people on ships, be they fishermen, or people in the Navy, merchant marine, cruise lines, or shipping industry.

Magical work: charm for safety for a sailor. Dress a red candle with rosemary oil: **Red for strength, power, health, and survival; rosemary for protection, health, and blessing.** In the wax, carve around it: **ᚦ Thorn for protection and safety; ᛖ Eh for safe journey; and ᛏ Tyr for success and a favorable outcome.** Add the sun sign and ruling planet of the person for whom the charm is made: **By** (sun sign) **and** (planet) **for** (Name). Light the working candle from the center altar candle. **This flame burns to keep the sailor** (Name) **strong and safe!** Lay out a six-inch square of dark blue cloth: **Dark Blue for the Goddess and the sea, for protection and safety!** Set out a six-inch-long narrow gold ribbon to tie the charm bundle (or gold thread if sewing it): **Gold for the God and the Sun, for physical strength, skill, and safety!** One at a time, hold up a bit of each herb over the pentacle, state the intention, and place on the cloth: **Fennel for the God for protection and deflecting negativity! Carnation for the Goddess for protection and strength! I call upon you comfrey for safe travel! I call upon you peppercorns for protection and warding negativity! I call upon you rosemary for protection, blessing, and health! I call upon you mustard seed for protection, health, and good luck! And I call upon you garlic for protection and power!** Add a small agate to the herbs: **With the power of agate do I draw these energies together to gain these goals!** Using black ink: **Black to ward negativity!** Draw on a piece of paper or parchment: 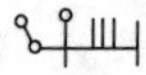 **Sealed with Algol for protection and victory, ♄ with Saturn for self-preservation, and with ♃ Jupiter for honor!** Lay this on top of the herbs and stone. Gather the cloth together so the contents are secure inside. Tie the bundle with the ribbon (or sew shut) and set it on the pentacle. Charge the charm. With wand or athame, gather energy deosil: **Through the Goddess and the God; through the Moon and the Sun; through the Elementals, planets, and stars; through runes, herbs, and stone; with the energy of Amixiel in Athoray; this charm keeps** (Name) **safe from all harm!** Direct and release the energy into the charm: **SAFETY! So Mote It Be!** Leave the charm on the pentacle for thirty minutes to an hour. Snuff the candle and dispose of the remains. Place, carry, or wear the charm as desired, or give it to the sailor to take to sea, or tie it where the Elementals may release the energy into the wind.

New Moon Waxing

• **ALDEBARAN, the Eye of Taurus** (8 ♉ 34 to 21 ♉ 25) **ruled by AZARIEL for favorable outcome in important things, and seeking substantial items**

This is used to direct energy into work or other enterprise so that what is initiated will be successful, such as with opening a new business.

Magical work: talisman for a favorable outcome. Dress a red working candle with bergamot oil: **Red for power; bergamot for success.** Light the working candle from the center altar candle: **This flame burns for long-term success!** Consecrate a polished carnelian and set it on the pentacle: **I call upon you carnelian to bring a favorable outcome in the important matters I undertake!** Using a black marker: **Black for protection and removing discord!** Draw on one side of the stone: ᛟ **Osa for a favorable outcome and** ᚠ **Feoh for fulfillment and ambition satisfied!** On the reverse side of the stone draw: ♃ **Jupiter for opportunity and expansion and** ⊔⊔ **Bethor for honors and success! This talisman brings me success in the matters that are important to me!** Put the stone into a small opened pouch that is green, yellow, orange, red, or black. Set it on the pentacle. One at a time, hold up a pinch of each herb over the pentacle, state the intention, and add it to the pouch: **I call upon you woodruff to remove barriers and bring success to me in my endeavors! I call upon you bay to aid me in attaining my desires! I call upon you cinnamon for energy in attaining my goals and protecting my success!** Close and charge the pouch. With the wand or athame, gather energy deosil: **Through the Goddess and the God; through the Moon and the Sun; through the Elementals, stone, and herbs; with the power of Jupiter and Bethor, and the energy of Azariel in Aldebaran; this talisman brings me long-term success in important**

matters! Direct and release the energy into the talisman charm: **ENDURING SUCCESS! So Mote It Be!** Leave the talisman on the pentacle for thirty minutes to an hour. Snuff the candle and dispose of the remains. Carry the talisman when working on important or expansive matters, or set where desired.

Full Moon

- **ALDEBARAN, the Eye of Taurus** (8♉34 to 21♉25) **ruled by AZARIEL for favorable outcome in important things, and seeking big items**

This brings energy to bear for attaining immediate positive results in an important matter.

Magical work: candle spell for a favorable outcome. Dress a red working candle with patchouli oil: **Red for energy; patchouli for strength and power.** In the wax, carve around it: ᚹ **Wyn for success and fulfillment in important matters;** ᚱ **Rad to find what is sought; and** ᛉ **Eolh to gain aspirations.** Light the working candle from the center altar candle: **This flame burns for a favorable outcome in an important matter!** Consecrate an orange votive spell candle and dress with bay oil: **Orange for ambition achieved and attracting what is sought; bay for success in attaining what is desired.** In the wax, carve around it: ⚹ **Aldebaran for good fortune!** ♃ **Jupiter for expansion and opportunity!** ♄ **Saturn for ambition and self-preservation!** ⚹ **Algol for victory!** ♂ **Mars to gain what is sought!** ♀ **Venus for what is desired!** ᛏ **Tyr for victory!** ᚠ **Feoh for good fortune and ambition satisfied!** ᛋ **Sigel for success!** Charge the candle and set it in a cauldron on top of the pentacle. Light a taper from the working candle and use it to light the spell candle. One at a time, hold up a pinch of each herb over the pentacle, state the intention, and add it to the flame: **I call upon you bergamot for success! I call upon you cinnamon for success! I call upon you thyme to bring swift action! I call upon you basil for protection from negativity!** With the wand or athame, gather energy deosil: **Through the Goddess and the God; through the Moon and the Sun; through the Elementals, planets, and stars; through runes and herbs; with the energy of Azariel in Aldebaran; this candle brings me a favorable outcome in** (state the important matter)**!** Direct and release the energy into the candle: **VICTORY! So Mote It Be!** Let the candle burn for thirty minutes to an hour, then snuff it and look at the wax for images indicating the time frame for the results to manifest. Dispose of candle remains.

New Moon Waxing

• **ALBACHAY, the Head of Orion** (21 ♉ 25 to 4♊17) **ruled by GABIEL for gaining favors, having fun, health, scholarship, strong buildings, and safe trips**

This initiates a happy energy that will get you going for socializing, having fun, and feeling healthy.

Magical work: charm for instigating good health and fun. Dress a pink working candle with rosemary oil: **Pink for sociability; rosemary for health, clarity and energy.** In the wax, carve around it: ᛋᚨᛚᚷᛟᛚ **Algol for protection!** ⚹ **Aldebaran for good fortune!** ᛉ **Eolh for the life-force!** ᚹ **Wyn for happiness, joy, and well-being!** Light the working candle from the center altar candle: **This flame burns for good health and the enjoyment of life!** Lay out a six-inch square of pink cloth: **Pink for friendships, relationships, and good health.** Set out a six-inch-long narrow red ribbon to tie the charm bundle (or thread if sewing it): **Red for health and enthusiasm!** Use red ink: **Red for vibrant energy!** On a piece of paper or parchment, draw a double circle. I **draw this mandala for good health and enjoyment of life!** Between the lines around the circle write **ALBACHAY · GABIEL · ALGOL · ALDEBARAN ·** Inside the center of the circle draw a large heart: **Here is a joyful heart!** In the left lobe draw: ♄ **Saturn for self-preservation!** In the right lobe draw: ♃ **Jupiter for good health!** In the center of the heart draw: ♂ ♀ **with Mars and Venus for energy and sociability!** At the point of the heart draw your sun sign and ruling planet: **With** (sun sign) **and** (ruling planet) **for good health and enjoyment of life for me to have to hold!** Outside the tip of the heart on the right draw: and on the left side draw: **With the beneficial energies of** ⚹ **Aldebaran and** ᛋᚨᛚᚷᛟᛚ **Algol!** Lay the mandala on the cloth. One at a time, hold up some of each herb over the pentacle, state the intention, and place it on top of the mandala: **I call upon you hops for your energy of good health! I call upon you lavender for your energy of happiness!** If available, hold up a small loose green garnet over the pentacle: **I call upon you green garnet to add your energy of good health, vitality, and joy!** (or: **I call upon you ocean jasper for enjoyment in my life!**) Add the stone. Tie the bundle with the ribbon (or sew shut). On the outside of the charm bag, with red marker, draw: ᛟ **Osa for good fortune!** On the other side draw: ᚹ **Wyn for happiness!** Set it on the pentacle and charge the charm. With the wand or athame, gather energy deosil: **Through the Goddess and the God; through the Moon and the Sun; through the Elementals, the planets, and the stars; through runes, herbs, and stone; with the energy of Gabiel in Albachay; this charm brings me**

good health and enjoyment of life! Direct and release the energy into the charm: **JOY AND HEALTH! So Mote It Be!** Leave the charm on the pentacle for thirty minutes to an hour. Snuff the candle and dispose of the remains. Carry the charm bag or place where desired.

Full Moon

- **ALBACHAY, the Head of Orion** (21 ♉ 25 to 4 ♊ 17) **ruled by GABIEL for gaining favors, having fun, health, scholarship, strong buildings, and safe trips**

Use this to enhance your aura when you need a practical favor.

Magical work: oil for receiving a practical favor. Dress a yellow working candle with bay oil: **Yellow for self-promotion and gains; bay to attain what is desired.** In the wax, carve around it: ᛟ **Osa for a favorable outcome;** ᚨ **as for convincing speech and luck;** ᛗ **Mannaz for cooperation; and** ᚠ **Feoh for fulfillment and ambition satisfied.** Light the working candle from the center altar candle: **This flame burns to gain a practical favor!** In a small glass bottle with lid, blend the following essential oils: 4 parts bay: **I call upon you bay to bring success to me that I attain the favor I seek!** 1 part lemon: **I call upon you lemon to invigorate and bring joy from the favor I seek!** 2 parts ylang-ylang: **I call upon you ylang-ylang for success in gaining the favor I seek!** ½ part pine: **I call upon you pine to clear away any barrier to my gaining the favor I seek!** Add 4 parts grapeseed, saffron, or canola oil. Put the lid on the bottle, shake: **All are blended to work together for my purpose!** Use a brown marker or ink: **Brown for special favors granted.** Draw on the bottle: ♉ **Taurus for practical accomplishment!** ♀ **Venus for sociability! and** ᚹ **Wyn for gains and fulfillment!** ☋╪ᛋ **Algol for victory!** ⌦ **Aldebaran for good fortune! Together these blended oils work to gain a practical favor for me!** On the opposite side of the bottle, draw the symbols of your sun sign and ruling planet: **With (sun sign) and (planetary ruler) is the favor I seek given to me!** Place the bottle on the pentacle and charge it. With the wand or athame, gather energy deosil: **Through the Goddess and the God; through the Moon and the Sun; through the Elementals, planets, and stars; through runes and herbs; with the energy of Gabiel in Albachay; this oil gains me whatever favors I seek!** Direct and release the energy into the bottle: **GRANTED! So Mote It Be!** Leave the oil bottle on the pentacle for thirty minutes to an hour. Snuff the candle and dispose of the remains. Use a dab of oil as needed.

GEMINI

The Moon in ♊ Gemini, the Twins, ruled by ☿ Mercury with the energy of versatility, wit, perception, rationality, and changeability, and the available energies of two fixed stars:

Capella, the Goat Star: Honors, favor of superiors; Jupiter and Saturn; Gemini; sapphire; thyme

Cauda Ursa, the Tail of the Bear (Polaris): Protection from personal violence and thieves; Venus and Moon; Gemini; lodestone; endive

In the Mansion of the Moon called:

New Moon Waxing

• **ALBACHAY, the Head of Orion** (21 ♉ 25 to 4♊17) **ruled by GABIEL for gaining favors, having fun, health, scholarship, strong buildings, and safe trips**

This is good for students at any level and may be carried or placed in a study area for focus and clarity of thought.

Magical work: charm for beginning successful studies. Dress an orange working candle with clove oil: **Orange for a clear mind and success in attaining my goals; clove for good memory. In the wax, carve around it: ♊ Gemini for rationality; ☿ Mercury for a quick mind; Capella for honors; with Cauda Ursa for protection of my work from theft; with ♃ Jupiter and ♄ Saturn for opportunity and ambition satisfied; and with ♀ Venus and the ☽ Moon that my successful studies bring me harmony.** Light the working candle from the center altar candle: **This flame burns for my successful studies!** Lay out a six-inch square of yellow cloth: **Yellow for mental alertness, intellect, memory, and learning!** Set out a six-inch long narrow red ribbon to tie the charm bundle (or red thread if sewing it): **Red for energy and power!** Use a blue marker or ink: **Blue for understanding!** Draw on the cloth: ♊ **With the versatile energy of Gemini! And with the energy of Bethor for honors!** One at a time, hold up over the pentacle some of each of the following herbs, state the intention, then place on the cloth: **I call upon you sage for inspiration and wisdom! I call upon you bay for wisdom! I call upon you mace for mental alertness! I call upon you bergamot for success! I call upon you thyme to bring swift action for this charm!** Hold up a small hematite (or aquamarine, or clear quartz crystal) over the pentacle, state the intention, and add it to the herbs on the cloth: **I call upon you hematite for reasoning and communication skills!** (or: **I call upon you aquamarine for success in tests!** or **I call upon you crystal for insight and attainment of my goals!**). Tie the bundle with the ribbon (or sew shut) and set it on the pentacle. Charge the charm. With the wand or athame, gather energy deosil: **Through the Goddess and the God; through the Moon and the Sun; through the Elementals, planets, and stars; through runes, herbs, and stones; with the power of Bethor, and the energy of Gabiel in Albachay; this charm brings me unhindered success in my studies!** Direct and release the energy into the charm: **SCHOLARSHIP! So Mote It Be!** Leave the charm bag on the pentacle for thirty minutes to an hour. Snuff the candle and dispose of the remains. Place, carry, or wear the charm as desired.

Full Moon

• **ALBACHAY, the Head of Orion** (21 ♉ 25 to 4 ♊ 17) **ruled by GABIEL for gaining favors, having fun, health, scholarship, strong buildings, and safe trips**

Savor a cup of this tea as a tonic for good health.

Magical work: tea for good health. Dress a light blue working candle with rosemary oil: **Blue for health; rosemary for health and vigor.** In the wax, carve around it: ↾ **Lagu for life-force vitality;** ↿ **As for magical energy;** ⟨ **Ken for opening healing energy;** ⋎ **Eolh for a strong life-force;** ⭍ **Sigel for health and vital energy;** ♭ **and Beorc for health brought to fruition.** Light the working candle from the center altar candle: **This flame burns for good health!** Set on the pentacle a clean bowl in which to blend herbs. Add to the bowl ½ cup of loose black tea leaves. **I call upon you black tea for vigor and strength!** One at a time, hold up over the pentacle ⅛ cup of each herb, state the intention, and add it to the bowl: **I call upon you hops for good health! I call upon you dandelion root for cleansing! I call upon you elderflower for healing energy!** Blend the herbs and black tea with a wooden spoon. Charge the blend. With the wand or athame, gather energy deosil: **Through the Goddess and the God; through the Moon and the Sun; through the Elementals and planets; through runes and herbs; with the energy of Gabiel in Albachay; this tea brings good health to all who drink it!** Direct and release the energy into the tea: **HEALTHY TEA! So Mote It Be!** Leave the tea blend on the pentacle for thirty minutes to an hour. Snuff the candle and dispose of the remains. Put the tea blend in a tightly covered jar and store away from light. Brew a cup or pot of tea when desired.

New Moon Waxing

• **ALCHAYA, the Little Star of Great Light** (4♊17 to 17♊8) **ruled by DIRACHIEL for love between two people, friendships, hunting, links, and gaining power**

Enjoy a cup of this tea for socializing and gaining new friends.

Magical work: tea for initiating friendships. Dress a pink working candle with lemon oil: **Pink for friendships; lemon for joy and energy.** In the wax, carve around it: ⚹ **Capella to generate honors and the favor of others toward me; ᛗ Daeg for new beginnings; ᛃ Gera for tangible results; ᚹ Wyn for happiness and harmony; ᛉ and Eolh to promote friendship.** Light the working candle from the center altar candle: **This flame burns to initiate friendships!** Set a clean bowl on the pentacle. Add to the bowl ½ cup of loose black tea leaves. **I call upon you black tea for power and energy!** One at a time, hold up over the pentacle ⅛ cup of each herb, state the intention, and add it to the bowl: **I call upon you chamomile for peace and balance! I call upon you rose hips for happiness, love, and positive energy!** Blend the herbs and black tea with a wooden spoon: **I call upon Dirachiel in Alchaya, to generate friendships with the drinking and sharing of this tea!** Add a pinch of thyme and stir: **I call upon you thyme to enhance this tea with the energy of Capella to draw the favor of others toward me!** With the wand draw ☽ in the tea: **I call upon the energy of the Moon to initiate friendships through this tea!** Charge the blend. With the wand or athame, gather energy deosil: **Through the Goddess and the God; through the Moon and the Sun; through the Elementals, planets, and stars; through runes and herbs; with the energy of Dirachiel in Alchaya; this tea brings friendship to all who drink it!** Direct and release the energy into the tea: **FRIENDSHIP TEA! So Mote It Be!** Leave the tea blend on the pentacle for thirty minutes to an hour. Snuff the candle and dispose of the remains. Put the tea blend in a tightly covered jar and store away from light. Brew a cup or pot of tea as desired.

Full Moon

• **ALCHAYA, the Little Star of Great Light** (4♊17 to 17♊8) **ruled by DIRACHIEL for love between two people, friendships, hunting, links, and gaining power**

This is good for those who seek advancement or a position of power and authority in a field of endeavor.

Magical work: Amulet for gaining power. Dress a red working candle with patchouli oil: **Red for energy and power; patchouli for power and protection.** In the wax, carve around it: ⟩ **Eoh for power and action;** ⟩ **Ing for the power to achieve goals;** ⟩ **Gera for good rewards and tangible results;** ⟩ **Sigel for power and achievement; and** ↑ **Tyr for victory.** Light the working candle from the center altar candle: **This flame burns for gaining power!** One at a time, hold up each small stone over the pentacle, state the intention, and set it in the center of the pentacle: **I call upon you opal for power and self-confidence! I call upon you agate for gaining my goal of power! I call upon you lapis lazuli to boost the power of these stones and infuse them with authority! I call upon you pumice to bring this power into manifestation!** Charge the stones. With the wand or athame, gather energy deosil: **Through the Goddess and the God; through the Moon and the Sun; through the Elementals; through rune and stone and candle flame; with the energy of Dirachiel in Alchaya; these stones gain power for me!** Direct and release the energy into the stones: **POWER! So Mote It Be!** Leave the stones on the pentacle for thirty minutes to an hour. Snuff the candle and dispose of the remains. Set the stones in the four corners of the place where you want your power felt, or put the stones in a pouch to carry with you.

New Moon Waxing

- **ALARZACH, the Arm of Gemini** (17♊8 to 0♋0) **ruled by SELHIEL for acquisitions, gains and favors, good travel, love, and contacts**

    Use this for catching the favors and things you desire.

Magical work: amulet for acquisitions and favors. Dress a brown working candle with bay oil: **Brown for favors and physical objects; bay oil for success and attaining what is desired.** In the wax, carve around it: **⟨ Ken for opening energy; ♃ Jupiter for opportunity; ♄ Saturn for ambition; ♀ Venus for luxuries; ☽ the Moon for nurture; the ☉ Sun for honor; and ⱷ Wyn for material gain and well-being.** Light the working candle from the center altar candle: **This flame burns to start bringing acquisitions and favors to me!** Hold up over the pentacle a clean, dry crab claw or a representation of one: **I call upon you claw of the crab to catch and to hold for me that which I seek!** Using brown marker: **Brown for favors and earth riches!** Draw on the claw: ✕ **Capella for favors and honors!** ⌇⌇✕⌐ **Cauda Ursa to protect me and my acquisitions from violence and thieves!** Shellac or paint it with clear nail polish as a preservative. When dry, set the claw on the pentacle: **I call upon you crab claw to start catching and bringing to me the favors and acquisitions I desire!** Charge the claw. With the wand or athame, gather energy deosil: **Through the Goddess and the God; through the Moon and the Sun; through the Elementals, planets, and stars; through sea and runes; with the energy of Selhiel in Alarzach; this claw brings favors and acquisitions to me!** Direct and release the energy into the claw: **FAVORS FOR ME! So Mote It Be!** Leave the claw on the pentacle for thirty minutes to an hour. Snuff the candle and dispose of the remains. Carry or place the claw where desired.

Full Moon

• **ALARZACH, the Arm of Gemini** (17♊8 to 0♋0) **ruled by SELHIEL for acquisitions, gains and favors, good travel, love, and contacts**

Burn this candle for manifesting what is desired.

Magical work: candle spell for acquiring what is desired. Dress a brown working candle with bay oil: **Brown for favors and physical objects; bay oil for success and attaining what is desired.** In the wax, carve around it: ↑ **Tyr for victory in getting what I desire;** ᚹ **Wyn for success and material gain;** ᚠ **Feoh for gains; and** ᛉ **Ethel for acquisitions and protection of possessions.** Light the working candle from the center altar candle: **This flame burns for me to acquire what I desire!** Consecrate an orange votive spell candle and carefully dress with cinnamon oil, then wipe your hands clean (this oil is a burning irritant, so keep it out of your eyes, nose, and mouth): **Orange to attract what I desire; cinnamon oil for success and gains.** In the wax, carve around it: ⌖ **Omeliel for ambition achieved!** ⊗ **Netoniel for expansion and prosperity! and** ⨳ **Habondia for abundance! all bring fulfillment to me** (carve your initials) **as I acquire what I desire!** Set the spell candle in a cauldron on top of the pentacle and wipe your hands clean again. Light a taper from the working candle and use it to light the spell candle. One at a time, hold up a pinch of each herb over the pentacle, state the intention, and drop into the candle flame: **I call upon you bergamot for success in gaining what I desire! I call upon you ginger for success in acquiring what I desire! I call upon you lemon balm for good luck and success in getting what I desire!** Charge the candle. With the wand or athame, gather energy deosil: **Through the Goddess and the God; through the Moon and the Sun; through the Elementals; through runes and herbs; through the power of Omeliel, Netoniel, and Habondia; and with the energy of Selhiel in Alarzach; this candle brings to me what I desire!** Direct and release the energy into the candle: **DESIRE ACHIEVED! So Mote It Be!** Let the candle burn for thirty minutes to an hour, then snuff and look at the wax for images indicating the time frame for the results to manifest. Dispose of candle remains.

CANCER

The Moon in ♋ Cancer, the Crab, ruled by ☽ Moon, with the psychic energy of intuition, introspection, nurturing, and family, and the available energy of two fixed stars:

Canis Major, the Greater Dog Star (Sirius): Communication, favor of Earth and Air Spirits, marital peace; Venus; Cancer; beryl; juniper

Canis Minor, the Lesser Dog Star (Procyon): Magic power, good health; Mercury and Mars; Cancer; agate; buttercup

In the Mansion of the Moon called:

New Moon Waxing

• **ALNAZA, Misty Clouds** (0♋0 to 12♋51) **ruled by AMNEDIEL for love and friendship, companions, safe travel, and battle victory**

  Use these bath salts to generate from within an aura that attracts love.

Magical work: bath salts for initiating love energy. Dress a pink working candle with jasmine oil: **Pink for love and caring; jasmine for love and confidence.** In the wax, carve around it: ᚷ **Gefu for love and partnership;** ᚲ **Ken for opening energy to be free to receive, love; and** ᚹ **Wyn for fulfillment in love and well-being;** **Canis Major for the favor of Earth and Air spirits to bring me loving energy; and** **Canis Minor for adding magic power.** Light the working candle from the center altar candle: **This flame burns to initiate love energy!** Set on the pentacle a clean bowl in which to blend the bath salt. Add to the bowl 2 cups of sea salt. **I call upon you salt of the sea to bring love energy to me!** Hold up over the pentacle ½ teaspoon of rose oil: **I call upon you rose to initiate loving energy for me!** Add the oil to the salt and stir together until the salt and rose oil are blended. Charge the salts. With the wand or athame, gather energy deosil: **Through the Goddess and the God; through the Moon and the Sun; through the Elementals and stars; through runes, herbs, and the sea; with the energy of Amnediel in Alnaza; these bath salts bring loving energy!** Direct and release the energy into the salts: **LOVE FOR ME! So Mote It Be!** Leave the bath salt on the pentacle for thirty minutes to an hour. Snuff the candle and dispose of the remains. Store salts in a tightly covered jar away from light. Add to tub water or rub on in the shower.

Full Moon

- **ALNAZA, Misty Clouds** (0♋0 to 12♋51) **ruled by AMNEDIEL for love and friendship, companions, safe travel, and battle victory**

  Use this oil for healing upsets and nurturing love in family and friendships.

Magical work: oil for family love and friendship. Dress a pink working candle with vetiver oil: **Pink for nurturing and healing emotions; vetiver for love and internal alignment in the family.** In the wax, carve around it: ᛒ **Beorc for the family;** ᚷ **Gefu for love and partnership;** ᚲ **Ken for well-being;** ᛜ **Ing for family unity;** ᛟ **Ethel for home and heritage; and** ᚹ **Wyn for love, joy, and happiness in the family.** Light the working candle from the center altar candle: **This flame burns for love and friendship in the family!** In a small glass bottle with lid, blend the following essential oils: 4 parts vetiver: **I call upon you vetiver for love and alignment!** 1 part rose: **I call upon you rose for love, happiness, and peace!** 3 parts jasmine: **I call upon you jasmine for love, confidence, and good health!** ½ part sandalwood: **I call upon you sandalwood to cleanse and protect the love and friendship in the family!** Add 4 parts grapeseed, saffron, or canola oil. Put the lid on the bottle, shake: **All are blended to work together for my purpose!** With a red marker or ink, draw on the bottle: **With** ✕◇⫲⟨ **Canis Major for family peace!** ⊞⊟ **Hagith for love and friendship! and** ♀ **Venus for love and companionship! There is love and friendship in the family!** Place the bottle on the pentacle and charge the oil. With the wand or athame, gather energy deosil: **Through the Goddess and the God; through the Moon and the Sun; through the Elementals, planets, and stars; through runes and herbs; with the power of Hagith and the energy of Amnediel in Alnaza; this oil brings family love and friendship!** Direct and release the energy into the bottle: **LOVE AND HARMONY! So Mote It Be!** Leave the oil on the pentacle for thirty minutes to an hour. Snuff the candle and dispose of the remains. Use a dab of oil as needed.

New Moon Waxing

- **ARCAPH, the Eye of the Lion** (12♋51 to 25♋42) **ruled by RAUBIEL for self-defense, helping others, empathy, and abilities**

Use this protective powder to increase your self-defense against psychic attack.

Magical work: powder for boosting psychic self-defense. Dress a white working candle with frankincense oil: **White for protection and purity; frankincense for cleansing and psychic protection.** In the wax, carve around it: ♆ **Neptune for psychic awareness, the subconscious, and spirits;** ⤙⚗⤚ **Canis Minor for magic power and good psychic health;** ✕◇⚏(**Canis Major for the favor of Earth and Air spirits in psychic protection;** ♭ **with Thorn for defense against psychic attack; and** ↓ **Eoh for protection with communications from other worlds.** Light the working candle from the center altar candle: **This flame burns to increase psychic self-defense!** One at a time, hold up an equal amount of each herb over the pentacle, state the intention, and drop into a mortar with pestle: **I call upon you thyme to strengthen psychic power! I call upon you bay for psychic awareness! I call upon you fennel for protection against psychic drain! I call upon you cinnamon for protection of psychic powers! And I call upon you lavender for cleansing psychic energy!** Grind the herbs together into a powder, bottle it, and set the powder on the pentacle. Charge the powder. With the wand or athame, gather energy deosil: **Through the Goddess and the God; through the Moon and the Sun; through the Elementals, planets, and stars; through runes and herbs; with the energy of Raubiel in Arcaph; this powder aids psychic self-defense!** Direct and release the energy into the powder: **PSYCHIC PROTECTION! So Mote It Be!** Leave the powder on the pentacle for thirty minutes to an hour. Snuff the candle and dispose of the remains. Sprinkle the powder where desired or add to charms or oils.

Full Moon

- **ARCAPH, the Eye of the Lion** (12♋51 to 25♋42) **ruled by RAUBIEL for self-defense, helping others, empathy, and abilities**

    This is for compassion, insight, and understanding the feelings of other people.

Magical work: talisman for enhancing empathy. Dress a light blue working candle with lavender oil: **Light blue for psychic awareness and understanding; lavender for calm balance and psychic awareness.** In the wax, carve on it: ⅄⚹⅄ **Canis Minor for magic power;** ⚹ **Hasmodai for sensitivity;** ᚺ **as for new awareness and magical energy;** ᛇ **Eoh for a channel and removal of obstacles to communication;** ᚲ **and Ken for opening energy to receive well-being.** Light the working candle from the center altar candle: **This flame burns for enhancing empathy!** Consecrate a piece of moonstone. Use a thin point blue marker: **Blue for psychic understanding!** Draw on a piece of moonstone: ♆ **Neptune for psychic and subconscious awareness! And the** ☽ **Moon for compassion! This moonstone enhances empathy for me!** Set the moonstone on the pentacle. Charge the talisman. With wand or athame, gather energy deosil: **Through the Goddess and the God; through the Moon and the Sun; through the Elementals and stars; with the power of Hasmodai and the energy of Raubiel in Arcaph; this talisman increases compassion and empathy!** Direct and release the energy into the moonstone talisman: **EMPATHY! So Mote It Be!** Leave the talisman on the pentacle for thirty minutes to an hour. Snuff the candle and dispose of the remains. Place, carry, or wear the moonstone talisman as desired.

New Moon Waxing

• **ALGEBH, the Forehead of the Lion** (25♋42 to 8♌34) **ruled by ARDESIEL for love and benevolence, the goodwill of allies, and strengthening buildings**

Light this candle to open the way for drawing the goodwill of others who are important to you or necessary for your advancement in any area.

Magical work: candle for initiating goodwill. Dress a red working candle with rose oil: **Red for energy; rose for attraction and goodwill.** Light the working candle from the center altar candle: **This flame burns to initiate the goodwill of others toward me!** Consecrate a pink votive spell candle and dress with ginger oil: **Pink for goodwill and nurturing sociability; ginger for goodwill and success.** In the wax, carve around it: ⋉▷⫢(**Canis Major for communication!** ⋏⋇⋎ **Canis Minor for magic power!** ᚠ **Eolh for goodwill and friendship!** ᚹ **Wyn for harmony and fulfillment!** ⊞ **Hagith for friendship! Here is goodwill initiated!** Set the spell candle in a cauldron on top of the pentacle. Charge the candle. Light a taper from the working candle and use it to light the spell candle. With the wand or athame, gather energy deosil: **Through the Goddess and the God; through the Moon and the Sun; through the Elementals and stars; with the power of Hagith and the energy of Ardesiel in Algebh; this candle initiates the goodwill of others toward me!** Direct and release the energy into the candle: **GOODWILL! So Mote It Be!** Let the candle burn for thirty minutes to an hour, then snuff it and look at the wax for images indicating the time frame for the results to manifest. Dispose of candle remains.

Full Moon

• **ALGEBH, the Forehead of the Lion** (25♋42 to 8♌34) **ruled by ARDESIEL for love and benevolence, the goodwill of allies, and to strengthen buildings**

Burn this incense to establish the goodwill of your associates to assist in your projects and needs.

Magical work: herbal incense for goodwill of allies. Dress a brown working candle with frankincense oil: **Brown to influence friends and gain special favors; rose to promote peace and goodwill.** In the wax, carve around it: ⊞ **Hagith for friends;** ᛉ **Eolh for friends and help that comes;** ᚲ **Ken to be open to receive;** ᛗ **Mannaz for cooperation and help from others; and** ᚹ **Wyn for success, harmony and well-being.** Light the working candle from the center altar candle: **This flame burns for the goodwill and help of allies!** One at a time, hold up an equal amount of each herb over the pentacle, state the intention, and drop into a mortar with pestle: **I call upon you rose hips for the kindness and help of friends! I call upon you coltsfoot for faithfulness in friends! I call upon you fir to manifest the goodwill and help of friends! I call upon you ginger for success in generating the goodwill and help of friends! And I call upon you woodruff to open the way for allies to express or demonstrate their goodwill toward me!** Grind the herbs together into a powder, bottle it, and set it on the pentacle. Charge the powder. With the wand or athame, gather energy deosil: **Through the Goddess and the God; through the Moon and the Sun; through the Elementals, runes, and herbs; with the power of Hagith and the energy of Ardesiel in Algebh; this incense generates goodwill and the help of friends!** Direct and release the energy into the powder: **SUCCESS THRU GOODWILL! So Mote It Be!** Leave the incense on the pentacle for thirty minutes to an hour. Snuff the candle and dispose of the remains. Burn incense on a charcoal diskette as needed.

LEO

The Moon in ♌ Leo, the Lion, ruled by ☉ Sun, with the energy of success, individuality, power, optimism, vitality, and sociability, and the available energy of one fixed star:

Cor Leonis, the Heart of the Lion (Regulus): Strength, nobility; Jupiter and Mars; Leo; granite; mugwort

in the Mansion of the Moon called:

New Moon Waxing

• **ALGEBH, the Forehead of the Lion** (25♋42 to 8♌34) **ruled by ARDESIEL for love and benevolence, the goodwill of allies, and to strengthen buildings**

When looking for love and kindness, this amulet will help push things into action.

Magical work: amulet for attracting love and benevolence. Dress a pink working candle with rose oil: **Pink for kindness and love; rose for love and affection.** In the wax, carve around it: ⟨ **Ken for opening energy for receiving love;** ↓ **Eoh for dynamic action and channeling love and benevolence;** ⋈ **Daeg for new beginnings in love and kindness;** ✕ **Gefu for attracting love and partnership;** ◊ **and Gera for drawing good rewards and results in love and kindness toward me.** Light the working candle from the center altar candle: **This flame burns for attracting love and benevolence to me!** Consecrate a piece of rose quartz. Hold up the rose quartz over the pentacle, state the intention, and set it in the center of the pentacle: **I call upon you rose quartz to draw love and benevolence to me!** Charge the stone. With the wand or athame, gather energy deosil: **Through the Goddess and the God; through the Moon and the Sun; through the Elementals; through rune and stone and candle flame; with the energy of Ardesiel in Algebh; this stone attracts love and goodwill to me!** Direct and release the energy into the stones: **LOVE FOR ME! So Mote It Be!** Leave the rose quartz on the pentacle for thirty minutes to an hour. Snuff the candle and dispose of the remains. Carry, wear, or place the stone where desired.

Full Moon

• **ALGEBH, the Forehead of the Lion** (25♋42 to 8♌34) **ruled by ARDESIEL for love and benevolence, the goodwill of allies, and to strengthen buildings**

The solar cross is used to give protection and strength to buildings.

Magical work: charm for protective solar cross. Dress a red working candle with rosemary oil: **Red for energy; rosemary for protection.** In the wax, carve around it: ᚦ **Thorn for protection and** ᛗ **Eh for safety.** Light the working candle from the center altar candle: **This flame burns for the protection and strength of a building!** Set out a six-inch long narrow red ribbon to tie the charm: **Red for power!** and / or a black ribbon: **Black for protection!** Lay out two 2-inch long birch twigs and a 1 to 1½-foot-long slim stalk of mugwort: Hold up over the pentacle, state the intention, then set on the pentacle: **I call upon you birch for protection! I call upon you mugwort, herb of the Heart of the Lion, for strength and protection!** Bend and twist the mugwort stalk into a circle, wrapping one end around the other at the top of the loop. Tie the loop with ribbon(s). Place one stick across the back of the herbal loop horizontally, and place the other stick vertically from the upper part of the loop in front, crossing behind the horizontal stick, and coming forward to the bottom part of the loop in front of the circle, thus securing both sticks in place. Set the solar cross craft on the pentacle. Charge the charm. With the wand or athame, raise energy moving deosil: **Through the Goddess and the God; through the Moon and the Sun; through the Elementals, herbs, and runes; with the energy of Ardesiel in Algebh; this charm gives protection and strength!** Direct and release the energy into the charm: **PROTECTION! So Mote It Be!** Leave the charm on the pentacle for thirty minutes to an hour. Snuff the candle and dispose of the remains. Hang the charm indoors or outdoors as desired.

New Moon Waxing

- **AZOBRA, the Mane of the Lion** (8♌34 to 21♌25) **ruled by NECIEL for voyages, retail gains, the release of captives, and reverence**

This money jar can be used to generate sales or other retail gains, as well as to draw money as needed with just a good shaking to stir up the money drawing energies. When not in use, let it sit on a shelf and regenerate its energies.

Magical work: charm for generating money. Dress a green working candle with clove oil: **Green for money; clove for attracting wealth.** In the wax, carve around it: ᚠ **Feoh for increasing wealth;** ᛟ **Ethel for monetary gains;** ᛟ **Osa for good fortune;** ᛗ **Daeg for financial increase;** ᛃ **Gera for tangible results;** ᛗ **Eh for swift changes; and** ᚹ **Wyn for material gains.** Light the working candle from the center altar candle: **This flame burns to generate money!** Set out a glass or pottery jar with lid. Use a green acrylic paint: **Green for money and prosperity!** Paint the jar so the contents cannot be seen. Next, use a brush and gold paint: **Gold for wealth!** On the jar, paint: ᚲ **Ken for opening energy!** ᛉ **Ethel for monetary gains!** ᚠ **Feoh for increasing wealth!** ᛟ **Osa for good fortune!** ᛗ **Daeg for financial increase!** ᛃ **Gera for tangible results!** ᛗ **Eh for swift changes!** ᚹ **Wyn for material gains!** ᛏ **Tyr for victory!** Set the jar on the pentacle. Hold up some of each item over the pentacle, state the intention, and place it in the jar: **I call upon you allspice for prosperity and money! I call upon you chamomile for prosperity! I call upon you cinquefoil for prosperity and good fortune! I call upon you coriander seed for money! I call upon you peridot for prosperity! I call upon you iron pyrite for wealth! I call upon you agate for gaining goals!** On the lid, paint: ⊞ **Bethor for wealth!** ♃ **Jupiter for finances! Sealed with** ⊠ **Netoniel!** Put the lid on the jar and seal around the edge of the lid with wax: **Blended and stored to draw wealth to me whenever I shake it, this jar brings money and prosperity!** Charge the charm on the pentacle. With the wand or athame, raise energy moving deosil: **Through the Goddess and the God; through the Moon and the Sun; through the Elementals, herbs, stones, and runes; with the power of Bethor and Netoniel; with the energy of Neciel in Azobra; this charm gives protection and strength!** Direct and release the energy into the charm: **MONEY FOR ME! So Mote It Be!** Leave the money jar on the pentacle for thirty minutes to an hour. Snuff the candle and dispose of the remains. Shake the bottle whenever needed.

Full Moon

• **AZOBRA, the Mane of the Lion** (8♌34 to 21♌25) **ruled by NECIEL for voyages, retail gains, the release of captives, and reverence**

Use this tea to aid with internal spiritual alignment and communion with the Full Moon in this mansion.

Magical work: tea for spiritual reverence. Dress a purple working candle with frankincense oil: **Purple for spirituality; frankincense for blessing and sacredness.** In the wax, carve around it: ♇ **Pluto for spirituality;** ☽ **the Moon for sensitivity;** ᛞ **Daeg for spiritual awakening;** ᚨ **As for deep awareness;** ᛇ **Eoh to channel energy and communication;** ᛗ **Mannaz for meditation; and** ᛃ **Gera for a good outcome to endeavors.** Light the working candle from the center altar candle: **This flame burns for reverence!** Set on the pentacle a clean bowl in which to blend herbs. Add to the bowl ½ cup of loose black tea leaves. **I call upon you black tea for truth, strength, and protection!** One at a time, hold up over the pentacle ⅛ cup of each herb, state the intention, and add it to the bowl: **I call upon you jasmine for spirituality! I call upon you lemon balm for success!** Blend the herbs and black tea with a wooden spoon. Charge the blend. With the wand or athame, gather energy deosil: **Through the Goddess and the God; through the Moon and the Sun; through the Elementals and planets; through runes and herbs; with the energy of Neciel in Azobra; this tea brings spiritual reverence to whoever drinks it!** Direct and release the energy into the tea: **SPIRITUAL TEA! So Mote It Be!** Leave the tea blend on the pentacle for thirty minutes to an hour. Snuff the candle and dispose of the remains. Put the tea blend in a tightly covered jar and store away from light. Brew a cup of tea when desired, especially before ritual or meditation.

New Moon Waxing

• **ALZARPHA, the Tail of the Lion** (21♌25 to 4♍17) **ruled by ABDIZUEL for a prosperous harvest, starting a building, and improvements for those in service or labor**

This charm utilizes the initiating energy of the lunar phase to encourage beneficial changes for your area of work.

Magical work: charm for improvement in work situation. Dress a red working candle with pine oil: **Red for energy; pine for courage and clear action.** In the wax, carve around it: ↓ **Eoh to open channels for improvement;** ↑ **Uruz to initiate changes;** ᛒ **Beorc for initiating improvements;** ᛗ **Daeg for a breakthrough for betterment;** ᚲ **Ken for opening energy for improvements;** ᛗ **Eh for growth and quick change; with** ⏹ **Cor Leonis, the Heart of the Lion, for courage and strength.** Light the working candle from the center altar candle: **This flame burns to open the way to improvements!** Lay out a six-inch square of dark blue cloth: **Blue for change!** Set out a six-inch long narrow red ribbon to tie the charm bundle (or red thread if sewing it): **Red for power!** One at a time, hold up over the pentacle some of each of the following herbs, state the intention, and place on the cloth: **I call upon you sunflower seeds for a bright prospect and positive changes! I call upon you bergamot for success in bettering my situation! I call upon you allspice for energy in improvements! I call upon you mugwort, herb of the Lion's Heart, for strength and protection for bettering my situation!** Add 3 small drops of pine oil to a cotton ball: **With the power of pine for strength and clear action do I draw these energies together to work my will!** Place on the herbs, tie the bundle with the ribbon (or sew shut) and set it on the pentacle. Charge the charm. With the wand or athame, raise energy moving deosil: **Through the Goddess and the God; through the Moon and the Sun; through the Elementals, herbs, runes, and star; with the energy of Abdizuel in Alzarpha; this charm initiates improvements for my situation!** Direct and release the energy into the charm: **IMPROVEMENT! So Mote It Be!** Leave the charm on the pentacle for thirty minutes to an hour. Snuff the candle and dispose of the remains. Carry or place the charm where desired.

Full Moon

• **ALZARPHA, the Tail of the Lion** (21♌25 to 4♍17) **ruled by ABDIZUEL for a prosperous harvest, starting a building, and improvements for those in service or labor**

   Use this charm for reaping a prosperous harvest or rewarding results in any area.

Magical work: charm for a prosperous harvest. Dress a green working candle with almond oil: **Green for fertility and prosperity; almond for a prosperous harvest.** In the wax, carve around it: ◊ **Gera for a good harvest with tangible results;** ᛗ **Osa for a favorable outcome;** ᚠ **Feoh for fulfillment;** ᚹ **Wyn for success and reward; and** ᛝ **Ing for a satisfactory conclusion;** ♌ **with Leo for success;** ☉ **and the Sun for vitality.** Light the working candle from the center altar candle: **This flame burns for a prosperous harvest!** Lay out a foot of wide orange ribbon: **Orange for success and vitality!** One at a time, hold up over the pentacle each of the following items, state the intention, and set on the pentacle: eight stalks of wheat: **Wheat for fertility, a good harvest, and good fortune!** 6 stalks of rosemary: **Rosemary to protect and bless!** four stalks of fennel: **Fennel for protection of what is gained!** 2 stalks of lavender: **Lavender for peace and creativity!** 9 green or brown feathers: **Bound with the power of three times three, with feathers for prosperity!** Tie the stalks and feathers securely with the ribbon, making a loop for hanging the bundle. A hot glue gun may be used if needed to secure the feathers to the stalks. Lay the bundle on the pentacle. Charge the charm. With the wand or athame, gather energy deosil: **Through the Goddess and the God; through the Moon and the Sun; through the Elementals, planets, and stars; through runes and flame; through herbs and feathers; with the energy of Abdizuel in Alzarpha; this charm brings a prosperous harvest to me!** Direct and release the energy into the charm: **REWARDS! So Mote It Be!** Leave the charm on the pentacle for thirty minutes to an hour. Snuff the candle and dispose of the remains. Hang the charm indoors or outdoors as desired.

VIRGO

The Moon in ♍ Virgo, the Virgin, ruled by ☿ Mercury, with the skillful and agile energy of analysis, service, modesty, and perfectionism

In the Mansion of the Moon called:

New Moon Waxing

• **ALZARPHA, the Tail of the Lion** (21♌25 to 4♍17) **ruled by ABDIZUEL for a prosperous harvest, starting a building, and improvements for those in service or labor**

This talisman instigates improvement for those in service or labor areas of work by enhancing the aura for pay increase, bonus, or advancement of position.

Magical work: talisman for improvements for service or labor. Dress a red working candle with clove oil: **Red for energy; clove for attraction and wealth.** In the wax, carve around it: ᛒ **Beorc for ideas brought to fruition;** ᛜ **Daeg for a breakthrough in transformation for financial increase;** ᛗ **Eh for gaining security in a position;** ᚲ **Ken for opening energy; and** ᛣ **Eolh for gaining aspirations in employment.** Light the working candle from the center altar candle: **This flame burns to initiate improvements for service or labor!** Charge a piece of rhodonite. Set the rhodonite on the pentacle: **Rhodonite for self-esteem, physical energy, self-actualization, and work!** Use a green marker: **Green for a good attitude, employment, and prosperity!** Draw on one side of the rhodonite: ♍ **Virgo for care with the details of work and perfection!** Draw on the other side of the stone: ☿ **Mercury for skill and agility!** Charge the talisman. With wand or athame, gather energy deosil: **Through the Goddess and the God; the Moon and the Sun; through the Elementals, runes, flame, and stone; with the energy of Abdizuel in Alzarpha; this talisman brings betterment for good service or labor!** Direct and release the energy into the talisman: **IMPROVEMENTS! So Mote It Be!** Leave the talisman on the pentacle for thirty minutes to an hour. Snuff the candle and dispose of the remains. Place, carry, or wear the talisman as desired.

Full Moon

• **ALZARPHA, the Tail of the Lion** (21♌25 to 4♍17) **ruled by ABDIZUEL for a prosperous harvest, starting a building, and improvement for those in service or labor**

This candle engages the Virgo energy of analysis for improvements through such forms as evaluations and favorable reports for recognition, pay raise, bonus, promotion, or other work advancements.

Magical work: candle for rewarding service or labor. Dress a yellow working candle with bay oil: **Yellow for mental alertness and employment; bay for clear vision and success.** Light the working candle from the center altar candle: **This flame burns for evaluation of service!** Consecrate an orange votive spell candle and dress with rosemary oil: **Orange for business and work success; rosemary for clarity and vigor.** In the wax, carve around it: ᛚ **Lagu for successful evaluation;** ᛗ **Mannaz for cooperation;** ᚱ **Rad to find what is sought;** ᚺ **Haegl to get results in a timely manner;** ᛝ **Ing for a satisfactory conclusion;** ♍ **Virgo for favorable analysis;** ☿ **Mercury for skill and communication.** Set the spell candle in a cauldron on top of the pentacle. Light a taper from the working candle and use it to light the spell candle. Charge a piece of carnelian. Hold up the stone over the pentacle: **I call upon you carnelian for self-confidence, success, and rewards for my work!** Set it to the left of the candle. Charge a piece of hematite. Hold up the stone over the pentacle: **I call upon you hematite for aid in communication and good evaluation of my work!** Set it to the right of the candle. With the wand or athame, gather energy deosil: **Through the Goddess and the God; through the Moon and the Sun; through the Elementals, runes, oil, and stones; with the energy of Abdizuel in Alzarpha; this candle brings a positive evaluation of my service for reward!** Direct and release the energy into the candle: **WORK REWARDED! So Mote It Be!** Let the candle burn for thirty minutes to an hour, then snuff and look at the wax for images indicating the time frame for the results to manifest. Take the stones and place, carry, or wear as desired. Dispose of candle remains.

New Moon Waxing

- **ALHAIRE, the Wings of Virgo** (21♌25 to 4♍17) **ruled by JAZERIEL for increase in trade and harvests, liberation of captives, agreement in marriage, restoration of potency, gain, clever financial dealings, voyages**

   Burn this incense to clear the air and bring peace and harmony into a marriage.

Magical work: incense for agreement in marriage. Dress a white working candle with rose oil: **White for peace and protection; rose to promote peace and goodwill.** In the wax, carve around it: ☽ **the Moon for sensitivity and harmony in the home;** ☿ **Mercury for communication;** ♀ **Venus for loving sociability;** ⟨ **Ken for receptivity;** ᛗ **Mannaz for cooperation;** ᚹ **Wyn for harmony; and** ⊞ **Hagith for love and stability.** Light the working candle from the center altar candle: **This flame burns for a loving, peaceful home!** One at a time, hold up an equal amount of each herb over the pentacle, state the intention, and drop into a mortar with pestle: **I call upon you rose hips for kindness and love! I call upon you fennel for protection of the marriage! I call upon you lavender for peace in the home! I call upon you rosemary for love and blessing in the home!** Grind the herbs together into a powder, bottle it, and set it on the pentacle. Charge the powder. With the wand or athame, gather energy deosil: **Through the Goddess and the God; through the Moon and the Sun; through the Elementals and planets; through runes, and herbs; with the power of Hagith and the energy of Jazeriel in Alhaire; this powdered incense prompts love and agreement in marriage!** Direct and release the energy into the powder: **MARITAL ACCORD! So Mote It Be!** Leave the incense on the pentacle for thirty minutes to an hour. Snuff the candle and dispose of the remains. Burn the incense on a charcoal diskette as needed.

Full Moon

- **ALHAIRE, the Wings of Virgo** (4♍17 to 17♍8) **ruled by JAZERIEL for increase in trade and harvests, liberation of captives, agreement in marriage, restoration of strength and power**

This powder may be sprinkled in a cash drawer or around a business area to increase trade and good results.

Magical work: powder for increasing in trade and harvest. Dress a green working candle with clove oil: **Green for fertility and prosperity; clove for attracting success and wealth.** In the wax, carve around it: **ᛄ Gera for an increase in rewards and tangible results for efforts; ᚹ Wyn to increase success and well-being; ᛞ Daeg for financial increase; ᛋ Sigel for energy and achievement; ᛈ Perth for gain from investments; ᛒ Beorc for growth; ᚩ Osa for a favorable outcome.** Light the working candle from the center altar candle: **This flame burns to increase trade, harvests, and business!** One at a time, hold up an equal amount of each herb over the pentacle, state the intention, and drop into a mortar with pestle: **I call upon you bergamot to bring increase in success and prosperity! I call upon you cinnamon for a successful increase in business and a good harvest! I call upon you mint for a prosperous increase in business!** Grind the herbs together into a powder, bottle it, and set the powder on the pentacle. Charge the powder. With the wand or athame, gather energy deosil: **Through the Goddess and the God; through the Moon and the Sun; through the Elementals, runes and herbs; with the energy of Jazeriel in Alhaire; this powder increases trade, harvests, and business!** Direct and release the energy into the powder: **INCREASE! So Mote It Be!** Leave the powder on the pentacle for thirty minutes to an hour. Snuff the candle and dispose of the remains. Sprinkle the powder where desired, add to a charm, blend with oils, or burn as incense.

New Moon Waxing

• **AZIMETH, the Flying Spike** (17♍8 to 0♎0) **ruled by ERGEDIEL for marital love, curing the sick, and profitable sailing**

Burn this candle to enhance healing energies in the early autumn months when the changing seasons may bring illness.

Magical work: candle for healing energies. Dress a red working candle with frankincense oil: **Red for power and energy; frankincense cleansing and protection.** In the wax, carve around it: ᛚ **Lagu for vitality and good health;** ᚠ **Feoh for energy and good health;** ᚲ **Ken for opening healing energy.** Light the working candle from the center altar candle: **This flame burns to promote healing energy!** Consecrate a light blue votive spell candle and dress with rosemary oil: **Blue for health; rosemary for invigoration and health.** In the wax, carve around it: **With the energies of** (your sun sign symbol) **and** (the ruling planet) **to represent me!** ᛋ **Sigel for strength, wholeness, healing, and vital energy!** ᚢ **Uruz for strength and physical health!** ᚹ **Wyn for well-being!** ᛟ **Osa for a favorable outcome!** Set the spell candle in a cauldron on top of the pentacle. Charge the candle. Light a taper from the working candle and use it to light the spell candle. With the wand or athame, gather energy deosil: **Through the Goddess and the God; through the Moon and the Sun; through the Elementals and planets; through rune and flame; with the energy of Ergediel in Azimeth; this candle enhances healing energies for me!** Direct and release the energy into the candle: **HEALTHY ME! So Mote It Be!** Let the candle burn for thirty minutes to an hour, then snuff and look at the wax for images indicating the time frame for the results to manifest. Dispose of candle remains.

Full Moon

• **AZIMETH, the Flying Spike (17♍8 to 0♎0) ruled by ERGEDIEL for marital love, curing the sick, and profitable sailing and travels**

This oil may be worn or dabbed on the marital bed to enhance romance and love in the marriage.

Magical work: oil for marital love. Dress a red working candle with jasmine oil: **Red for vitality and sexuality; jasmine for love.** In the wax, carve around it: X **Gefu for partnership and love;** ⟨ **Ken for love and stability;** ♦ **Eoh for a channel to good communication;** M **Mannaz for cooperation;** ⋏ **Ethel for the home;** ℬ **Beorc for the family;** ℞ **Osa for a favorable outcome.** Light the working candle from the center altar candle: **This flame burns for marital love!** In a small glass bottle with lid, blend the following essential oils: 4 parts rosemary: **I call upon you rosemary for blessings in marital love!** 1 part vetiver: **I call upon you vetiver to enhance marital love!** 3 parts ginger: **I call upon you ginger to strengthen marital love!** ½ part orange: **I call upon you orange to add good fortune to marital love!** Add 2 parts grapeseed, saffron, or canola oil. Put the lid on the bottle, shake: **All are blended to work together for marital love!** Use a red marker: **Red for passion!** Draw on the bottle: ⊟ **Hagith for love!** ⊞ **Phaleg for passion!** ☽ **The Moon for home and marital love.** Place the bottle on the pentacle and charge the oil. With the wand or athame, gather energy deosil: **Through the Goddess and the God, the Moon and the Sun; through the Elementals, planets, and stars; through runes and herbal oils; with the power of Hagith and Phaleg; with the energy of Ergediel in Azimeth; this oil enhances marital love!** Direct and release the energy into the bottle: **LOVING MARRIAGE! So Mote It Be!** Leave the oil on the pentacle for thirty minutes to an hour. Snuff the candle and dispose of the remains. Use a dab of oil as desired.

LIBRA

The Moon in ♎ Libra, the Scale, ruled by ♀ Venus, with the energy of affection, harmony, balance, and uncertainty, and the available energy of three fixed stars:

Ala Corvi, the Wing of the Crow (Gienah): Strength of will, induce sleep, create hostility, bind another's magic; Saturn and Mars; Libra; onyx; burdock root

Spica, the Ear of Grain: Resolve disputes, bind enemies, protect from danger, enhance telepathy, reap abundance; Venus and Mercury; Libra; emerald; sage

Alchameth (Arcturus): Good health, heal wounds and fever; Mars and Jupiter; Libra; jasper; snakeweed (common plantain)

In the Mansion of the Moon called:

New Moon Waxing

• **AGRAPHA, Covered or Covered Flying (0♎0 to 12♎51) ruled by ACHALIEL for extracting treasure, using or promoting new opportunities through goodwill or friendship**

This is especially good to use when cultivating the help of others for opening a new opportunity, advancement, or beneficial transfer in work or career.

Magical work: oil for promoting new opportunities through goodwill. Dress a red working candle with rose oil: **Red for energy and enthusiasm; rose for attraction and cooperation.** In the wax, carve around it: ᛗ **Mannaz for cooperation;** ᚨ **As for convincing speech and communication;** ᚲ **Ken for receptivity;** ᚦ **Thorn for protection; and** ᛟ **Osa for a favorable outcome.** Carve by the wick: **With Spica to reap abundance;** ♀ **with Venus for sociability and friendship; and with** ☿ **Mercury for communication, is goodwill initiated to promote new opportunities for me.** Light the working candle from the center altar candle: **This flame burns to promote new opportunities through goodwill toward me!** In a small glass bottle with lid, blend the following essential oils: 4 parts bay: **I call upon you bay to attain my desires!** 3 parts clove: **I call upon you clove to attract what I seek!** 1 part rose: **I call upon you rose for harmony and cooperation!** ½ part ginger: **I call upon you ginger for success in gaining opportunities through goodwill toward me!** Add 2 parts grapeseed, saffron, or canola oil. Put the lid on the bottle, shake: **All are blended to work together to promote goodwill toward me!** With a red marker or ink: **Red for energy!** Draw on the bottle the symbol of your sun sign and ruling planet: **With** (sun sign) **and** (ruling planet) **is goodwill initiated toward me for new opportunities!** Set the bottle on the pentacle. Charge the oil. With the wand or athame, gather energy deosil: **Through the Goddess and the God, the Moon and the Sun; through the Elementals, planets, and stars; through runes and herbal oils; with the energy of Achaliel in Agrapha; this oil promotes new opportunities through goodwill toward me!** Direct and release the energy into the bottle: **GOODWILL! So Mote It Be!** Leave the oil on the pentacle for thirty minutes to an hour. Snuff the candle and dispose of the remains. Use a dab of oil as needed.

Full Moon

- **AGRAPHA, Covered or Covered Flying** (0♎0 to 12♎51) **ruled by ACHALIEL for extracting treasure, promoting and using new opportunities through goodwill or friendship**

Use this amulet to open the door to a new opportunity for success in any area.

Magical work: amulet for using new opportunities. Dress a light blue working candle with bergamot oil: **Light blue for opportunities; bergamot oil for success in using new opportunities.** In the wax, carve around it: ᚲ **Ken for opening energy;** ♃ **Jupiter for opportunity;** ♄ **Saturn for ambition;** ☿ **Mercury for agility and skillful communication;** ᛃ **Gera for tangible results from efforts;** ᚢ **Uruz for changes from new situations;** ♎ **Libra for balance and harmony;** [Bethor sigil] **Bethor for success, honors, and wealth;** ᚠ **Feoh for ambition satisfied; and** ᚹ **Wyn for material gain and well-being.** Light the working candle from the center altar candle: **This flame burns to aid me in the successful use of new opportunities!** Take a large, clean, dry tonka bean and set it on the pentacle: **I call upon you tonka bean to aid me in the successful use of new opportunities!** Charge the tonka bean. With the wand or athame, gather energy deosil: **Through the Goddess and the God; through the Moon and the Sun; through the Elementals, planets, and stars; through runes, herb, and candle flame; with the power of Bethor and the energy of Achaliel in Agrapha; this amulet aids me to suc-**

cessfully use new opportunities! Direct and release the energy into the tonka bean: **SUCCESS! So Mote It Be!** Leave the tonka bean on the pentacle for thirty minutes to an hour. Snuff the candle and dispose of the remains. Carry or place the tonka bean where desired.

New Moon Waxing

• **AZUBENE, the Horns of Scorpio** (12♎51 to 25♎42) **ruled by AZERUEL for liberation, universal friendship, opportunities, and increasing possessions**

This is a good talisman for opportunities, whether seeking work, advancement, or any type of beneficial occasion.

Magical work: talisman to initiate opportunities. Dress a red working candle with dragon's blood oil: **Red for energy; dragon's blood for power and to initiate change.** In the wax, carve around it: **〈 Ken for opening energy; ⌁ Eoh for dynamic action to remove obstacles and open a path; ᛗ Daeg to initiate a fresh start; ᚹ Wyn for success and gains; and ↑ Tyr for victory, success, and a favorable outcome.** Light the working candle from the center altar candle: **This flame burns to initiate opportunities for me!** On a piece of parchment or paper no more than 3 inches square, use blue ink: **Blue to open opportunities!** to draw a double ring circle: in the center of the circle, draw: ⊗ **With Netoniel for opportunity!** In the ring around the circle, write: **NETONIEL · JOHPHIEL · AZERUEL ·** (your sun sign symbol) · (your ruling planet symbol) · On the back of the paper, draw:

4	14	15	1
9	7	6	12
5	11	10	8
16	2	3	13

34

With the Square of Jupiter! Across the center of the square draw: ⇌ **With Johphiel are opportunities initiated for me!** Turn the talisman face up. Charge the talisman. With wand or athame, gather energy deosil: **Through the Goddess and the God; the Moon and the Sun; through the Elementals and the runes; with the power of Netoniel and Johphiel and the energy of Azeruel in Azubene; this talisman initiates opportunities for me!** Direct and release the energy into the talisman: **OPPORTUNITIES! So Mote It Be!** Leave the talisman on the pentacle for thirty minutes to an hour. Snuff the candle and dispose of the remains. Place, carry, or wear the talisman in a locket as desired.

Full Moon

- **AZUBENE, the Horns of Scorpio** (12♎51 to 25♎42) **ruled by AZERUEL for liberation, opportunities, increasing possessions, and universal friendship**

The sign adds balancing energy to this charm for universal friendship so that the friendship is calm, equitable, and genuine.

Magical work: charm for universal friendship. Dress a pink working candle with lavender oil: **Pink for friendship and loving emotions; lavender for balance and affection.** In the wax, carve around it: **ᚷ Gefu for partnership and equilibrium while yet retaining individuality; ᚲ Ken for opening energy to affection and stability; ᚨ As for communication in friendship; ᛉ Eolh to promote friendship; and ᚹ Wyn for harmony in friendship.** Light the working candle from the center altar candle: **This flame burns for balance in friendship!** Lay out a six-inch square of pink cloth: **Pink for nurturing friendship!** Set out a six-inch long narrow white ribbon to tie the charm bundle (or thread if sewing it): **White for peace and sincerity!** One at a time, hold up over the pentacle some of each of the following herbs, state the intention, then place on the cloth: **I call upon you lavender for balance and calm! I call upon you chamomile for balance and affection! I call upon you basil for optimism and joy! I call upon you orris root for good companionship!** Add two small drops of vetiver oil to a cotton ball: **With the power of vetiver are these energies drawn together for balanced universal friendship!** Set the cotton ball on top of the herbs. Gather and tie the bundle with the ribbon(s) (or sew shut) and set it on the pentacle. Charge the charm. With the wand or athame, raise energy moving deosil: **Through the Goddess and the God; through the Moon and the Sun; through the Elementals, herbs and runes; with the energy of Azeruel in Azubene; this charm brings universal friendship!** Direct and release the energy into the charm: **FRIENDSHIP! So Mote It Be!** Leave the charm on the pentacle for thirty minutes to an hour. Snuff the candle and dispose of the remains. Carry or place the charm where desired.

New Moon Waxing

• **ALCHIL, the Crown of Scorpio** (25♎42 to 8♏34) **ruled by ADRIEL for strengthening love, strengthening buildings, improving fortune, and helping sailors**

This charm draws helpful energies together to initiate improvements in any area of your life that you choose for its focus.

Magical work: charm for improving fortune. Dress a red working candle with dragon's blood oil: **Red for energy; dragon's blood for power and protection.** In the wax, carve around it: ☉ **The Sun for success;** ☿ **Mercury for skill and communication;** ♃⚳ **Spica for reaping abundance;** ♃ **Jupiter for opportunity and expansion; and** ↑ **Tyr for victory and a favorable outcome.** Light the working candle from the center altar candle: **This flame burns for improving fortune!** Lay out a six-inch square of orange cloth: **Orange for attracting success and achieving objectives!** Set out a six-inch long narrow red ribbon to tie the charm bundle (or thread if sewing it): **Red for power and enthusiasm!** One at a time, hold up over the pentacle some of each of the following herbs, state the intention, then place on the cloth: **I call upon you bay for success, improving fortune, and attaining my desire! I call upon you clove for attracting good fortune! I call upon you ginger for success and attainment of improving fortune!** Tie the bundle with the ribbon (or sew shut) and set it on the pentacle. Charge the charm. With the wand or athame, raise energy moving deosil: **Through the Goddess and the God; through the Moon and the Sun; through the Elementals, planets and star; through runes and herbs; with the energy of Adriel in Alchil; this charm improves my fortune!** Direct and release the energy into the charm: **IMPROVEMENT! So Mote It Be!** Leave the charm on the pentacle for thirty minutes to an hour. Snuff the candle and dispose of the remains. Carry or place the charm where desired.

Full Moon

• **ALCHIL, the Crown of Scorpio** (25♎42 to 8♏34) **ruled by ADRIEL for strengthening love, strengthening buildings, improving fortune, and helping sailors**

   Burn this incense to strengthen your ability to give and receive love and affection.

Magical work: incense for love and harmony. Dress a pink working candle with ginger oil: **Pink for nurture and affection; ginger for love and success.** In the wax, carve around it: ♀ **Venus for love and sociability;** ♎ **Libra for balance and harmony;** ᛗ **Mannaz for cooperation;** ᚷ **Gefu for love and partnership;** ᚲ **Ken for affection and stability; and** ᚹ **Wyn for harmony and love.** Light the working candle from the center altar candle: **This flame burns for affection and harmony!** One at a time, hold up an equal amount of each herb over the pentacle, state the intention, and drop into a mortar with pestle: **I call upon you rose hips for harmony and love! I call upon you lavender for calm and affection! I call upon you rosemary for happiness and love! I call upon you yarrow for happiness and love! And I call upon you vetiver for unifying energy for love and harmony!** Grind the herbs together into a powder, bottle it, and set it on the pentacle. Charge the powder. With the wand or athame, gather energy deosil: **Through the Goddess and the God; through the Moon and the Sun; through the Elementals and planets; through runes, and herbs; with the energy of Adriel in Alchil; this incense strengthens love and harmony!** Direct and release the energy into the powder: **LOVING ME! So Mote It Be!** Leave the incense on the pentacle for thirty minutes to an hour. Snuff the candle and dispose of the remains. Burn the incense on a charcoal diskette.

SCORPIO

The Moon in ♏ Scorpio, the Scorpion, ruled by ♇ Pluto, with the guarded energy of order, transformation, passion, and the available energy of one fixed star:

Alphecca Lucida Corone (Elpheia): love and honor, restoration of purity; Venus and Mars; Scorpio; topaz; rosemary

In the Mansion of the Moon called:

New Moon Waxing

• **ALCHIL, the Crown of Scorpio** (25♎42 to 8♏34) **ruled by ADRIEL for strengthening love, strengthening buildings, improving fortune, and helping sailors**

Burn this candle to increase the strength of your love.

Magical work: candle for strengthening love. Dress a red working candle with ginger oil: **Red for energy and passion; ginger for love and power.** In the wax, carve around it: **ᛈ Wyn for love, joy, and harmony; ᚷ Gefu for loving partnership and union; ↑ Tyr for victory; ᛃ Gera for a good outcome from endeavors; and ᚲ Ken for love and stability.** Light the working candle from the center altar candle: **This flame burns to strengthen love!** Consecrate a pink votive spell candle and dress with rosemary oil: **Pink for caring, love, and partnership; rosemary for strength and love.** In the wax, carve around it: **Elpheia for love and honor! ♀ Venus for love! ♂ Mars for energy and passion! ☉ The Sun for happiness and energy! ☽ The Moon for sensitivity!** Set the spell candle in a cauldron on top of the pentacle. Charge the candle. Light a taper from the working candle and use it to light the spell candle: **This candle burns for strengthening love!** With the wand or athame, gather energy deosil: **Through the Goddess and the God; through the Moon and the Sun; through the Elementals, planets, and stars; through rune and herbs; with the energy of Adriel in Alchil; this candle strengthens love!** Direct and release the energy into the candle: **LOVE IS STRONG! So Mote It Be!** Let the candle burn for thirty minutes to an hour, then snuff and look at the wax for images indicating the time frame for the results to manifest. Dispose of candle remains.

Full Moon

- **ALCHIL, the Crown of Scorpio** (25♎42 to 8♏34) **ruled by ADRIEL for strengthening love, strengthening buildings, improving fortune, and helping sailors**

  Burn this candle to realize improved fortune in any area of your life you choose.

Magical work: candle to improve fortune. Dress a red working candle with bergamot oil: **Red for energy and power; bergamot for success and good fortune.** In the wax, carve around it: ᚲ **Ken for transforming energy and well-being;** ᛋ **Sigel for energy, success, and achievement;** ᛞ **Daeg for transformation and increase of fortune;** ᚠ **Feoh for energy and fulfillment; and** ᛏ **Tyr for victory and a favorable outcome.** Light the working candle from the center altar candle: **This flame burns to improve fortune!** Consecrate an orange votive spell candle and dress with dragon's blood oil: **Orange for vitality and success; dragon's blood for power.** In the wax, carve around it: ♏ **Scorpio for transformative energy!** ♇ **Pluto for evolution!** ☉ **The Sun for energy and success! With Phul for transformation! And Bethor for Fortune!** Charge the candle and set it in a cauldron on top of the pentacle. Light a taper from the working candle and use it to light the spell candle. With the wand or athame, gather energy deosil: **Through the Goddess and the God; through the Moon and the Sun; through the Elementals, planets, stars and runes; with the power of Phul and Bethor; and with the energy of Adriel in Alchil; this candle brings into fruition improved fortune!** Direct and release the energy into the candle: **FORTUNATE ME! So Mote It Be!** Let the candle burn for thirty minutes to an hour, then snuff and look at the wax for images indicating the time frame for the results to manifest. Dispose of candle remains.

New Moon Waxing

• **ALCAB, the Heart of Scorpio** (8♏34 to 21♏25) **ruled by EGRIBIEL for victory over enemies, strengthening buildings, freedom, and healing fevers and stomach pain**

Sprinkle this water onto buildings and structures you seek to strengthen against structural damage caused by storms and other acts of nature.

Magical work: water for strengthening a building and protecting it from damage. Dress a black working candle with dragon's blood oil: **Black for a binding protection; dragon's blood for strength and power.** In the wax, carve around it: **♄ Saturn for structures; ᚦ Thorn for protection and safety; ᚢ Uruz for strength; ᚯ Ethel for protection of structures and possessions; ᛋ and Sigel for success, wholeness, and victory.** Light the working candle from the center altar candle: **This flame burns to strengthen a building against damage!** Charge 2 cups of spring water in a jar with a lid. Hold up over the pentacle a leafy sprig of rue (some people have an allergic skin reaction to rue, so use disposable gloves if sensitive): **I call upon you rue, herb of the Craft and bountiful protection, to strengthen buildings and structures against all harm!** Place the rue plant in the water. Hold up over the pentacle rue oil: **I call upon you rue oil to increase the strength and protection of buildings and structures!** Add 9 drops of rue oil to the bottle. Put the lid on the bottle, shake: **Water, herb, and oil blend to strengthen and protect buildings and structures!** Place the bottle on the pentacle. Charge the oil. With the wand or athame, gather energy deosil: **Through the Goddess and the God, the Moon and the Sun; through the Elementals, planets, and stars; through runes, water, herb, and oil; with the energy of Egribiel in Alcab; this water strengthens and protects buildings and structures!** Direct and release the energy into the bottle: **STRONG AND SAFE! So Mote It Be!** Leave the bottle on the pentacle for thirty minutes to an hour. Snuff the candle and dispose of the remains. Store away from light and sprinkle or squirt the water on buildings, trees, fences, and other property to protect from storm damages.

Full Moon

- **ALCAB, the Heart of Scorpio** (8♏34 to 21♏25) **ruled by EGRIBIEL for victory over enemies, strengthening buildings, freedom, and healing fevers and stomach pain**

  Take a warm bath with these bath salts for gentle healing energy.

Magical work: bath salt for good health and healing energy. Dress a yellow working candle with rosemary oil: **Yellow for good health; rosemary for health and protection.** In the wax, carve around it: ♃ **Jupiter for good health;** ⊣⊢ **Och for healing energy;** ⟨ **Ken for physical well-being;** ⚡ **Sigel for healing energy; and** ᚢ **Uruz for physical health.** Light the working candle from the center altar candle: **This flame burns for good health!** Set on the pentacle a clean non-plastic or metal bowl in which to blend the bath salt. Add to the bowl 2 cups of sea salt: **I call upon you salt of the sea for healing strength!** Hold up over the pentacle 1 teaspoon of rosemary leaf: **I call upon you rosemary for healthy energy!** Add the rosemary to a mortar, grind to a powder with the pestle, and add to the sea salt. Hold up over the pentacle ¼ teaspoon of rosemary oil: **I call upon the energy of rosemary to infuse this salt with healing energy!** Add the oil to the salt and stir together until the salt, powder, and oil are well blended. Charge the bath salt. With the wand or athame, gather energy deosil: **Through the Goddess and the God; through the Moon and the Sun; through the Elementals and planet; through runes, herbs, and the sea; with the power of Och and the energy of Egribiel in Alcab; this bath salt brings healing energy!** Direct and release the energy into the salts: **HEALING ENERGY! So Mote It Be!** Leave the bath salts on the pentacle for thirty minutes to an hour. Snuff the candle and dispose of the remains. Store salts in a tightly covered jar away from light. Add to tub as water is running or rub on in the shower.

New Moon Waxing

- **AXAULAH, the Tail of Scorpio** (21♏25 to 4♐17) **ruled by ANUCIEL for military gains, capturing fugitives, easing birth, and starting the menses**

    This talisman is good for people in military service to achieve their goals.

Magical work: talisman for initiating military gains. Dress a red working candle with dragon's blood oil: **Red for energy; dragon's blood for power and strength.** In the wax, carve around it: ♂ **Mars for dynamic energy;** ♄ **Saturn for military structure and protection;** ⟨ **Ken for opening energy;** ᛝ **Ing for the potential to achieve the goals set; and** ᛋ **Sigel for the energy and will to gain success.** Light the working candle from the center altar candle: **This flame burns for initiating military gains!** Hold over the pentacle a piece of carnelian: **Carnelian for fast action, protection, and success!** Use a red marker or paint: **Red for power and energy!** Draw on the carnelian: ⟨⟨ᛏ⟩⟩ **Phaleg for valor and victory!** On the reverse side of the stone, draw: ⟨⟩ **Ithuriel for military gains!** Charge the talisman. With wand or athame, gather energy deosil: **Through the Goddess and the God; the Moon and the Sun; through the Elementals and the runes; with the power of Phaleg and Ithuriel; with the energy of Anunciel in Axaulah; this talisman initiates military achievement!** Direct and release the energy into the talisman: **GAINS! So Mote It Be!** Leave the talisman on the pentacle for thirty minutes to an hour. Snuff the candle and dispose of the remains. Place, carry, or wear the talisman as desired.

Full Moon

- **AXAULAH, the Tail of Scorpio (21♏25 to 4♐17) ruled by ANUCIEL for military gains, capturing fugitives, easing birth, and starting the menses**

    Light this candle to help bring a criminal fugitive into custody and thereby protect society at large.

Magical work: candle spell for capturing a criminal. Dress a red working candle with dragon's blood oil: **Red for courage and action; dragon's blood for power.** In the wax, carve around it: ᚺ **Haegl to limit the criminal fugitive's movement;** ᛁ **Is to bring inertia to the criminal;** ᚾ **Nyd to constrain the criminal;** ᛗ **Daeg for a breakthrough in capturing the criminal fugitive;** ᚱ **Rad to find the fugitive that is sought;** ᛡ **Gera for rewarding results in capturing the criminal;** ᛝ **Ing to hold the fugitive in a successful capture.** Light the working candle from the center altar candle: **This flame burns for the capture of a criminal fugitive!** Consecrate a black votive spell candle and dress with bay oil: **Black to bind the movements of a criminal, and bay for justice.** In the wax, carve around it: ⊞ **Aratron for knowing where the criminal hides!** ♏ **Scorpio for order!** ♇ **Pluto for transformation!** ♄ **Saturn for institutions and restrictions!** ♂ **Mars to gain what is sought!** ↑ **Tyr for victory!** ⚡ **Sigel for successful capture!** Charge the candle and set it in a cauldron on top of the pentacle. Light a taper from the working candle and use it to light the spell candle. One at a time, hold up a bit of each herb over the pentacle, state the intention, and add it to the flame: **I call upon you bergamot for justice and success! I call upon you bay for justice and success! I call upon you lemon balm for justice and success! I call upon you thyme for swift action! I call upon you basil to thwart negative forces!** With the wand or athame, gather energy deosil: **Through the Goddess and the God; through the Moon and the Sun; through the Elementals and planets; through runes and herbs; with the power of Aratron and with the energy of Anunciel in Axaulah; this candle brings a criminal fugitive to justice!** Direct and release the energy into the candle: **CAPTURED! So Mote It Be!** Let the candle burn for thirty minutes to an hour, then snuff and look at the wax for images indicating the time frame for the results to manifest. Dispose of candle remains.

SAGITTARIUS

The Moon in ♐ Sagittarius, the Centaur, ruled by ♃ Jupiter, with the jovial energy of idealism, independence, education, opportunity, and expansion, and the available energy of one fixed star:

Cor Scorpini, the Heart of the Scorpion (Antares): Aid memory, restore good health, defense, protection; Venus and Jupiter; Sagittarius; sardonyx; birthwort (snakeroot or Aristolochia)

In the Mansion of the Moon called:

New Moon Waxing

• **AXAULAH, the Tail of Scorpio** (21 ♏ 25 to 4 ♐ 17) **ruled by ANUCIEL for military gains, capturing fugitives, easing birth, and starting the menses**

Use this amulet for an easy delivery at birth.

Magical work: amulet for easing birth. Dress a light blue working candle with jasmine oil: **Light Blue for tranquility and health; jasmine oil for health and love.** In the wax, carve around it: ᛒ **Beorc for family and a gentle new beginning brought to fruition;** ᚲ **Ken for opening energy;** ᛚ **Lagu for vitality of the life-force of the mother;** ᚱ **Rad for the safe journey of the child; and** ᛃ **Gera for a good outcome and the tangible results from the pregnancy.** Light the working candle from the center altar candle: **This flame burns to ease birth and restore good health!** Hold up over the pentacle a clean, wooden (or plastic) egg: **Egg for creation and birth!** With yellow acrylic: **Yellow for good health!** Paint the egg (or use a yellow plastic egg). Let it dry, and with blue paint or marker: **Blue for good health!** draw: **Cor Scorpini to restore good health!** Tie a red string around the egg: **This is the birthing;** loosen the string and slip it off: **This is the ease of delivery.** Place the string and the egg together and wrap in white cloth: **White for purity and protection!** Set the wrapped egg and string on the pentacle: **Mother and child, how they beguile! With ease comes the babe with mother to lay!** Charge the bundle. With the wand or athame, gather energy deosil: **Through the Goddess and the God; through the Moon and the Sun; through the Elementals, planets, and stars; through runes and herbs; with the energy of Anunciel in Axaulah; this amulet brings an ease of birth!** Direct and release the energy into the bundle: **EASY BIRTH! So Mote It Be!** Leave the bundle on the pentacle for thirty minutes to an hour. Snuff the candle and dispose of the remains. Place the wrapped egg and string in a safe place. After delivery, open the bundle and place the egg and string in a tree to release the energies to the wind; give the cloth to the mother as a keepsake.

Full Moon

• **AXAULAH, the Tail of Scorpio (21 ♏ 25 to 4 ♐ 17) ruled by ANUCIEL for military gains, capturing fugitives, easing birth, and starting the menses**

Light this candle six weeks after a birthing to bring the mother's body back into a natural rhythm.

Magical work: candle for starting the menses. Dress a red working candle with cedar oil: **Red for energy; cedar for cleansing and strength.** In the wax, carve around it: ᛒ **Beorc for motherhood and gentle new beginnings;** ᚷ **Gefu for loving energy;** ᛃ **Gera for a good outcome to endeavors;** ᚲ **Ken for healing energy and physical well-being; and** ᚹ **Wyn for harmony, love, and joy!** Light the working candle from the center altar candle: **This flame burns for restoring the natural rhythm after giving birth!** Consecrate a yellow votive spell candle and dress with cypress oil: **Yellow for good health; cypress for calm and stability.** In the wax carve around it: ᛉ **Eolh for strengthening the life-force!** ᚢ **Uruz for strength and physical well-being!** ᛏ **Tyr for quick recuperation!** At the top of the candle by the wick carve: ᛏᛁᛏ **With Cor Scorpii, the Heart of the Scorpion, to restore natural health!** Set the spell candle in a cauldron on top of the pentacle. Light a taper from the working candle and use it to light the spell candle. Charge a piece of sardonyx and drop it into the candle: **I call upon you sardonyx, stone of Cor Scorpii, for purification, strength, and removal of any obstacle to restoring natural good health!** Charge the candle. With the wand or athame, gather energy deosil: **Through the Goddess and the God; through the Moon and the Sun; through the Elementals and star; through runes, herbs, and stone; with the energy of Anunciel in Axaulah; this candle restores the natural rhythm!** Direct and release the energy into the candle: **RESTORED! So Mote It Be!** Let the candle burn for thirty minutes to an hour, then snuff and look at the wax for images indicating the time frame for the results to manifest. Remove the sardonyx and clean it to place, carry, or wear as desired. Dispose of candle remains.

New Moon Waxing

• **ABNAHAYA, the Beam (4♐17 to 17♐8) ruled by KYHIEL for taming animals, hunting, compelling one to a place, and fortifying bondages**

This charm will aid with communication to make it easier to work with animals.

Magical work: charm for communicating with animals. Dress a brown working candle with sandalwood oil: **Brown for the Earth and for animals; sandalwood to open psychic awareness and honor the spirits of nature.** In the wax, carve around it: ᛟ **Osa for the God and a favorable outcome;** ᛒ **Beorc for the Goddess and fruition;** ᛗ **Eh for telepathic communication;** ᛇ **Eoh for a channel of communication;** ᚨ **As for communication, new awareness, and magical power;** ☿ **with Mercury for skilled communication; and** ♆ **Neptune for psychic awareness.** Light the working candle from the center altar candle: **This flame burns to enhance communication with animals!** Lay out a six-inch square of green cloth: **Green for the deities of nature, Elemental Earth, and the animals of nature!** Set out a six-inch long narrow yellow ribbon to tie the charm bundle (or thread if sewing it): **Yellow for intuitive insight and communication!** One at a time, hold up over the pentacle some of each of the following herbs, state the intention, then place on the cloth: **I call upon you woodruff, Master of the Woods, to remove barriers and to enhance communication with animals! I call upon you elderflower for the blessing of the spirits of nature! I call upon you orris root to enhance communication! I call upon you rose for gentle psychic awareness!** Hold up over the pentacle a piece of turquoise: **I call upon you turquoise to actualize intuitive communication with animals!** Put it on top of the herbs. Tie the bundle with the ribbon (or sew shut) and set it on the pentacle. Charge the charm. With the wand or athame, raise energy moving deosil: **Through the Goddess and the God, through the Moon and the Sun, through the Elementals and the planets; through runes, herbs, and stone; with the energy of Kyhiel in Abnahaya; this charm opens communication with animals!** Direct and release the energy into the charm: **COMMUNICATION! So Mote It Be!** Leave the charm on the pentacle for thirty minutes to an hour. Snuff the candle and dispose of the remains. Carry or place the charm where desired.

Full Moon

- **ABNAHAYA, the Beam** (4♐17 to 17♐8) **ruled by KYHIEL for taming animals, hunting, compelling one to a place, and fortifying bondages**

This charm is mainly for hunters to bring home game meat, but can be focused on any hunt, such as for a new job, home, partner, etc.

Magical work: charm for a good hunt. Dress a red working candle with dragon's blood oil: **Red for energy, strength, and vigor; dragon's blood for power and energy.** In the wax, carve around it: ᛟ **Osa for a favorable outcome;** ᛒ **Beorc for endeavors coming to fruition;** ᛖ **Eh for safe journey;** ᛃ **Gera for tangible results from efforts;** ᛜ **Ing to achieve objectives;** ᛊ **Sigel for success and achievement; and** ᛏ **Tyr for victory and action with a favorable outcome.** Light the working candle from the center altar candle: **This flame burns for a good hunt!** Lay out a six-inch square of brown cloth: **Brown for the bounty of the Earth!** Set out a six-inch long narrow green ribbon to tie the charm bundle (or thread if sewing it): **Green for the bounty of nature!** One at a time, hold up over the pentacle some of each of the following herbs, state the intention, then place on the cloth: **I call upon you woodruff, Master of the Woods, for protection and success in the hunt! I call upon you star anise for good fortune in the hunt! I call upon you peppermint for alertness an action in the hunt!** Hold up over the pentacle a piece of tiger's eye stone: **I call upon you tiger's eye for luck, good instincts, and protection in the hunt!** Put it on the herbs. Tie the bundle with the ribbon (or sew shut) and set it on the pentacle. Charge the charm. With the wand or athame, raise energy moving deosil: **Through the Goddess and the God; through the Moon and the Sun; through the Elementals and runes; through herbs and stone; with the energy of Kyhiel in Abnahaya; this charm bring success to the hunt!** Direct and release the energy into the charm: **GOOD HUNTING! So Mote It Be!** Leave the charm on the pentacle for thirty minutes to an hour. Snuff the candle and dispose of the remains. Carry or place the charm where desired.

New Moon Waxing

- **ALBELDA, Defeat** (17♐8 to 0♑0) **ruled by BETHNAEL for strengthening buildings, good harvests, good travel, and gains**

This tea is especially good for business trips. Drink a cup to encourage the accomplishment of your travel goals.

Magical work: tea for good travel and gains. Dress a red working candle with rosemary oil: **Red for energy and strength; rosemary for protection, power, and blessing.** In the wax, carve around it: ☉ **The Sun for success;** ᛗ **Eh for safe journey and progress;** ᚱ **Rad for safe journey, travel, and gaining what is sought;** ᛋ **Sigel for success and achievement;** ⸸ **and Cor Scorpii for protection.** Light the working candle from the center altar candle: **This flame burns for good travel and gains!** Set on the pentacle a clean non-plastic or metal bowl in which to blend herbs. Add to the bowl ½ cup of loose black tea leaves. **I call upon you black tea for vigor and strength!** One at a time, hold up over the pentacle ⅛ cup of each herb, state the intention, and add it to the bowl: **I call upon you burdock root for protection and to ward negativity! I call upon you hops for relaxing travel! I call upon you lemon balm for success! I call upon you rosehips for goodwill and cooperative energy**! Blend the herbs and black tea with a wooden spoon. Charge the blend. With the wand or athame, gather energy deosil: **Through the Goddess and the God; through the Moon and the Sun; through the Elementals and star; through runes and herbs; with the energy of Bethnael in Albelda; this tea brings good travel and gains!** Direct and release the energy into the tea: **GOOD TRAVEL! So Mote It Be!** Leave the tea blend on the pentacle for thirty minutes to an hour. Snuff the candle and dispose of the remains. Put the tea blend in a tightly covered jar and store away from light. Brew a cup prior to travel, or take along in a thermos.

Full Moon

• **ALBELDA, Defeat** (17♐8 to 0♑0) **ruled by** ~~BECNEL~~ **for strengthening buildings, good harvests, good travel, and gains**

This versatile powder may be used for reaping rewards in any area of life, and may be sprinkled in the work area, burned as incense, added to a candle, or used in a charm bag.

Magical work: powder for a good harvest. Dress a green working candle with patchouli oil: **Green for fertility and abundance; patchouli for strength, power, and prosperity.** In the wax, carve around it: ᚠ **Feoh for prosperity and fulfillment;** ᛃ **Gera for harvest and tangible results from efforts;** ᛝ **Ing for fertility and satisfactory conclusions;** ᛋ **Sigel for success and achievement; and** ᚹ **Wyn for success and material gain.** Light the working candle from the center altar candle: **This flame burns for a good harvest!** One at a time, hold up an equal amount of each herb over the pentacle, state the intention, and drop into a mortar with pestle: **I call upon you allspice for prosperity and a good harvest! I call upon you bergamot for success and a prosperous harvest! I call upon you clove to attract a good harvest! I call upon you ginger for success and a good harvest!** Grind the herbs together into a powder, bottle it, and set the powder on the pentacle. Charge the powder. With the wand or athame, gather energy deosil: **Through the Goddess and the God; through the Moon and the Sun; through the Elementals, runes, and herbs; with the energy of Bethnael in Albelda; this powder brings a good harvest!** Direct and release the energy into the powder: **GOOD HARVEST! So Mote It Be!** Leave the powder on the pentacle for thirty minutes to an hour. Snuff the candle and dispose of the remains. Sprinkle the powder where desired or add to charms or oils.

CAPRICORN

The Moon in ♑ Capricorn, the Sea Goat, ruled by ♄ Saturn, with the energy of materialism, industry, discipline, and solitude, and the available energy of one fixed star:

 Vega, the Vulture Falling: avert fears, talk with animals, avert/end nightmares; Mercury and Venus; Capricorn; chrysolite (golden peridot); winter savory

In the Mansion of the Moon called:

New Moon Waxing

• **ZODEBOLUCH, a Pastor** (0 ♑ 0 to 12 ♑ 51) **ruled by GELIEL for curing illness, useful and profitable partnership, putting on new clothes/jewelry, and escaping captivity**

This talisman is good for business partnerships and successfully working with others.

Magical work: talisman for useful and profitable partnership. Dress a red working candle with dragon's blood oil: **Red for strength; dragon's blood for power and energy.** In the wax, carve around it: ᚨ **As for awareness and communication;** ᛞ **Daeg for a beneficial breakthrough;** ᛗ **Eh for progress;** ᚠ **Feoh for fulfillment and ambition satisfied;** ᚷ **Gefu for self-confidence and partnership.** Light the working candle from the center altar candle: **This flame burns for useful and profitable partnership!** On a piece of parchment or paper no more than 3 inches square, draw a double ring circle in red ink: **Red for power!** In the center of the circle, draw: ⤧⤸ **With the Seal of Omeliel for business structure!** Under or through the Seal of Omeliel, draw: ⟳ **With the Seal of Agiel for self-preservation!** In the ring around the circle, write: **OMELIEL · AGIEL · GELIEL ·** (the symbol of your sun sign) · (the symbol of your ruling planet) · In the center of the mandala, draw: ♀ **Venus for sociability in partnership!** ☿ **Mercury for communication skills!** On the back of the paper draw:

4	9	2
3	5	7
8	1	6

15

With the Square of the Saturn I initiate ambition and structure for successful business partnership! Turn the talisman over so the mandala is face up. Charge the talisman. With wand or athame, gather energy deosil: **Through the Goddess and the**

God; the Moon and the Sun; through the Elementals and planets; through runes
and flame; with the power of Omeliel and Agiel; and with the energy of Geliel in
Zodeboluch; this talisman initiates useful and profitable partnership! Direct and
release the energy into the talisman: **SUCCESS! So Mote It Be!** Leave the talisman on
the pentacle for thirty minutes to an hour. Snuff the candle and dispose of the remains.
Place, carry, or wear the talisman as desired.

Full Moon

• **ZODEBOLUCH, a Pastor** (0♑0 to 12♑51) **ruled by GELIEL for curing illness, useful
and profitable partnership, putting on new clothes/jewelry, and escaping captivity**

As a talisman for social advancement, this magical work blends the energies for social
success found in putting on new clothes/jewelry with networking ability with influential
people for useful partnerships.

Magical work: talisman for social advancement. Dress a pink working candle with vetiver:
**Pink for sociability and goodwill; vetiver for enhancing personality and opening
the way to profitable social success.** In the wax, carve around it: ᚨ **As for communication skill;** ᛋ **Sigel for self-confidence;** ᛖ **Eoh for power and dynamic action;**
ᛗ **Daeg for a breakthrough and fresh start;** ᛉ **Eolh to promote friendships and
strengthen good luck.** Light the working candle from the center altar candle: **This
flame burns for career sociability!** Use a piece of carnelian: **Carnelian for self-confidence, motivation, and career success!** Hold it up over the pentacle: **I call upon you
carnelian to open the way to confident social interactions for useful partnerships
and career success!** Use red marker: **Red for power!** Draw on one side of the stone:
With ⊟ **Aratron for business success!** On the other side of the stone, draw: **And
with ᚹ Wyn for happiness and fulfillment in career!** Charge the talisman. With wand
or athame, gather energy deosil: **Through the Goddess and the God; the Moon and
the Sun; through the Elementals and the runes; through the power of Aratron and
with the energy of Geliel in Zodeboluch; this talisman brings social advancement!**
Direct and release the energy into the talisman: **USEFUL PARTNERSHIPS! So Mote
It Be!** Leave the talisman on the pentacle for thirty minutes to an hour. Snuff the candle
and dispose of the remains. Place, carry, or wear the talisman as desired.

New Moon Waxing

• **ZABADOLA, Swallowing** (12 ♑ 51 to 25 ♑ 42) **ruled by ZEQUIEL for curing the ill, marriage, revealing secrets, and liberating captives**

This oil blends energies for aid with the healing process in an illness.

Magical work: oil for healing illness. Dress a yellow working candle with rosemary oil: **Yellow for good health; rosemary for good health and protection.** In the wax, carve around it: ᛉ **Ethel for good health;** ᚢ **Uruz for physical strength and health;** ᛋ **Sigel for vitality of the life force;** ᛜ **Ing for the power to achieve the goal of healing;** ᛟ **Osa for a favorable outcome to treatment.** Carve by the wick: **With the energies of** (patient's sun sign symbol) **and** (the ruling planet) **to represent** (name or me)! Light the working candle from the center altar candle: **This flame burns to augment the curing of illness!** In a small glass bottle with lid, blend the following essential oils: 2 parts rosemary: **I call upon you rosemary for physical purification and renewal of health!** 1 part amber: **I call upon you amber for successful healing!** 1 part lotus oil: **I call upon you lotus for healing and good health!** Add 2 parts grapeseed, saffron, or canola oil. Hold up over the pentacle 1 chip of yellow calcite: **I call upon you calcite for healing energy!** Add it to the oil, put the lid on the bottle, and shake: **All blended to work together for healing illness and bringing good health!** Place the bottle on the pentacle. Charge the oil. With the wand or athame, gather energy deosil: **Through the Goddess and the God, the Moon and the Sun; through the Elementals, planets, and stars; through runes, herbs, and stones; with the energy of Zequiel in Zabadola; this oil aids with the healing of illness!** Direct and release the energy into the bottle: **HEALING! So Mote It Be!** Leave the oil on the pentacle for thirty minutes to an hour. Snuff the candle and dispose of the remains. Dab on patient if possible or on the bed or in a sick room.

Full Moon

• **ZABADOLA, Swallowing** (12♑51 to 25♑42) **ruled by ZEQUIEL for revealing secrets, curing the ill, marriage, and liberating captives**

The Full Moon energy pushes curing the ill into the accomplishment of good health.

Magical work: amulet for good health. Dress a red working candle with bay oil: **Red for energy; rosemary for wellness.** In the wax, carve around it: ♃ **Jupiter for health;** ⟨ **Ken for opening energy;** ᚢ **Uruz for strength and physical health;** ᛋ **Sigel for vitality and the life-force; and** ᚹ **Wyn for well-being.** Light the working candle from the center altar candle: **This flame burns for curing illness and restoring good health!** Hold up over the pentacle a small, clean, dry pine cone: **I call upon you pine cone for good health and longevity!** Hold up over the pentacle a container of gold glitter: **Gold for energy, physical strength, and wellness!** Hold up a container of glue: **Glue for wellness and good health to stick!** Paint the pine cone with the glue and roll the pine cone in the glitter. When the pine cone is dry, set it on the pentacle. Charge the pinecone. With the wand or athame, gather energy deosil: **Through the Goddess and the God; through the Moon and the Sun; through the Elementals, planets, and runes; with the energy of Zequiel in Zabadola; this pine cone promotes wellness!** Direct and release the energy into the pine cone: **HEALTHY! So Mote It Be!** Leave the pine cone on the pentacle for thirty minutes to an hour. Snuff the candle and dispose of the remains. Carry or place the pine cone where desired, or use as an addition to a potted plant.

New Moon Waxing

- **SADABATH, the Star of Fortune** (25 ♑42 to 8 ♒34) **ruled by ABRINIEL for peace between couples, winning a war, and increasing trade/herds**

Add these bath salts to the tub with warm running water for relieving stress and restoring peace in a relationship.

Magical work: bath salts for peaceful relations. Dress a white working candle with lavender oil: **White to ward fears and bring peace; lavender for calm and peaceful relations.** In the wax, carve around it: ᚲ **Ken for transforming energy to release fears and initiate peace;** ᛗ **Mannaz for self-improvement and cooperation in a relationship; and** ᚹ **Wyn for well-being; with** ⚹ **Vega, the Vulture Falling, to avert fears;** ♑ **Capricorn for self-discipline;** ☿ **Mercury for communication skills; and** ♀ **Venus for love and camaraderie.** Light the working candle from the center altar candle: **This flame burns to restore peace in a relationship!** Set on the pentacle a clean bowl in which to blend the bath salt. Add to the bowl 2 cups of sea salt. **I call upon you salt of the sea for personal cleansing that peaceful relations are restored!** Hold up over the pentacle ½ teaspoon of lavender oil: **I call upon you lavender for calm and peace!** Add the oil to the salt and stir together until the salt and lavender oil are blended. Charge the salts. With the wand or athame, gather energy deosil: **Through the Goddess and the God; through the Moon and the Sun; through the Elementals, planets, and stars; through runes, herbs, and the sea; with the energy of Abriniel in Sadabath; these bath salts bring emotional cleansing and inspire peace in a relationship!** Direct and release the energy into the salts: **PEACE! So Mote It Be!** Leave the bath salts on the pentacle for thirty minutes to an hour. Snuff the candle and dispose of the remains. Store salts in a tightly covered jar away from light. Add to tub water or rub on in the shower.

Full Moon

• **SADABATH, the Star of Fortune** (25 ♑42 to 8 ♒34) **ruled by ABRINIEL for peace between couples, winning a war, and increasing trade/herds**

This charm is useful to those who work in a trade, are merchants, or are in a retail business.

Magical work: charm for increasing trade. Dress an orange working candle with pine oil: **Orange for business and trade; pine for strength and energy in material matters.** In the wax, carve around it: ᚠ **Feoh to protect valuables and increase wealth;** ᛟ **Ethel for monetary gains;** ᛈ **Perth for gains from investments and speculations;** ᚹ **Wyn for success and gains;** ♑ **with Capricorn for business discipline;** ☿ **Mercury for skill and communication; and** ♀ **Venus for sociability with the public and coworkers.** Light the working candle from the center altar candle: **This flame burns for increase in trade!** Lay out a six-inch square of orange cloth: **Orange for career goals, business and vitality!** Use red marker: **Red for energy and power!** In the center of the cloth, draw: ⚹ **Vega, the Vulture Falling, for fearlessness in business and trade!** Set out a six-inch long narrow red ribbon to tie the charm bundle (or thread if sewing it): **Red for drive and vigor!** One at a time, hold up over the pentacle a bit of each of the following, state the intention, then place on the cloth: **I call upon you mint for business growth! I call upon you winter savory for increasing commercial skills! I call upon you chrysolite, stone of the Vulture Falling, for fearlessness in business!** Put the stone on top of the herbs. Add 1 drop of pine oil to a cotton ball: **The energy of pine for strength and clear action for increase of trade!** Set this on top of the bundle. Tie the bundle with the ribbon (or sew shut) and set it on the pentacle. Charge the charm. With the wand or athame, raise energy moving deosil: **Through the Goddess and the God; through the Moon and the Sun; through the Elementals, planets, and star; through runes, herbs, and stone; with the energy of Abriniel in Sadabath; this charm increases trade!** Direct and release the energy into the charm: **INCREASE! So Mote It Be!** Leave the charm on the pentacle for thirty minutes to an hour. Snuff the candle and dispose of the remains. Carry or place the charm where desired.

AQUARIUS

The Moon in ♒ Aquarius, the Water Bearer, ruled by ♅ Uranus, with the energy of originality, individuality, idealism, and unpredictability

In the Mansion of the Moon called:

New Moon Waxing

- **SADABATH, the Star of Fortune** (25 ♑ 42 to 8 ♒ 34) **ruled by ABRINIEL for peace between couples, winning a war, and increasing trade/herds**

This candle can be lit when you need to increase sales in a trade or business.

Magical work: candle for increasing trade. Dress a red working candle with patchouli oil: **Red for energy; patchouli for power and financial gains.** In the wax, carve around it: ᚨ **As for creative ideas;** ᛒ **Beorc to bring ideas into fruition;** ᚠ **Feoh for prosperity and increasing wealth;** ᛟ **Ethel for monetary gains and secure possessions;** ᛈ **Perth for gain from investments;** ↑ **Tyr for victory and a favorable outcome; and** ᛜ **Ing for the power to achieve goals and hold the benefits.** Light the working candle from the center altar candle: **This flame burns to increase trade and business!** Consecrate a yellow votive spell candle and dress with ginger oil: **Yellow for creativity, mental alertness, and gainful work; ginger for creativity, increase of trade, business, and riches.** In the wax carve around it: **With the energies of** (your sun sign symbol) **and** (the ruling planet) **to represent me!** ᚩ **Osa for a good outcome!** ᚹ **Wyn for success and well-being!** ♅ **Uranus for originality!** ⊠ **Vehiel, the Seal of Mercury for commerce skills and trade!** ⬏ **Tiriel, the Intelligence of Mercury to increase trade and business!** Set the spell candle in a cauldron on top of the pentacle. Light a taper from the working candle and use it to light the spell candle. Charge the candle. With the wand or athame, gather energy deosil: **Through the Goddess and the God; through the Moon and the Sun; through the Elementals and planets; through runes and herbs; with the power of Vehiel and Tiriel; and with the energy of Abriniel in Sadabath; this candle increases trade and business!** Direct and release the energy into the candle: **INCREASE! So Mote It Be!** Let the candle burn for thirty minutes to an hour, then snuff and look at the wax for images indicating the time frame for the results to manifest. Dispose of candle remains.

Full Moon

- **SADABATH, the Star of Fortune (25 ♑42 to 8 ♒34) ruled by ABRINIEL for peace between couples, winning a war, and increasing trade/herds**

    Take the time to enjoy tea for two while keeping peace in a relationship.

Magical work: tea for peaceful relations. Dress a pink working candle with rose oil: **Pink for health peace, goodwill, and healing emotions; rose for peace and happiness.** In the wax, carve around it: ᛇ **Eoh for opening the way to peace;** ᛗ **Mannaz for cooperation and curbing excessive emotions;** ᚱ **Rad for good communication;** ᛉ **Eolh for optimism and promoting friendship; and** ᚹ **Wyn for harmony and comfort.** Light the working candle from the center altar candle: **This flame burns for peaceful relations!** Set on the pentacle a clean non-plastic or metal bowl in which to blend herbs. Add to the bowl ½ cup of black tea. **I call upon you black tea for energy and power!** One at a time, hold up over the pentacle 1 teaspoon of the following herbs, state the intention, and add it to the bowl: **I call upon you burdock root for the purification of any negativity! I call upon you rose hips for love and goodwill! I call upon you chamomile for calm! I call upon you hops for relaxation!** Blend the herbs and black tea with a wooden spoon. Charge the blend. With the wand or athame, gather energy deosil: **Through the Goddess and the God; through the Moon and the Sun; through the Elementals and planets; through runes and herbs; with the energy of Abriniel in Sadabath; this tea brings peace in a relationship to all who drink it!** Direct and release the energy into the tea: **PEACE TEA! So Mote It Be!** Leave the tea blend on the pentacle for thirty minutes to an hour. Snuff the candle and dispose of the remains. Put the tea blend in a tightly covered jar and store away from light. Brew a cup or pot of tea when desired.

New Moon Waxing

• **SADALAHBIA, a Butterfly** (8♒34 to 21♒25) **ruled by AZIEL for repairing structures, protecting trees/crops, destroying enemies, and getting fast news**

Use this incense when awaiting important news or results in a matter.

Magical work: incense for urging news to come quickly. Dress a red working candle with frankincense oil: **Red for energy to bring news quickly; frankincense for power and blessing for good news.** In the wax, carve around it: ♅ **Uranus for news;** ⚹ **Ophiel for speed;** ᛖ **Eh for swift communication;** ᛇ **Eoh for dynamic action;** ᚱ **Rad for communication;** ᛗ **Mannaz for cooperation and help from others to receive news quickly; and** ᚹ **Wyn for success, harmony and well-being with news.** Light the working candle from the center altar candle: **This flame burns to bring news quickly!** One at a time, hold up an equal amount of each herb over the pentacle, state the intention, and drop into a mortar with pestle: **I call upon you thyme for swift action! I call upon you woodruff to remove any barriers to receiving news quickly! I call upon you allspice for luck in bringing news quickly! I call upon you clove to attract good news!** Grind the herbs together into a powder, bottle it, and set it on the pentacle. Charge the powder. With the wand or athame, gather energy deosil: **Through the Goddess and the God; through the Moon and the Sun; through the Elementals and planets; through runes and herbs; with the power of Ophiel and the energy of Aziel in Sadalahbia; this powdered incense brings news quickly!** Direct and release the energy into the powder: **NEWS COMES! So Mote It Be!** Leave the incense on the pentacle for thirty minutes to an hour. Snuff the candle and dispose of the remains. Burn the incense on a charcoal diskette.

Full Moon

• **SADALAHBIA, a Butterfly** (8♒34 to 21♒25) **ruled by AZIEL for repairing structures, protecting trees/crops, destroying enemies, and getting fast news**

Use this oil to anoint areas where crops, orchards, or trees are growing or stored to protect them from harm.

Magical work: oil for protecting crops and trees. Dress a green working candle with pine oil: **Green for agriculture and plants; pine for protection and strength.** In the wax, carve around it: ᛒ **Beorc for fertility, growth, and protection;** ᛟ **Ethel for protection of lands, crops, and trees;** ᚦ **Thorn for protection of crops and trees;** ᚢ **Uruz for the strength and physical health of crops and trees; and** ᛃ **Gera for tangible results and a good harvest.** Light the working candle from the center altar candle: **This flame burns to protect crops and trees!** In a small glass bottle with lid, blend the following essential oils: 1 part patchouli: **I call upon you patchouli for fertility of the Earth and the crops and trees!** 1 part rosemary: **I call upon you rosemary for protection and the blessing of Earth spirits!** 2 parts bergamot: **I call upon you bergamot to bring me success and wealth!** Add 4 parts grapeseed, saffron, or canola oil. Put the lid on the bottle, shake: **All are blended to protect crops and trees!** Place the bottle on the pentacle. Charge the oil. With the wand or athame, gather energy deosil: **Through the Goddess and the God, the Moon and the Sun; through the Elementals, runes, and herbs; with the energy of Aziel in Sadalahbia; this oil protects crops and trees!** Direct and release the energy into the bottle: **PROTECTED PLANTS! So Mote It Be!** Leave the oil on the pentacle for thirty minutes to an hour. Snuff the candle and dispose of the remains. Use a dab of oil to anoint trees, garden tools, farm equipment, fence posts at a field, silos, and so forth, as desired.

New Moon Waxing

- **ALPHARG, the Spout of the Urn** (21♒25 to 4♓17) **ruled by TAGRIEL for unity and goodwill, and instigating love and favor**

    Use this amulet to commence a period of unity bringing goodwill, love, and favor.

Magical work: amulet to initiate unity, goodwill, love, and favor. Dress a pink working candle with lavender oil: **Pink for goodwill, love, and unity; lavender for peace, favor, and balance. In the wax, carve around it: ⟨ Ken for opening energy; ᛞ Osa for good fortune in my endeavors and a favorable outcome; ᛉ Eolh to promote goodwill; ♀ Venus for affection and camaraderie; and ᛈ Wyn for harmony, well-being, love, and favor.** Light the working candle from the center altar candle: **This flame burns to prompt unity, goodwill, love and favor for me!** Place a small bottle on the pentacle. Knot a short piece of red sting or ribbon: **Red for love and strength!** One at a time, hold up each of the following over the pentacle, state the intention, and put it into the bottle: **I call upon you hematite for goodwill and unity! I call upon you clove to bring loving energy! I call upon you apple seed to draw unity, goodwill, and love to me! I call upon you knot to instigate unity and love!** Cap the bottle with lid or cork. Use red marker: **Red for strength and enthusiasm!** On the bottle, draw: ᛗ **Mannaz for cooperation and help from others!** Then draw on the bottle: ᚷ **Gefu for unity, goodwill, love, and favor!** Charge the bottle. With the wand or athame, gather energy deosil: **Through the Goddess and the God; through the Moon and the Sun; through the Elementals and planets; through runes and herbs; with the energy of Tagriel in Alpharg; this amulet brings unity, goodwill, love, and favor to me!** Direct and release the energy into the bottle: **UNITY! So Mote It Be!** Leave the bottle on the pentacle for thirty minutes to an hour. Snuff the candle and dispose of the remains. Carry or place the bottle where desired.

Full Moon

- **ALPHARG, the Spout of the Urn** (21♒25 to 4♓17) **ruled by TAGRIEL for unity and goodwill, and instigating love and favor**

  This charm is good for manifesting unity and goodwill.

Magical work: charm for unity and goodwill. Dress a red working candle with ginger oil: **Red for power and strength; ginger for goodwill and success.** In the wax, carve around it: ᛇ **Eoh for a channel to unity and goodwill;** ᚲ **Ken for opening energy for unity and goodwill;** ᚫ **As for skillful communication;** ᛗ **Mannaz for cooperation and gaining the goodwill of others; and** ᚷ **Gefu for unity and partnership.** Light the working candle from the center altar candle: **This flame burns for manifesting unity and goodwill!** Lay out a six-inch square of white cloth: **White for unity, peace, and sincerity!** Set out a six-inch long narrow yellow ribbon to tie the charm bundle (or thread if sewing it): **Yellow for harmony and alertness!** One at a time, hold up over the pentacle some of each of the following herbs, state the intention, then place on the cloth: **I call upon you woodruff for success to unity and goodwill! I call upon you lavender for peace and harmony! I call upon you lemon balm for unity and goodwill! I call upon you hazelnut for communication! I call upon you tansy for happiness!** Add 1 small drop of lemon oil to a cotton ball: **With lemon for joy and to invigorate these energies for unity and goodwill!** Set this on top of the bundle. Tie the bundle with the ribbon (or sew shut) and set it on the pentacle. Charge the charm. With the wand or athame, raise energy moving deosil: **Through the Goddess and the God; through the Moon and the Sun; through the Elementals, runes, and herbs; with the energy of Tagriel in Alpharg; this charm brings unity and goodwill!** Direct and release the energy into the charm: **UNITY! So Mote It Be!** Leave the charm on the pentacle for thirty minutes to an hour. Snuff the candle and dispose of the remains. Carry or place the charm where desired.

PISCES

The Moon in ♓ Pisces, the Fishes, ruled by ♆ Neptune, with the energy of mysticism, sensitivity, imagination, and intuition, and the available energy of one fixed star:

Cauda Capricorni, the Tail of the Sea-Goat (Deneb Algedi): Aid a Just Cause, Bring Peace, Protect From Harm; Saturn & Mercury; Pisces; Chalcedony; Marjoram.

In the Mansion of the Moon called:

New Moon Waxing

• **ALPHARG, the Spout of the Urn** (21♒25 to 4♓17) **ruled by TAGRIEL for unity and goodwill, and instigating love and favor**

Light this candle when you are feeling closed off from people so that the way for receiving love and favor may be opened.

Magical work: candle for instigating love and favor. Dress a red working candle with orange (or neroli) oil: **Red for passion and enthusiasm; orange for love and favor.** In the wax, carve around it: ⟨ **Ken for opening energy to receive love;** ᛗ **Eh for progress in prompting love and favor;** ᛇ **Gera for tangible results and a good outcome.** Light the working candle from the center altar candle: **This flame burns to instigate love and favor!** Consecrate a pink votive spell candle and dress with rose oil: **Pink for love, caring, and nurturing; rose for love and happiness.** In the wax, carve around it: **With the energies of** (your sun sign symbol) **and** (the ruling planet) **to represent me!** ᚷ **Gefu for partnership with love and favor!** ᚹ **Wyn for happiness and fulfillment in love!** Add to prompt the love of a woman: ᛒ **Beorc to attract new beginnings and fulfillment with a woman!** *or* add to prompt the love of a man: ᛜ **Ing to attract love and favor with a man!** Set the spell candle in a cauldron on top of the pentacle. Light a taper from the working candle and use it to light the spell candle. Charge a piece of rose quartz and drop it into the candle flame: **With rose quartz to open the way to love and favor for me!** Charge the candle. With the wand or athame, gather energy deosil: **Through the Goddess and the God; through the Moon and the Sun; through the Elementals, runes, and stone; with the energy of Tagriel in Alpharg; this candle instigates love and favor!** Direct and release the energy into the candle:

LOVE FOR ME! So Mote It Be! Let the candle burn for thirty minutes to an hour, then snuff and look at the wax for images indicating the time frame for results to manifest. Remove the rose quartz and clean it to place, carry, or wear as desired. Dispose of candle remains.

Full Moon

• **ALPHARG, the Spout of the Urn** (21♒25 to 4♓17) **ruled by TAGRIEL for unity and goodwill, and instigating love and favor**

Light this candle for manifesting unity and goodwill with others in any area of your life.

Magical work: candle spell for unity and goodwill. Dress a red working candle with rose oil: **Red for energy and power; rose for peace and goodwill.** In the wax, carve around it: ᛟ **Osa for good fortune and a favorable outcome;** ᚷ **Gefu for unity and equilibrium; and** ᛗ **Mannaz for help from others and cooperation.** Light the working candle from the center altar candle: **This flame burns for unity and goodwill!** Consecrate a pink votive spell candle and dress with lavender oil: **Pink for unity and goodwill; lavender for balance, peace, unity, and goodwill.** In the wax, carve around it: ⚹⚏ **Cauda Capricorni, the Tail of the Sea-goat to bring peace and protection me from harm!** ♄ **Saturn to remove inner restrictions to unity and goodwill!** ☿ **Mercury for good communication skills!** ᛇ **Eoh to channel unity and goodwill!** ᛋ **Sigel for success!** Charge the candle and set it in a cauldron on top of the pentacle. Light a taper from the working candle and use it to light the spell candle. One at a time, hold up a pinch of each herb over the pentacle, state the intention, and add it to the flame: **I call upon you marjoram to enhance the power of Cauda Capricorni for peace and protection! I call upon you basil for goodwill! I call upon you bergamot for success! I call upon you thyme for quick results! I call upon you High John the Conqueror for harmony and goodwill!** With the wand or athame, gather energy deosil: **Through the Goddess and the God; through the Moon and the Sun; through the Elementals, planets, and stars; through runes and herbs; with the energy of Tagriel in Alpharg; this candle brings unity and goodwill!** Direct and release the energy into the candle: **UNITY! So Mote It Be!** Let the candle burn for thirty minutes to an hour, then snuff and look at the wax for images indicating the time frame for the results to manifest. Dispose of candle remains.

New Moon Waxing

- **ALCHARYA, the Lip of the Urn** (4ℋ17 to 17ℋ8) **ruled by ABLEMIEL for increasing the harvest, increasing income, increasing gain, healing the sick, and psychic power**

Use this charm to draw upon the intuitive energy of the sign for attracting more income through pay raises, bonuses, sales, gifts, investments, speculations, etc.

Magical work: charm for increasing income. Dress a green working candle with patchouli oil: **Green for prosperity and money; patchouli for increase of money.** In the wax, carve around it: ♆ **Neptune for intuition;** ᚠ **Feoh for prosperity and material wealth;** ᚯ **Ethel for acquisition of monetary gains;** ᚲ **Perth for hidden forces to bring opportunity and financial gain; and** ᚹ **Wyn for success and material gain.** Light the working candle from the center altar candle: **This flame burns to increase income!** Lay out a six-inch square of green cloth: **Green for prosperous income!** Set out a six-inch long narrow purple ribbon to tie the charm bundle (or thread if sewing it): **Purple for intuitive ability!** One at a time, hold up over the pentacle some of each of the following herbs, state the intention, then place on the cloth: **I call upon you allspice for prosperity and money! I call upon you jasmine for intuition to increase my income! I call upon you clove to attract wealth! I call upon you cinnamon for intuitive power and financial success! I call upon you bay for intuitive success in attaining an increase of my income!** Put them on the cloth. Add 1 small drop of almond oil to a cotton ball: **With the power of almond for a prosperous harvest to blend these energies for an increase of income!** Set this on top of the bundle. Add a piece of iron pyrite to the bundle: **With iron pyrite for intuitive insight in drawing wealth!** Tie the bundle with the ribbon (or sew shut) and set it on the pentacle. Charge the charm. With the wand or athame, raise energy moving deosil: **Through the Goddess and the God; through the Moon and the Sun; through the Elementals and planet; through runes, herbs, and stone; with the energy of Ablemiel in Alcharya; this charm gives insight to increasing income!** Direct and release the energy into the charm: **INCREASE! So Mote It Be!** Leave the charm on the pentacle for thirty minutes to an hour. Snuff the candle and dispose of the remains. Carry or place the charm where desired.

Full Moon

- **ALCHARYA, the Lip of the Urn** (4)(17 to 17)(8) **ruled by ABLEMIEL for increasing the harvest, increasing income, increasing gain, healing the sick, and psychic power**

  Burn this incense in conjunction with divination for psychic awareness.

Magical work: incense for psychic power. Dress a light blue working candle with frankincense oil: **Light blue for psychic awareness; rose for divination and psychic power.** In the wax, carve around it: ᚲ **Ken for opening energy to psychic ability;** ᚨ **As for psychic power;** ᛗ **Daeg for working between the worlds;** ᛚ **Lagu for psychic awareness;** ᛇ **Eoh for a channel of communicate with other worlds.** Light the working candle from the center altar candle: **This flame burns for psychic power!** One at a time, hold up an equal amount of each herb over the pentacle, state the intention, and drop into a mortar with pestle: **I call upon you woodruff to open the way to psychic ability! I call upon you clove for vision! I call upon you cinnamon for psychic power! I call upon you mace for psychic awareness! I call upon you bay for psychic power and divination skill! I call upon you mugwort for psychic ability and divination skill! I call upon you star anise for psychic power and good fortune!** Grind the herbs together into a powder, bottle it, and set it on the pentacle. Charge the powder. With the wand or athame, gather energy deosil: **Through the Goddess and the God; through the Moon and the Sun; through the Elementals, runes, and herbs; with the energy of Ablemiel in Alcharya; this incense brings psychic power!** Direct and release the energy into the powder: **PSYCHIC POWER! So Mote It Be!** Leave the incense on the pentacle for thirty minutes to an hour. Snuff the candle and dispose of the remains. Burn the incense on a charcoal diskette.

New Moon Waxing

• **ALBOTHAM, the Belly of the Fish** (17♓8 to 0♈0) **ruled by ANUXIEL for increase of harvest, increase of trade, safe travel, marital joy, and gathering in fish**

Use this amulet for increasing your trade or harvest. This is especially good for people working in any area of sales and production.

Magical work: amulet for increasing harvest or trade. Dress an orange working candle with almond oil: **Orange for attracting sales, luck, and success; almond oil for prosperity and good rewards.** In the wax, carve around it: ◊ **Gera for rewards and tangible results;** ᚠ **Feoh for prosperity and fulfillment;** ᚲ **Perth to initiate good fortune and gains;** ᚹ **Wyn for success and material gain;** ᚮ **Osa for a favorable outcome.** Light the working candle from the center altar candle: **This flame burns to increase harvest or trade!** Hold up over the pentacle a clean, dry turkey feather: **With the feather of the turkey, symbol of abundance and well-being, I do summon abundance and good rewards to me!** Tie to the feather the following six-inch ribbons: **Red for power and energy to attain my goal! Yellow for prosperity! Orange for ambition and attaining success!** Set the feather on the pentacle: **I call upon you to increase my harvest and trade!** Charge the feather. With the wand or athame, gather energy deosil: **Through the Goddess and the God; through the Moon and the Sun; through the Elementals and runes; with the energy of Anuxiel in Albotham; this amulet increases my harvest and trade!** Direct and release the energy into the feather: **INCREASE! So Mote It Be!** Leave the feather on the pentacle for thirty minutes to an hour. Snuff the candle and dispose of the remains. Carry or place the feather where desired.

Full Moon

• **ALBOTHAM, the Belly of the Fish** (17♓8 to 0♈0) **ruled by ANUXIEL for increase of harvest, increase of trade, safe travel, marital joy, and gathering in fish**

This is a charm that can be placed anywhere within a vehicle for safe travel.

Magical work: charm for safe travel in a car. Dress a red working candle with rosemary oil: **Red for energy; rosemary for protection.** In the wax, carve around it: ⚹⚑ **Cauda Capricorni for protection from harm;** ᚦ **Thorn for protection;** ᛗ **Eh for safety; and** ♄ **Saturn for self-preservation.** Light the working candle from the center altar candle: **This flame burns for safe travel in the automobile!** Lay out a six-inch square of black cloth: **Black for protection!** Set out a six-inch long narrow black ribbon to tie the charm bundle (or thread if sewing it): **Black to seal this charm of protection!** One at a time, hold up over the pentacle some of each of the following herbs, state the intention, then place on the cloth: **I call upon you marjoram to enhance the power of Cauda Capricorni for protection from harm! I call upon you comfrey for safe travel! I call upon you rosemary for protection! I call upon you basil for protection and safe keeping! I call upon you burdock root for protection and well-being! I call upon you cumin to protect my automobile and belongings! I call upon you fennel for protection and security**! Hold up over the pentacle a piece of jade: **I call upon you jade for protection and safe travel!** Set the stone on top of the bundle. Tie the bundle with the ribbon (or sew shut) and set it on the pentacle. Charge the charm. With the wand or athame, raise energy moving deosil: **Through the Goddess and the God; through the Moon and the Sun; through the Elementals, planets, and star; through runes, herbs, and stone; with the energy of Anuxiel in Albotham; this charm protects my vehicle and gives safe travel!** Direct and release the energy into the charm: **SAFETY! So Mote It Be!** Leave the charm on the pentacle for thirty minutes to an hour. Snuff the candle and dispose of the remains. Place the charm in a vehicle.

Part Four

WANING MOON TO
DARK MOON

TABLE OF CONTENTS FOR MAGICAL WORKS

GEMINI . . . 147

ALBACHAY, the Head of Orion (21 ♉ 25 to 4♊17) ruled by GABIEL for destroying alliances or friendships

> *New Moon Waning:* amulet to avert energies destructive to friendships and alliances
>
> *Dark Moon:* Tarot divination for weaknesses in friendships or alliances

ALCHAYA, the Little Star of Great Light (4♊17 to 17♊8) ruled by DIRACHIEL for destroying business empires, cities, crops, or health, and for revenge

> *New Moon Waning:* candle to ward against health destructive energy
>
> *Dark Moon:* stone transfer spell

ALARZACH, the Arm of Gemini (17♊8 to 0♋0) ruled by SELHIEL for the destruction of high offices, and the cooperation of flies

> *New Moon Waning:* oil to repel flies and insects
>
> *Dark Moon:* meditation to keep away flies

CANCER . . . 153

ALNAZA, Misty Clouds (0♋0 to 12♋51) ruled by AMNEDIEL for the maltreatment of captives, and for controlling mice

> *New Moon Waning:* talisman to control mice
>
> *Dark Moon:* meditation to cleanse the feelings that lead to maltreatment of others

ARCAPH, the Eye of the Lion (12♋51 to 25♋42) ruled by RAUBIEL for destroying harvests, hindering travel, and creating discord or infirmities

> *New Moon Waning:* charm to deflect hindrances to travel
>
> *Dark Moon:* star candle to ward discord

ALGEBH, the Forehead of the Lion (25♋42 to 8♌34) ruled by ARDESIEL to destroy enemies, ease childbirth, and banish illness

> *New Moon Waning:* candle spell to banish illness
>
> *Dark Moon:* Tarot reading on enemies

LEO . . . 160

ALGEBH, the Forehead of the Lion (25♋42 to 8♌34) ruled by ARDESIEL to destroy enemies, ease childbirth, banish illness

New Moon Waning: amulet to banish illness

Dark Moon: candle to ease childbirth

AZOBRA, the Mane of the Lion (8♌34 to 21♌25) ruled by NECIEL for attacking, aggression, and inspiring fear

New Moon Waning: elixir to overcome an adversary or competitor

Dark Moon: rune reading to find the cause of fear

ALZARPHA, the Tail of the Lion (21♌25 to 4♍17) ruled by ABDIZUEL for hindering sailing, loss of investment, and separation

New Moon Waning: incense to banish loss of investment

Dark Moon: meditation to separate from the functional that which is worthless and release it

VIRGO . . . 167

ALZARPHA, the Tail of the Lion (21♌25 to 4♍17) ruled by ABDIZUEL for hindering sailing, loss of investment, and separation

New Moon Waning: candle spell to ease separation

Dark Moon: Meditation to ease separation

ALHAIRE, the Wings of Virgo (4♍17 to 17♍8) ruled by JAZERIEL for diminishing gains or the status quo, and for clever financial dealings

New Moon Waning: candle to ward against diminishing gains

Dark Moon: candle meditation to ward against diminishing status quo

AZIMETH, the Flying Spike (17♍8 to 0♎0) ruled by ERGEDIEL for destroying harvests, destroying desires, hindering land journeys, for divorce, and for separations

New Moon Waning: talisman to banish hazards to a harvest

Dark Moon: meditation for banishing desires for unhealthy foods when dieting

LIBRA . . . 175

AGRAPHA, Covered or Covered Flying (0♎0 to 12♎51) ruled by ACHALIEL for hindering travelers, promoting divorce, promoting discord, destroying houses, and destroying enemies

> *New Moon Waning:* oil to repel domestic discord
> *Dark Moon:* rune reading to banish discord

AZUBENE, the Horns of Scorpio (12♎51 to 25♎42) ruled by AZERUEL for hindering journeys or trips, hindering wedlock, and hindering harvests or merchandise

> *New Moon Waning:* oil for candle to avert hindrance
> *Dark Moon:* tarot reading for revealing the source of hindrances

ALCHIL, the Crown of Scorpio (25♎42 to 8♏34) ruled by ADRIEL to drive away thieves and robbers, seek redress

> *New Moon Waning:* incense to banish thieves and robbers
> *Dark Moon:* rune divination for seeking redress

SCORPIO . . . 181

ALCHIL, the Crown of Scorpio (25♎42 to 8♏34) ruled by ADRIEL to drive away thieves and robbers, seek redress

> *New Moon Waning:* oil seeking redress
> *Dark Moon:* rune reading on removing obstacles to seeking redress

ALCAB, the Heart of Scorpio (8♏34 to 21♏25) ruled by EGRIBIEL for discord, sedition, conspiracy, and destroying friendships

> *New Moon Waning:* elixir to ward against destroying friendships
> *Dark Moon:* tarot reading to expose what is destroying a friendship

AXAULAH, the Tail of Scorpio (21♏25 to 4♐17) ruled by ANUCIEL for destroying ships, and for the ruination of captives

> *New Moon Waning:* charm bag to bind ruination energy
> *Dark Moon:* meditation to reveal the source of current captivity from a past life

SAGITTARIUS . . . 188

AXAULAH, the Tail of Scorpio (21♏25 to 4♐17) ruled by ANUCIEL for destroying ships, and for the ruination of captives

New Moon Waning: amulet to ward against the destruction of ships

Dark Moon: tarot reading to reveal enmity behind the ruination of captives

ABNAHAYA, the Beam (4♐17 to 17♐8) ruled by KYHIEL for destroying social wealth, and creating arguments among friends

New Moon Waning: elixir to restrict arguments among friends

Dark Moon: meditation to banish argumentative energy

ALBELDA, Defeat (17♐8 to 0♑0) ruled by BERTHNAEL for causing divorce and destroying a person

New Moon Waning: charm bag to ward against the energy for destroying a person

Dark Moon: mirror charm to deflect destructive energy

CAPRICORN . . . 194

ZODEBOLUCH, a Pastor (0♑0 to 12♑51) ruled by GELIEL for creating discord between two people, breaking an engagement or enduring constant marital conflicts

New Moon Waning: candle to banish discord between two people

Dark Moon: rune divination to uncover the source of discord in a relationship

ZABADOLA, Swallowing (12♑51 to 25♑42) ruled by ZEQUIEL for destruction, laying waste, and divorce

New Moon Waning: powder to repel destructive energy

Dark Moon: rune divination on hidden threats to security in any area

SADABATH, the Star of Fortune (25♑42 to 8♒34) ruled by ABRINIEL for gaining power over enemies, and hindering governance or rule

New Moon Waning: oil to banish the power of foes

Dark Moon: tarot reading to reveal those who seek power over another

AQUARIUS . . . 201

SADABATH, the Star of Fortune (25♑42 to 8♒34) ruled by ABRINIEL for gaining power over enemies, and hindering governance or rule

> *New Moon Waning:* elixir to restrict others from gaining power over you
> *Dark Moon:* meditation for overcoming hindrances to governance or rule

SADALAHBIA, a Butterfly (8♒34 to 21♒25) ruled by AZIEL for divorce, revenge, besieging, and binding someone against their duty

> *New Moon Waning:* candle to banish besieging energies
> *Dark Moon:* meditation to release revenge energy

ALPHARG, the Spout of the Urn (21♒25 to 4♓17) ruled by TAGRIEL for breaking barriers, and destroying buildings and prisons

> *New Moon Waning:* candle spell to remove barriers
> *Dark Moon:* rune divination for breaking the barriers to gaining goals

PISCES . . . 208

ALPHARG, the Spout of the Urn (21♒25 to 4♓17) ruled by TAGRIEL for breaking barriers, and destroying buildings and prisons

> *New Moon Waning:* candle to break psychic barriers
> *Dark Moon:* tea to remove barriers to psychic ability

ALCHARYA, the Lip of the Urn (4♓17 to 17♓8) ruled by ABLEMIEL for obstructing the construction of buildings, endangering sailors, destroying springs and wells, destroying baths and medicinal waters, and sending mischief as desired

> *New Moon Waning:* charm bag for protection and warding against mischief
> *Dark Moon:* tarot reading to reveal mischief.

ALBOTHAM, the Belly of the Fish (17♓8 to 0♈0) ruled by ANUXIEL for strengthening captivity, and instigating loss of wealth and/or treasures

> *New Moon Waning:* amulet to ward against loss of wealth
> *Dark Moon:* rune divination on threatened loss of wealth

INTRODUCTION

This section contains the activities for magical works performed during the Crone Moon and Veiled Moon Esbats. These works involve magic for banishing, restricting, binding, reducing, diminishing, ending, and cleansing, as well as for communication, journey, meditation, divination, and psychic development. While the mansion energies in the Waning to Dark Moon phases are generally negative, malevolent, or diminishing, some of these can ultimately provide a positive result, and the others can be warded, banished, or counteracted through magical works. Creativity and focus are part of the magical process in turning the negative energies to beneficial use.

The symbols and items I use within the magical works are drawn from the correspondences that are part of my practice, but you may substitute from your own customary correlations as long as you understand the energy being moved in the working. To better facilitate this, I state the purpose or function at the beginning of each magical work. There are some mansions that overlap zodiac signs, so these will have magical works relevant to the influence of both signs.

NOTES FOR THE MAGICAL WORKS

Refer to Part Two for cleansing candles, consecrations, and charging materials. The working candle may be a votive, small pillar, or taper candle. I do not recommend tapers or bottle candles for spell candles, but if bottle candles are used for working or spell candles, draw the images on the glass with a marker. When drawing a mandala (a double-ring circle: ◯) leave space in the center of the circle for symbols and space between the rings for writing or symbols. For carving symbols on candles, mandalas, and meditations, the bold print in the text shows the words that are spoken as the images are drawn. A votive spell candle should have an appropriate container (such as a cauldron) that can hold melted wax and burning herbs without breaking or damaging the pentacle. Have a cover or lid to smother the flame. Use a candle snuffer to extinguish the working candle and altar candles, but if blown out, say: **With the breath of life.** For activities making an incense or powder, the herbs may be ground prior to the ritual and blended during the activity. Use glass, china, or pottery bowls and bottles to prepare and store herbal, tea, and oil blends. Label the stored bottles. Loose black tea leaves normally form the base of herbal tea blends. Green tea leaves have a cleansing energy whereas the black is associated with strength and power.

START AND FINISH FOR MEDITATIONS

Rather than repeat the opening and closing portions of the meditations that come under the Mansions of the Moon magical workings, I am placing them here. Each mansion meditation will state at the start: (*Go to MEDITATION BEGINNING*) and state at the end: (*Go to MEDITATION ENDING*). Thus, when the magical work is a meditation, the only portion under the mansion heading will be the actual meditation, so you will have to turn to this part for the beginning, turn to the mansion for the meditation, and return to this part for the ending before proceeding to the Cakes and Wine of the Esbat ritual. The **spoken words** are in bold print.

MEDITATION BEGINNING

Sit comfortably, with eyes closed if desired, and relax to ground and center. Feel the stress and chaotic energies of the day drain away down from the top of the head, down the neck, from the arms and hands and where it all collects in the torso . . . feel the energy drain down the body, through the legs, passing from the feet into the ground below. Let the tensions of the day drain away until there is stillness within, at the center of the body.

Take a deep breath 1, 2; hold 1, 2; and release 1, 2, letting any remaining extraneous energies and confusions of the day drain away with that breath, feeling that calmness spreading throughout the body. Take a second deep breath 1, 2, feeling the inrush of cleansing air; hold 1, 2, feeling the fresh energy; and release 1, 2, feeling a sense of balance throughout the body. Take a third deep breath 1, 2, feeling the energy of the cosmos; hold 1, 2, feeling peace spreading throughout the body; and release 1, 2, feeling a oneness with the universe. Now breathe normally.

Toes, ankles, feet, and legs are feeling relaxed; the body is feeling relaxed; the fingers, hands, and arms are feeling relaxed; the neck and head are feeling relaxed. Envision roots growing from the bottoms of the feet, plunging through any obstacle to reach deep into the rich earth. The roots now pull in the green, vibrant energy of the earth. Just like a tree draws in water, the roots draw this powerful earth energy up into the feet, up into the legs, up through the torso, into the arms and hands, up through the neck and to the top of the head.

Envision a shaft of white light, of cosmic energy, entering into the top of the head, cascading down the body, cleansing and bringing the chakras—the energy points of

the body—into balance. The energy gathers at the feet and rises again, interweaving with the earth energy, back to the top of the head and down again, blending and harmonizing serene cosmic energy with invigorating earth energy. Feel calmness, feel energy, feel relaxed and comfortable in this blend, knowing more energy from the earth and the cosmos can be drawn in as needed to remain calm and relaxed, but also energized. Feel relaxed in the toes, in the ankles, in the lower legs, in the upper legs, in the lower body, in the upper body, in the fingers, the lower arms, the upper arms, in the shoulders, and in the neck; the body is totally relaxed.

Think now of a place where you feel safe and secure. This is a personal and private place; a special place of comfort and peace. Look around and see the familiar surroundings of this private haven, knowing this is a personal inner sanctuary. This is a place visited before or for the first time, but this is the starting point for all meditations; a place that becomes clearer and more detailed with every visit; a place that becomes familiar and exactly what is desired. It is from here that inner visions begin and expand; it is from here that travels and explorations to other regions and worlds begin and end, from where to start a journey and where to return when the journey is over.

(INSERT MEDITATION FROM THE MANSION OF THE MOON.)

MEDITATION ENDING

Now, it is time to return to the private place of security and safety; time to return to the personal sanctuary. Remember the inner sanctuary; see yourself returning to the place of peace and comfort. Now, you enter into the safe haven, remembering what has passed and what has been learned.

Take a deep breath and slowly release the breath, moving away from the sanctuary now. Take another deep breath, and slowly release the breath, and feel the returning of normal awareness. Take a third deep breath, slowly release it, and begin moving the arms and shoulders while returning closer to normal awareness. At the count of three, full awareness returns mentally alert and fully refreshed. One, two, three. Be awake and refreshed. Remember what was seen at the personal sanctuary, and what occurred in the meditation.

MANSIONS OF THE MOON

ARIES

Tonight the Moon is in ♈ Aries, the Ram, ruled by ♂ Mars with the aggressive energy for leadership, vitality, focus, and exactitude

In the Mansion of the Moon called:

New Moon Waning

- **ALNATH, the Horns of Aries** (0♈0 to 12♈51) **ruled by GENIEL for discord and destroying a foe**

   Light this candle to repel the discord energy of the mansion in this lunar phase.

Magical work: candle to halt discord. Dress a red working candle with dragon's blood oil: **Red for energy; dragon's blood for power.** In the wax, carve around it: | **Is to halt negative energies and discord;** ᛗ **Eh for security;** ᛇ **Eoh for protection and banishing discord;** ᚾ **Nyd for protection and constraining discord; and** ᛉ **Eohl for protection against discord.** Light the working candle from the center altar candle: **This flame burns to transmute discord into positive vitality!** Consecrate a black votive spell candle and dress with myrrh oil: **Black for protection, warding negativity, and repelling discord; myrrh for protection, warding negativity, and binding discord.** Carve in the wax around it: ᚺ **Haegl to halt discord throughout the waning and dark phases of the Moon!** ᚦ **Thorn for protection and safety!** ᛒ **Beorc to protect family!** ᛟ **Ethel to protect possessions!** ᛋ **Sigel for power and success in halting discord!** Set the spell candle in a cauldron on top of the pentacle. Light a taper from the working candle and use it to light the spell candle. Charge a piece of red jasper, then drop it into the candle flame: **With red jasper to deflect negative energy!** Charge the candle. With the wand or athame, gather energy deosil: **Through the Goddess and the God; through the Moon and the Sun; through the Elementals, runes, herbs, and stone; this candle halts the discord energy of Geniel in Alnath!** Direct and release the energy into the candle: **DISCORD STOPS! So Mote It Be!** Let the candle burn for thirty minutes to an hour, then snuff and scry the wax for relevant images. Remove the red jasper and clean it to place, carry, or wear as desired. Dispose of candle remains.

Dark Moon

• **ALNATH, the Horns of Aries** (0♈0 to 12♈51) **ruled by GENIEL for discord and destroying a foe**

Drink a tablespoon of this elixir to ward against discord and restore calm.

Magical work: elixir to ward against discord. Rub a red working candle with sandalwood oil: **Red for energy and power; sandalwood for protection and warding negativity.** In the wax, carve around it: ⚏ **Phul for defeating evil; and** ⚏ **Phaleg for power and victory.** Light the working candle from the center altar candle: **This flame burns to ward against discord and negativity!** Hold up a piece of peridot over the pentacle: **I call upon you peridot for protection and warding discord!** Place the stone in a small jar of spring water. Set the jar on the pentacle and cup your hands over the top of the water: **This elixir gives protection and wards discord!** Hold up a teaspoon of vodka, brandy, whiskey, or rum over the pentacle, state the intention, and add the alcohol to the jar of water: **This elixir fixed and sealed!** Charge the blend. With the wand or athame, gather energy deosil: **Through the guidance of the Veiled Goddess and the God; through the hidden Moon and the setting Sun; through the Elementals, planets, and stone; with the power of Phul and Phaleg, this elixir wards against the discord energy of Geniel in Alnath!** Direct and release the energy into the elixir: **DISCORD WARDED! So Mote It Be!** Leave the elixir on the pentacle for thirty minutes to an hour. Snuff the candle and dispose of the remains. Remove the stone and cleanse. Store the tightly covered jar of elixir away from light. Sip a tablespoon of the elixir as needed or sprinkle in an area to repel discord.

New Moon Waning

• **ALBOTAYN, the Belly of Aries** (12♈51 to 25♈42) **ruled by ENEDIEL for destroying buildings under construction and creating arguments**

This charm bag protects against those who deliberately instigate arguments.

Magical work: charm bag to ward against arguments. Dress a black working candle with vetiver oil: **Black to ward against and bind negativity; Vetiver to ward negativity and exorcise ill will from others.** In the wax, carve around it: ♈ **Aries for strong leadership;** ♂ **Mars for dynamic energy;** ᚼ **As for skillful communication;** ᛒ **Beorc for protection and safety of family;** ᚾ **Nyd for protection and self-control against argumentative people; and** ᛉ **Eolh for protection from enemies and for controlling**

emotions. Light the working candle from the center altar candle: **This flame burns to ward arguments instigated by others!** Lay out a six-inch square of black cloth: **Black for protection and warding negative energies!** Set out a six-inch long narrow red ribbon to tie the charm bundle (or thread if sewing it): **Red for power!** One at a time, hold up over the pentacle some of each of the following seven herbs, state the intention, and place on the cloth: **I call upon you basil for protection and repelling negativity! I call upon you burdock for protection and to ward negativity! I call upon you fennel to deflect negative energies! I call upon you peppercorn for protection and warding negativity! I call upon you yarrow for defense, protection, and warding negativity! I call upon you agrimony to return argumentative energy to the sender! I call upon you thyme for swift action in warding negativity and arguments!** Add 1 small drop of vetiver oil to a cotton ball: **With the power of vetiver are these energies blended to ward argumentative energy and discord!** Set this on top of the bundle. Tie the bundle with the ribbon (or sew shut) and set it on the pentacle. Charge the charm. With the wand or athame, raise energy moving deosil: **Through the Goddess and the God, through the Moon and the Sun, through the Elementals, runes, and herbs; this charm wards against the argumentative energy of Enediel in Albotayn!** Direct and release the energy into the charm: **ARGUMENTS STOPPED! So Mote It Be!** Leave the charm bag on the pentacle for thirty minutes to an hour. Snuff the candle and dispose of the remains. Carry or place the charm where desired.

Dark Moon

• **ALBOTAYN, the Belly of Aries** (12 ♈ 51 to 25 ♈ 42) **ruled by ENEDIEL for destroying buildings under construction and creating arguments**

   Use this meditation to uncover the source of argumentative energy in order to better deal with the real issues.

Magical work: meditation for ending arguments. Dress a purple working candle with frankincense oil: **Purple for progress and protection; frankincense for protection and psychic energy.** Light the working candle from the center altar candle: **This flame burns for progress and protection!** (*Go to MEDITATION BEGINNING.*)

   Pose in your mind a question, a problem, a situation where you need the advice, guidance, or direction from the Veiled Goddess to uncover the source of arguments in order to find workable solutions. Formulate your thought and let it slip into the depths of your mind.

Take a few steps from your safe place, and see that you are standing in a pleasant, broad, sunlit meadow bordered by a deep forest. In the distance you see tall mountains, and you remember that you have walked in the woods before, but have not climbed the mountain before. You walk now toward the forest. The woods are shady and dark, with a coolness you can feel as you approach. It is very inviting to enter the shadowy forest and leave the heat of the sun behind you. You see a narrow dirt path and remember this was one you followed before, but now you notice another trail winding away in another direction, toward the mountains you can no longer see, but know are nearby. You follow this trail, and soon the woods thin out so you can see the snowy peaks of the mountain range beyond the woodlands. The trail is easy to walk, and you hear the twittering of birds around you. Your totem animal or your guide is coming to walk with you. The air is crisp and clean, and a slight breeze fans your face as, together with your companion, you follow the trail away from the trees and past large boulders where the trail winds up toward a snowcapped mountaintop.

The air is cool, but not unpleasant as the Sun shines brightly in the clear blue sky. With tour totem animal or guide, you climb the gentle slope, following the dirt path that threads a passage among tall boulders. Brush is sparse, and now you are walking on patches of snow. You pause and look down to see the tops of trees blotting out the forest floor. The meadow is an opening in the forest, and you see the rivulets of water from melting snow meandering down the mountain to disappear into the woods.

Now, you look up and continue with your companion, passing rocks, snowy patches, and little streams until you notice that the snowcap on top of the mountain conceals a small, dry cave, and this is where your guide is leading you. You move along a ledge of rock, and come to the opening of the cave. You look inside. At first it may appear dark, but as your eyes adjust, you see that is clean and tidy. There is a bearskin rug on the ground, a small fire pit with a fire burning, and a tripod with a cauldron hanging from it over the fire.

Your guide motions you to enter, and you brush past some overhanging grasses, wet with the melting snow, which drizzles on you as enter the cave. You turn to look out and discover the view is panoramic, taking in forest, meadow, and the circling mountain ranges. You remember that ancient sages were known to meditate and commune with the Divine in places like this. You feel comfortable and secure here as the atmosphere of calm and compassion wraps gently around you. You turn back to look at the cauldron, and now you see that an old woman, cloaked and hidden in the shadows is moving to stir the contents of the pot with a dark, long-handled wooden spoon.

"Look within," she whispers, "and see what you will see. Listen to the steam and bubbles, and hear what you will hear."

You take a step to the cauldron, and gaze within, looking and listening. Is there a symbol in the cauldron? A rune? A sentence? An image? Look and see. (*Pause.*) **Do you hear a voice? A word? A song? A call? Listen and hear.** (Pause)

Remember what you have seen and heard. Look up from the cauldron. Your companion motions to you, and you know it is time to return down the mountain path. You nod to the ancient Crone, who smiles as you turn and walk out of the cave, past the overhanging, dripping, grasses, and into the bright sunlight. The path down the mountain is easy to tread, and you feel comfortable walking past the ancient stones and the little streams.

Now, you pass some trees, and the path takes you into the cool, dark forest. You know your way back to your safe place and quickly walk through the woods. Your companion leaves you at the edge of the woods as you return to the meadow. The Sun shines over the grasses and flowers of the meadow, and you brush your hand over the tall, soft grasses, moving back now to your sanctuary, your safe place. You gaze back at the forest and the mountains beyond, remembering what you have experienced. Remember your companion in the forest. Remember what you saw and heard in the cavern. Before you go to sleep tonight, ask the Earth spirits and the universe to make the meanings clear to you if need be. (*Go to MEDITATION END-ING.*) Snuff the candle and dispose of the remains.

New Moon Waning

• **ATHORAY, the Showering of Pleiades** (25 ♈ 42 to 8 ♉ 34) **ruled by AMIXIEL for curbing overindulgence**

This is used to help with moderation after indulging in too much of any good thing during the waxing aspect of this mansion, especially if this lead to bad habits or addictions or over-consumption of food or alcohol.

Magical work: charm to restrict overindulgence. Dress a red working candle with frankincense oil: **Red for energy; frankincense for protection and power.** In the wax, carve around it: ᛁ **Is to halt negative energies and unwanted forces;** ᛇ **Eoh to remove ob-stacles to moderation;** ᛗ **Mannaz for self-improvement and curbing excesses;** ᛞ **Daeg for a breakthrough in ending overindulgence;** ᛚ **Lagu for the energy needed for long term success;** ᚲ **and Ken for opening the way to well-being.** Light the work-ing candle from the center altar candle: **This flame burns to restrict overindulgence!** Lay out a six-inch square of orange cloth: **Orange for vitality, healing, encourage-ment, and success!** Set out a six-inch long narrow yellow ribbon to tie the charm bun-dle (or thread if sewing it): **Yellow for health, changes, and harmony!** One at a time, hold up over the pentacle some of each of the following herbs, state the intention, then place on the cloth: **I call upon you nettle for protection against overindulgence and restoring balance! I call upon you mullein for good health and restricting overin-dulgence! I call upon you hyssop for warding negativity that leads to overindul-gence! I call upon you lemon balm for success in restricting overindulgence! I call upon you jasmine for good health!** Hold up over the pentacle a piece of iolite: **I call upon the energies of iolite for breaking bad habits and addictive behavior!** Put it on the cloth. Add 1 drop of dragon's blood oil to a cotton ball: **With dragon's blood for protection and power to make changes, all these energies are blended to restrict overindulgence!** Set this on top of the bundle. Tie the bundle with the ribbon (or sew shut) and set it on the pentacle. Charge the charm. With the wand or athame, raise en-ergy moving deosil: **Through the Goddess and the God; through the Moon and the Sun; through the Elementals, runes, herbs, and stone; with the energy of Amixiel in Athoray; this charm restricts overindulgence!** Direct and release the energy into the charm: **EXCESS RESTRICTED! So Mote It Be!** Leave the charm on the pentacle for thirty minutes to an hour. Snuff the candle and dispose of the remains. Carry or place the charm where desired.

Dark Moon

• **ATHORAY, the Showering of Pleiades** (25 ♈ 42 to 8 ♉ 34) **ruled by AMIXIEL for curb-ing overindulgence**

This is used to help restrain excesses in every good thing associated with the waxing man-sion, in whatever form it takes.

Magical work: meditation for restricting overindulgence. Dress a purple working candle with frankincense oil: **Purple for meditative work; frankincense for power, protection, and**

meditation. Light the working candle from the center altar candle: **This flame burns for restricting overindulgence!** (*Go to MEDITATION BEGINNING.*)

Through the wisdom of the Veiled Goddess, let Amixiel in Athoray open the way to understanding how to restrict a tendency for excess in a needed area of your life. What behavior needs to be curbed? Is it eating? Drinking? Gossiping? Taking risks? Arguing? Competing? In your mind, ask what spirits and entities of nature are willing to help you curb your intemperance. Let the thought slip away into the depths of your mind as you step away from your safe place and see that you are standing in a pleasant, broad, sunlit meadow bordered on one side by a forest. You feel content and secure here, and walk toward the forest. The woods are shady and dark, with a coolness you can feel as you approach. It is very inviting to enter the shadowy forest and leave the heat of the Sun behind you. You see a narrow dirt path and you follow it into the woods, winding past trees and leafy bushes deeper into the forest. The ground is moist and covered in leaf litter and you pause now to listen carefully—what sounds do you hear? You look around through the dense clusters of trees. What do you see? Are there animals? Birds? Small creatures? Large ones?

Look and see which one looks at you, and follow the one that beckons you with a nod of the head or a glance over the shoulder. You are moving deeper into the forest now, and the trail narrows and disappears, leaving only an animal path to follow. Your guide pauses and you look down. See the tiny trails of mice and rabbits creating tunnels in the underbrush. Now look up and continue following your guide, gently moving aside the branches of shrubs and saplings as you follow your guide deeper into the woods.

You hear the bubbling of a small stream as it meanders through the forest and you know you are nearing the center of the woods. The sound of the flowing water is louder now, and you realize there must be a pond close by where the stream gathers in a deep pool. You can smell the scent of a trout as it breaks the surface of the pool to snap up a careless fly.

Your guide leads you into a tiny clearing, and you see the pool, with its mossy banks, slippery rocks, and disheveled bits of tangled fall-wood and vines giving it a gently wild appearance. Around the pool are the low-hanging branches of hazel trees, their burden of nuts drooping down, some touching the water, and you know you are in a sacred place.

Your guide drinks from the clear, glistening pool, and you know you should look into the deep waters. Moving quietly, you feel a sensation of calm as you approach the pool. Now, you are standing beside your guide, and you look into the pool. There you see a large trout swimming gracefully in the depths, and the fish fixes an eye on you. The shimmering creature swims upward, breaking the surface of the water into gentle ripples. You recognize that this is the pool guarding the gateway to Faerie, and it is the home of the wise old trout who feeds upon the hazelnuts of wisdom.

You are not surprised when the fish opens its mouth and speaks to you about how to bring an unwanted excess under control and who might be of help and offer you advice. Listen and remember the words of the wise old trout. (*Pause.*) The trout turns suddenly and slips beneath the waters, disappearing behind old tree limbs at the bottom of the pool. Now, you look upon the shimmering water of this Faerie pool surrounded by hazel trees. A vision comes into focus for your eyes alone to see. Look and remember what you see. (*Pause.*)

Your guide moves closer and nudges you and you know it is time to go back. Moving quickly along back to the familiar trail, you follow your guide back to the edge of the forest. You see before you the sunlit meadow, and then your guide turns and disappears into the silent shadows of the deep woods. You walk into the meadow and stand gazing back at the forest; remembering what you have experienced. Remember the journey you undertook. Remember your guide into the forest. Remember the message of the trout. Remember the vision you saw in the pool. Before you go to sleep tonight, ask the Earth spirits and the universe to make the meanings clear to you if need be. (*Go to MEDITATION ENDING.*) Snuff the candle and dispose of the remains.

TAURUS

Tonight the Moon is in ♉ Taurus, the Bull, ruled by ♀ Venus, with energies for the values of stability, productivity, and practicality, and with the available energy of three fixed stars:

Algol, the Head of Algol: audacity, victory, protection; Saturn and Jupiter. Taurus; diamond; hellebore

Pleiades: secrets, talk to spirits; Moon and Mars; Taurus; crystal; fennel

Aldebaran: good fortune, create discord; Mars and Venus; Gemini; ruby or Garnet; milk thistle

In the Mansion of the Moon called:

New Moon Waning

• **ATHORAY, the Showering of Pleiades (25 ♈ 42 to 8 ♉ 34) ruled by AMIXIEL for curbing overindulgence**

This dieting tea uses the waning energy to restrict intemperance that may have come with the waxing energy of every good thing, so that moderation is restored.

Magical work: tea to banish overindulgence when dieting. Dress a light blue working candle with rosemary oil: **Blue for good health and warding depression; rosemary for cleansing, good health, and vigor. In the wax, carve around it: ⟩ Nyd for patience and self-control to achieve goals; ✕ Aldebaran for good fortune; Algol for protection and victory; ⟨ Gera for tangible results from efforts; and ⟨ Ken for transforming energy for physical well-being.** Light the working candle from the center altar candle: **This flame burns to banish overindulgence when dieting!** Set on the pentacle a clean non-plastic or metal bowl in which to blend herbs. Add to the bowl 1 cup of loose black tea leaves. I call upon you black tea for vigor and strength! One at a time, hold up over the pentacle ¼ teaspoon of each herb, state the intention, and add it to the bowl: **I call upon you milk thistle to deflect negativity and remove toxins! I call upon you fennel seed for purification and good health!** Hold up over the pentacle ⅛ cup of each herb, state the intention, and add it to the bowl: **I call upon you hops** for good health! I call upon you dandelion root for cleansing and good fortune! Blend the herbs and black tea leaves with a wooden spoon. Charge the blend. With the wand or athame, gather energy deosil: **Through the Goddess and the God; through the Moon and the Sun; through the Elementals and stars; through runes and herbs; this tea helps curb overindulgence energy of Amixiel in Athoray when dieting!** Direct and release the energy into the tea: **EXCESS STOPPED! So Mote It Be!** Leave the tea blend on the pentacle for thirty minutes to an hour. Snuff the candle and dispose of the remains. Put the tea blend in a tightly covered jar and store away from light. Brew a cup of tea when needed to halt intemperate eating or drinking.

Dark Moon

• **ATHORAY, the Showering of Pleiades** (25 ♈ 42 to 8 ♉ 34) **ruled by AMIXIEL for curbing overindulgence**

Use this meditation to remove overindulgence in any area of life. The waning energy can aid with restricting the excesses that came from the waxing energy of every good thing.

Magical work: meditation to release the cause for overindulgence. Dress a purple working candle with frankincense oil: **Purple for wisdom and power; frankincense for meditation and power.** Light the working candle from the center altar candle: **This flame burns for wisdom and power in meditation!** (*Go to MEDITATION BEGINNING.*)

With the wisdom of the Veiled Goddess and the energy of Amixiel in Athoray, consider those areas in your life where there is overindulgence. Do you eat too much? Drink too much? Spend too much? Engage in self-pity too much? Give up your time too much? What is it that you overindulge in? What prompts you into doing more than you should in this area of your life? While in your safe place, focus on each of your chakras to reveal the source of your excesses. At the root chakra at the base of the spine, what are the buried fears and insecurity? At the abdominal chakra, what causes fear? At the belly chakra, what causes the insatiable need for consumption? At the heart chakra, what are the causes of worry and emotional distress? At the throat chakra, what are the careless words that injure the self-image? At the third-eye chakra, what beneficial inner voice has been suppressed? At the crown chakra at the top of the head, what has caused the loving light of cosmic energy to be blocked?

You examine these issues, and now you gather together the negativity that activates your indulgence and excesses. You see an open dark blue velvet bag with a silver cord drawstring, and you know what to do. The energies you gathered are like a gauzy mist, like lint from a clothes dryer trap, and you peel the energies of excess from you, rolling them up on themselves until all are removed from you. You stuff the roll of negative energies and unhealthy habits into the bag, and close it by pulling the drawstring tight. Wrap the silver cord around the top of the bag and knot it. Now, you have to dispose of the bag.

Looking outward from your place, you see the vast expanse of the deep night sky, sprinkled with stars. So deep is the night, it is like black velvet. You see the Milky Way, filled with the sparkling stars, spiraling thru the darkness, and you realize that this reminds you of a glittering white road. You look down and see the bright lights at your feet, and you know that the white road begins at the entrance of your safe place. Looking up again, you see in the distance a waterfall of starlight coming from seven stars, and you know they are the Pleiades. From your safe place, you can see there is someone behind the cascading starlight and you understand that you may step onto the starry road to be whisked away to the waterfall. Take that step onto the starry road, and walk with swift steps that sweep you to the Pleiades and that starry cataract. You know you are safe, you have your bag of negative energies secure in your hand, and now you stand before the cascading starlight.

Behind the flowing light you see a large, glowing, friendly figure, and you know this is Amixiel in Athoray. He is crowned by nine stars: Algol for protection and victory, the Pleiades for secrets and talking to entities, and Aldebaran for good fortune. With the stars around his head and his smiling countenance, you are reminded that there are times for excess and times for control, and understanding this now, you hold out to him the bag you have carried. Amixiel opens his hands to receive it and you must pass the bag through the starlight cascade to him. You comprehend the significance of this action, for the stars cleanse away the negativity as you happily pass the burdensome bag through the showering light and into the hands of Amixiel. He sets the bag behind him, and you see now that there are many other bags there, all good in their proper time and place, but put aside until appropriate.

The light of the cascade becomes dazzling and brilliant, and you feel a rush of exhilaration as the light washes over you, cleansing you and releasing you from your burden. You take a step back, and with a smile, you bow slightly to Amixiel. He nods to you, and you feel yourself move swiftly back along the white road as the cascading starlight retreats far away from you. Take a quick look at the universe around you as you travel back, back, to the entrance of your safe place. The starry road is fading, and you take a voluntary step off the road and back into your safe place. The starry road vanishes now, and only the night sky is visible before you. Take a deep breath and draw into yourself the strength and power of the earth, blending it with the cosmic light within you, to bring your destiny into reality. Release the breath, and know that you are now able to bring your goals into manifestation without the burden of overindulgence. (*Go to MEDITATION ENDING.*) Snuff the candle and dispose of the remains.

New Moon Waning

• **ALDEBARAN, the Eye of Taurus** (8 ♉ 34 to 21 ♉ 25) **ruled by AZARIEL for discord, hindrance, revenge, enmity, and separation**

Light this candle to repel the energy of hindrance from any area of your life.

Magical work: candle spell to repel hindrance to goals. Dress a red working candle with sandalwood oil: **Red for energy and power; sandalwood for protection and warding negativity.** In the wax, carve around it: | **Is to halt negative energies and hindrances;** Ħ **Haegl to restrict the energies of hindrance;** ↑ **Nyd to overcome hindrances to objectives;** Y **Eolh to protect against enemies who create hindrances to my objectives;** ħ **Saturn to restrict energies that hinder self-preservation or ambition;** ♉ **and Taurus for strength and stability to repel hindrances.** Light the working candle from the center altar candle: **This flame burns to repel what hinders achievement of my objectives!** Consecrate a black votive spell candle and dress with bergamot oil: **Black to ward negativity and hindrances; bergamot to break hindrances.** In the wax, carve around it: Ϟ **Perth for revealing hindrances!** Ϻ **Daeg for a breakthrough against hindrances!** ↓ **Eoh for banishing and removing hindrances to my objectives!** ϟ **Sigel for success in repelling hindrances!** ♟ᵾⅢ⅃ **Algol for victory in repelling hindrances to my objectives!** Charge the candle and set it in a cauldron on top of the pentacle. Light a taper from the working candle and use it to light the spell candle. One at a time, hold up a pinch of each herb over the pentacle, state the intention, and add it to the flame: **I call upon you fennel to deflect** negative energies! I call upon you agrimony to return hindrance energy to whoever sends it to me! I call upon you vetiver to ward negativity and break hindrances to my goals! I call upon you thyme for swift action in repelling hindrances to my objectives! With the wand or athame, gather energy deosil: **Through the Goddess and the God; through the Moon and the Sun; through the Elementals, planets, and star; through runes and herbs; this candle repels the hindrance energy of Azariel in Aldebaran!** Direct and release the energy into the candle: **HINDRANCE REPELLED! So Mote It Be!** Let the candle burn for thirty minutes to an hour, then snuff it and look at the wax for relevant images. Dispose of candle remains.

Dark Moon

• **ALDEBARAN, the Eye of Taurus** (8 ♉ 34 to 21 ♉ 25) **ruled by AZARIEL for discord, hindrance, revenge, separations, enmity**

With knowledge of what hinders you in a matter, you can then work to remove that blockage.

Magical work: rune divination to reveal hindrances. Dress a black working candle with frankincense oil: **Black for truth, warding negativity, and removing confusion; frankincense for power, protection, and opening psychic awareness.** In the wax, carve around it: ⚹ **the Pleiades for opening the way to learning secrets and opening psychic communication;** ⚸ **Algol for victory and protection;** ╳ **Aldebaran for success and good fortune.** Light the working candle from the center altar candle: **This flame burns to reveal what hinders me in my objectives!** Charge a bag of runes and set it on top of the pentacle. Focus on a personal matter where energy seems blocked: **With the guidance of the Veiled Goddess, let these runes show me where the hindrance energy of Azariel in Aldebaran affects me in the matter of** (state hindered effort)! Shake the bag and pull out one rune: **This is the current situation.** Examine the symbol and consider how this relates to the matter. Pull out a second rune: **This is the foundation of the situation.** Consider how this relates to the background of the matter. Pull out a third rune: **This is what will unblock the hindrance.** Consider how to overcome the obstacle or redefine what is really desired. While a solution may not be given, understanding the possible source of the interference may be enough to determine how to handle the situation. Meditate on the runes, or draw one more for further guidance. Snuff the candle and dispose of the remains. If still uncertain, at bedtime, ask the universe for clarification. An answer should come through lucid dreaming within a few days, or by sudden insight upon awakening.

New Moon Waning

• **ALBACHAY, the Head of Orion** (21 ♉ 25 to 4 ♊ 17) **ruled by GABIEL for destroying alliances or friendships**

This oil may be worn, dabbed in an appropriate area, or added to a charm bag to remove the negative energy threatening to destroy alliances or friendships.

Magical work: oil to banish energies destructive to friendships or alliances. Dress a black working candle with sandalwood oil: **Black for warding negativity and removing discord; sandalwood for protection and warding negativity.** In the wax, carve around it: **| Is to halt negative energies and unwanted forces; ♀ Venus for sociability; ♉ Taurus for stability; ⊟ Hagith for friendship; ⸰⫯⫼ Algol for victory; ᛗ Mannaz for cooperation among friends; ᛉ Osa for a favorable outcome.** Light the working candle from the center altar candle: **This flame burns to banish energies destructive to friendships and alliances!** In a small glass bottle with lid, blend the following essential oils: 1 part vetiver: **I call upon you vetiver to exorcise destructive energies!** 2 parts myrrh: **I call upon you myrrh to bind destructive energies and protect friendships and alliances!** 1 part clove: **I call upon you clove to ward negativity from friends and alliances!** Add 2 parts grapeseed, saffron, or canola oil. Put the lid on the bottle, shake: **All are blended to work together for my purpose!** Place the bottle on the pentacle. Charge the oil. With the wand or athame, gather energy deosil: **Through the Goddess and the God; through the Moon and the Sun; through the Elementals, planets, and stars; through runes and herbs; with the power of Hagith; this oil banishes the energy of Gabiel in Albachay that is destructive to friendships and alliances!** Direct and release the energy into the bottle: **DESTRUCTION BANISHED! So Mote It Be!** Leave the oil on the pentacle for thirty minutes to an hour. Snuff the candle and dispose of the remains. Use a dab of oil as needed.

Dark Moon

• **ALBACHAY, the Head of Orion** (21♉25 to 4♊17) **ruled by GABIEL for destroying alliances or friendships**

Sip alone or share this meditative tea to deflect the energy that threatens to destroy friendships or alliances.

Magical work: tea to deflect negativity in friendships or alliances. Dress a black working candle with rosemary oil: **Black for warding negativity and deflecting discord and confusion; rosemary for protection of friendships or alliances.** In the wax, carve around it: ♀ **Venus to reinforce friendships, alliances, and sociability; ⎯ Hagith to reinforce friendships and alliances; and ☋♉♒ Algol for victory against energy that threatens to destroy friendships or alliances.** Light the working candle from the center altar candle: **This flame burns to deflect negativity in friendships or alliances!** Set on the pentacle a clean non-plastic or metal bowl in which to blend herbs. Add to the bowl ½ cup of loose black tea leaves. **Black tea for vigor and strength!** One at a time, hold up over the pentacle ¼ teaspoon of each herb, state the intention, and add it to the bowl: **Burdock root to ward negativity! Fennel to protect friendships and alliances!** Hold up over the pentacle ⅛ cup of each herb, state the intention, and add it to the bowl: **Chamomile for calm in friendships and alliances! Hops for relaxation in friendships and alliances!** Blend the herbs and black tea with a wooden spoon. Charge the blend. With the wand or athame, gather energy deosil: **Through the guidance of the Veiled Goddess and the God; through the hidden Moon and the setting Sun; through the Elementals, planets, stars, and herbs; with the power of Hagith; this tea deflects the energy of Gabiel in Albachay that is destructive to friendships and alliances!** Direct and release the energy into the tea: **DESTRUCTION DEFLECTED! So Mote It Be!** Leave the tea blend on the pentacle for thirty minutes to an hour. Snuff the candle and dispose of the remains. Store the tea blend in a closed jar away from light. Brew as needed.

GEMINI

Tonight the Moon is in ♊ Gemini, the Twins, ruled by ☿ Mercury, with the energy of versatility, wit, perception, rationality, and changeability, and the available energies of two fixed stars:

Capella, the Goat Star: honors, favor of superiors; Jupiter and Saturn; Gemini; sapphire; thyme

Cauda Ursa, the Tail of the Bear (Polaris): protection from personal violence and thieves; Venus and Moon; Gemini; lodestone; endive

In the Mansion of the Moon called:

New Moon Waning

• ALBACHAY, the Head of Orion (21♉25 to 4♊17) ruled by GABIEL for destroying alliances or friendships

Use this amulet to repel friend- or alliance-destroying energies during the waning to dark phases of the Moon in this mansion.

Magical work: amulet to avert energies destructive to friendships and alliances. Dress a red working candle with ginger oil: **Red for power and energy; ginger for success and goodwill.** In the wax, carve around it: **Hagith to deflect negativity from friendships and alliances; Ophiel for good communication skills; ♊ Gemini for wit and perception; Capella to preserve favor and esteem; ☽ the Moon for sensitivity to others; ☉ the Sun for success and joy; and ♃ Jupiter for optimism.** Light the working candle from the center altar candle: **This flame burns to avert energies destructive to friendships and alliances!** Hold up over the pentacle a clean piece of yellow calcite: **Yellow calcite to manifest goals!** Set the calcite on the pentacle: **I call upon you yellow calcite to banish blockages and avert destructive energies to friendships and alliances!** Charge the calcite. With the wand or athame, gather energy deosil: **Through the Goddess and the God; through the Moon and the Sun; through the Elementals, planets, and stars; through runes and stone; with the power of Hagith and Ophiel; this calcite averts the energies of Gabiel in Albachay that are destructive to friendships and alliances!** Direct and release the energy into the stone:

ILL WILL AVERTED! So Mote It Be! Leave the calcite on the pentacle for thirty minutes to an hour. Snuff the candle and dispose of the remains. Carry or place the calcite where desired.

Dark Moon

• **ALBACHAY, the Head of Orion** (21♉25 to 4♊17) **ruled by GABIEL for destroying alliances or friendships**

This divination will reveal weaknesses in friendships or alliances where destructive energies may manifest, thereby providing you the opportunity to take action to avert this.

Magical work: Tarot divination for weaknesses in friendships or alliances. Dress a purple working candle with frankincense oil: **Purple for protection and insight; frankincense for protection and psychic energy.** In the wax, carve around it: ♆ **Neptune for psychic awareness;** ☽ **the Moon for sensitivity and nurturing; and** ♀ **Venus for friendship and sociability.** Light the working candle from the center altar candle: **This flame burns to reveal weak areas in friendships or alliances!** Charge a tarot deck and set it on top of the pentacle. Focus on seeking weaknesses in friendships or alliances. **Through the wisdom of the Veiled Goddess, these cards reveal what energy of Gabiel in Albachay might destroy friendships or alliances!** Shuffle the deck, cut the deck and restack the cards or spread them on a table. Deal or select the first card: **This is how I see myself.** Deal or draw a second card. **This is how others see me.** Deal or draw a third card. **This is what interferes with friendships or alliances.** Interpret the cards as they relate to the question. If the answer seems unclear, deal or select another card, lay it on the one in question, and read the two together for more information. Now deal or select the solution card: **This is how I can strengthen friendships or alliances.** Interpret the card, adding another if needed to help clarify the answer. Understanding what might be causing the interference may be enough to determine how to handle the situation or deal with a weak area in a relationship. Snuff the candle and dispose of the remains. If still uncertain, at bedtime, ask the universe for clarification. An answer should come through lucid dreaming within a few days, or by sudden insight upon awakening.

New Moon Waning

- **ALCHAYA, the Little Star of Great Light** (4♊17 to 17♊8) **ruled by DIRACHIEL for destroying business empires, or cities, or crops, or health, and for revenge**

  Light this candle to ward energy that is destructive to health.

Magical work: candle to ward against health-destructive energy. Dress a red working candle with rosemary oil: **Red for energy, power, and health; rosemary for protection and health.** In the wax, carve around it: ↓ **Eoh to remove obstacles to good health;** | **Is to halt negative energies;** ⟨ **Ken to protect health;** ♂ **Mars for dynamic energy; and** ♃ **Jupiter for good health:** Light the working candle from the center altar candle: **This flame burns to ward against energy destructive to health!** Consecrate a light blue votive spell candle and dress with myrrh oil: **Light blue for health; myrrh for protection and warding negativity.** In the wax, carve around it: ▶ **Thorn for protection and neutralizing destructive energy!** ⋎ **Eolh to strengthen the life force!** ⟩⟩⟩⟨ **Cauda Ursa, the Tail of the Bear for protection and power!** ♄ **Saturn for self-preservation and restricting destructive energies!** ⛿ **Phul to defeat evil! and** ⊥ **Och for healing energy!** Charge the candle and set it in a cauldron on top of the pentacle. Light a taper from the working candle and use it to light the spell candle. One at a time, hold up a pinch of each herb over the pentacle. State the intention and drop it into the spell candle flame: **I call upon you basil for protection and repelling energies destructive to health! I call upon you juniper berry for protection from energies destructive to health! I call upon you mullein for protection from energies destructive to health!** With the wand or athame, gather energy widdershins: **Through the Goddess and the God; through the Moon and the Sun; through the Elementals, runes, herbs, and star; with the energy of Phul and Och; this candle wards the energy of Dirachiel in Alchaya that is destructive to health!** Direct and release the energy into the candle: **DESTRUCTION WARDED AGAINST! So Mote It Be!** Let the candle burn for thirty minutes to an hour, then snuff and look at the wax for relevant images. Bury the candle remains outdoors.

Dark Moon

• **ALCHAYA, the Little Star of Great Light** (4♊17 to 17♊8) **ruled by DIRACHIEL for destroying business empires, cities, crops, or health, or for revenge**

 Use this stone spell to transfer unhealthy revenge energy harmlessly out of your system.

Magical work: stone transfer spell. Dress a purple working candle with cypress oil: **Purple for protection and spiritual power; cypress for calm energy and soothed emotions.** Light the working candle from the center altar candle: **This flame burns to protect spirituality and calm the energy of revenge!** Consecrate an ordinary rock that can be held in the hands without difficulty. Set the stone on the pentacle and charge it. Hold the stone in your hands and while focusing on the center of the stone, consider a matter that generates anger, hostility, and a desire for revenge: **Into this stone I place my anger and hostility! I release into this stone the negativity that afflicts me! Let the revenge energy of Dirachiel in Alchaya speed my negative feelings into this stone!** Take the stone and set it on the ground outside: **Gentle stone, with my blessings, take these negative energies I have consigned into your care and release them into the ground.** Bury the stone under a mound of dirt: **Good earth, take this negative energy and transform it to your use, that nature be replenished. May the torch of the Veiled Goddess shed light to guide me on my path!** Snuff the candle and dispose of the remains. Leave the stone under the soil until the Waxing Crescent Moon, then remove, cleanse, and set aside to use again if needed.

New Moon Waning

- **ALARZACH, the Arm of Gemini** (17♊8 to 0♋0) **ruled by SELHIEL for the destruction of high offices, and the cooperation of flies**

   Use this oil to repel flies and other flying insects.

Magical work: oil to repel flies and insects. Dress a green working candle with lavender oil: **Green for Nature; lavender for balance and calm.** In the wax, carve around it: ᛗ **Mannaz for cooperation of flies and insects;** ᛃ **As for psychic power and communication skill with flies and insects;** ᛗ **Eh for empathic or telepathic communication with flies and insects;** ᛁ **Nyd for constraint of flies and insects;** ᚦ **Thorn to neutralize flies and insects.** Light the working candle from the center altar candle: **This flame burns for the cooperation of flies and insects to keep away!** In a small glass bottle with lid, blend the following essential oils: 2 parts rosemary: **I call upon you rosemary for protection and the repelling of flies and insects!** 3 parts eucalyptus: **I call upon you eucalyptus to keep away flies and insects!** 2 parts clover: **I call upon you clover to repel flies and insects!** Add 2 parts olive oil or soybean oil. Put the lid on the bottle and shake: **All are blended that flies and insects cooperate and be repelled!** Place the bottle on the pentacle. Charge the oil. With the wand or athame, gather energy deosil: **Through the Goddess and the God, the Moon and the Sun; through the Elementals, runes, and herbs; with the energy of Selhiel in Alarzach; this oil gains the cooperation of flies and insects to keep away!** Direct and release the energy into the bottle: **INSECTS REPELLED! So Mote It Be!** Leave the oil on the pentacle for thirty minutes to an hour. Snuff the candle and dispose of the remains. Dab on the oil as needed.

Dark Moon

• **ALARZACH, the Arm of Gemini (17♊8 to 0♋0) ruled by SELHIEL for the destruction of high offices, and the cooperation of flies**

With this meditation you gain an understanding of the insect's place in Nature and how to gain the cooperation of flies to stay away.

Magical work: meditation to keep away flies. Dress a green working candle with patchouli oil: **Green for nature; patchouli for the creatures of the earth.** Light the working candle from the center altar candle: **This flame burns for nature and the insect creatures of the earth!** (*Go to MEDITATION BEGINNING.*)

With the wisdom of the Veiled Goddess and the energy of Selhiel in Alarzach, consider the reason for insects in the world. From your safe place, you hear the distant drone of a variety of insects. You step out of your safe place and into a meadow in full bloom. Now the sound of insects is louder and you listen to the buzzing of bees, the noise of flies, mosquitoes, and other insects. Consider that each creature of nature has an ancestor that can be called the Grandfather or Grandmother of the species. Perhaps the Grandfather of the flies can tell you if flies are only an annoyance or do they serve a purpose in the cycle of life on earth?

As you consider this question, Selhiel in Alarzach sends Grandfather Fly to speak with you. Ask Grandfather Fly for the Truth about his family and listen to what he says. Does he tell you his people provide food for other animals, such as birds and frogs? Does he tell you his people help to decompose matter to return to the Earth? After you hear what he has to say, tell him that you understand and respect the place of flies in the cycles of the Earth, but that you would greatly appreciate it if he will ask his family to keep away from you in this life. Give Grandfather Fly your blessing that he may depart in peace. When you find flies are an annoyance, simply tell the flies that you have an agreement with Grandfather Fly that they should depart in peace.

Selhiel in Alarzach nods and Grandfather Fly departs. As you listen, the meadow becomes quieter, with only the distant buzzing of bees gathering nectar from the flowers. Now even that sound fades away, and you return to your safe place. (*Go to MEDITATION ENDING.*) Snuff the candle and dispose of the remains.

CANCER

Tonight the Moon is in ♋ Cancer, the Crab, ruled by ☽ Moon, with the psychic energy of intuition, introspection, nurturing, and family, and the available energy of two fixed stars:

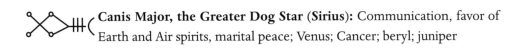

Canis Major, the Greater Dog Star (Sirius): Communication, favor of Earth and Air spirits, marital peace; Venus; Cancer; beryl; juniper

Canis Minor, the Lesser Dog Star (Procyon): magic power, good health; Mercury and Mars; Cancer; agate; buttercup

In the Mansion of the Moon called:

New Moon Waning

- **ALNAZA, Misty Clouds** (0♋0 to 12♋51) **ruled by AMNEDIEL for the maltreatment of captives, and for controlling mice**

    Place this talisman in an area where mice are likely to enter.

Magical work: talisman to control mice. Dress a red working candle with dragon's blood oil: **Red for energy; dragon's blood for power and strength.** In the wax, carve around it: ᚦ **Thorn for protection and neutralizing foes;** ᛟ **Ethel for protection of possessions and the home;** ᛇ **Eoh for protection of the home and banishing rodents.** Light the working candle from the center altar candle: **This flame burns to control mice!** On a piece of parchment or white paper no more than 3 inches square, draw in brown marker or ink a double ring circle to fill the space: **I draw this mandala ◯ in brown for control of rodents.** In the center of the circle, draw: **With 🜰 Azarel and the Seal of the Moon for protection of the home!** Above the image draw: **By ♒ Phul to defeat what is vile!** Below to the right of the image, draw: ⨯⊳Ⱶ⊂ **Canis Major, the Greater Dog Star, for the favor of earth and air spirits and for communication!** Below to the left of image of Phul, draw: ⅄⚹⋎ **Canis Minor, the Lesser Dog Star, for magic power and good health!** On the left side of the image, draw: ♋ **Cancer for protection of comfort and home!** In the ring around the circle, write: **PHUL · AZAREL · HASMODAI · YASHIEL ·** On the back of the paper, draw:

369

Over the Square, draw: **With ⚹ Hasmodai, the Spirit of the Moon! And with Yashiel, the Intelligence of the Intelligences of the Moon!** Turn the talisman over so the mandala is face up: **By Phul, Azarel, Hasmodai, and Yashiel are mice kept from the home! With the square of the Moon do I summon protection for the home from infestation by mice!** Charge the talisman. With wand or athame, gather energy deosil: **Through the Goddess and the God; the Moon and the Sun; through the Elementals, planets, stars, and runes; through the power of Phul, Azarel, Hasmodai, and Yashiel and with the energy of Amnediel in Alnaza; this talisman protects the home from infestation by mice!** Direct and release the energy into the talisman: **NO MICE! So Mote It Be!** Leave the talisman on the pentacle for thirty minutes to an hour. Snuff the candle and dispose of the remains. Place the talisman along the baseboard.

Dark Moon

• **ALNAZA, Misty Clouds** (0♋0 to 12♋51) **ruled by AMNEDIEL for the maltreatment of captives, and for controlling mice**

There are many types and degrees of captivity and ways to bully others, be they in a weaker position at work, the newcomer to a team or other group, or those simply timid by nature. This meditation aids with understanding the motivation behind being mean to someone, and offers a way to cleanse these feelings.

Magical work: meditation to cleanse the feelings that lead to maltreatment of others. Dress a black working candle with frankincense oil: **Black for truth and removing discord; frankincense to cleanse and bless through meditation.** Light the working candle from the center altar candle: **This flame burns for truth and cleansing!** (*Go to MEDITATION BEGINNING.*)

With the wisdom of the Veiled Goddess and the energy of Amnediel in Alnaza, consider those times in your life when it was within your power to mistreat another person. Was there someone who was under your control? Perhaps it was someone over whom you exercised authority; who was required to do as you commanded; who was a child, a student, a coworker, a subordinate, an employee, a person relying on your generosity. Did you take advantage of your position of

power in that situation? If so, now consider what motivated you to do this. Look back through time and in your memories; was there an incident where you felt you had been mistreated? Were you hurt? Frightened? Resentful? Angry? How long have you carried this pain within you, allowing it to smolder and fester? How often have you been hurtful to others when the opportunity arose?

In this time, the energy of Amnediel in Alnaza is strongest to provoke harm to another, but if you understand from where that desire arises within you, it can be conquered. Heal your own hurt and turn it into compassion. Being in a position to inflict harm on another leaves open the choice of whether or not you take that action or conquer that baneful desire.

In your safe place, there is no recrimination, only understanding. Just outside of your safe place you see a white light beginning to manifest. The light is growing, getting larger and brighter. You feel drawn to this light, and you know there is nothing harmful in this light. You move out of your safe place, drawn by the loving energy of the cosmic white light, and you know that this light is filled with healing energy. You look into your own past and see the sad person you once were when you were afflicted, and you gently caress your past self with a feeling of sympathy. But now the white light calls you back to deal with who you became from who you once were. You smile and turn to look into the light. The energy is pulsating and powerful, and you know that now that you understand your past, you can create your future. The light is streaming before you now as a cascade. You sense that if you enter into the cascade, the pain of the past will be washed away, and you will be cleansed, able to face the future with confidence and compassion.

You enter into the white light, and it feels like a shower of energy flowing around you. Washing yourself in the light, you see your past anger and self-recriminations burned away. You see your past hurts soothed and healed, and you know that you are loved by the Divine. A voice enters your mind: I am Amnediel in Alnaza, and I give you choice, for in another Moon, I am the energy of love and compassion. Release into me your pain, and I will take this from you so that you are cleansed by the starlight of Sirius and Procyon with communication, peace, and magical power. Cleanse yourself in this light.

You wash the light over yourself, from head to foot, and you step out of the cascade, feeling a sense of self-forgiveness and a desire to make right was set wrong so long ago. You resolve to be a better person, and release the petty one within you

who once demanded pain from others to compensate for your own past pain. With this understanding, the light immediately collapses in on itself and vanishes. You are at peace with your past and yourself. There is no need to inflict harm on others, for you now feel compassion for their situation. (*Go to MEDITATION ENDING.*) **Snuff the candle and dispose of the remains.**

New Moon Waning

- **ARCAPH, the Eye of the Lion** (12♋51 to 25♋42) **ruled by RAUBIEL for destroying harvests, hindering travel, and creating discord or infirmities**

This is a charm to deflect energies that hinder travel through whatever means, be it delays, disagreements, mechanical problems, or traffic.

Magical work: charm to deflect hindrances to travel. Dress a red working candle with pine oil: **Red for energy; pine for protection, strength, and clear action.** In the wax, carve around it: 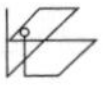 **Ophiel for quick travel;**  **Phul to overcome obstacles;**  **Tiriel for agility in working around difficulties swiftly;** 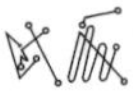 **Yashiel for safe travel.** Light the working candle from the center altar candle: **This flame burns for safe travel and overcoming hindrances!** Lay out a six-inch square of black cloth: **Black for protection and warding negativity!** Set out a six-inch long narrow red ribbon to tie the charm bundle (or thread if sewing it): **Red for power!** One at a time, hold up over the pentacle some of each of the following herbs, state the intention, then place on the cloth: **I call upon you vetiver to ward negativity and exorcise hindrances to travel! I call upon you fennel for protection and deflecting negative energies in travel! I call upon you burdock for protection and warding negativity in travel! I call upon you peppercorn for protection and warding negativity in travel! I call upon you nettle for protection and balance in travel!** Charge a piece of jade and hold it up over the pentacle: **I call upon you jade for protection and safety in travel!** Put the jade on the herbs. Tie the bundle with the ribbon (or sew shut) and set it on the pentacle. **Black and red, herbs and stone! Together deflect hindrances to travel!** Charge the charm. With the wand or athame, raise energy moving widdershins: **Through the Goddess and the God; through the Moon and the Sun; through the Elementals, herbs, and stones; with the powers of Ophiel, Phul, Tiriel, and Yashiel; this charm deflects the negative energy of Raubiel in Arcaph that nothing hinders travel!** Direct and release the energy into the charm: **HINDRANCE-FREE! So Mote It Be!** Leave the charm on the pentacle for thirty minutes to an hour. Snuff the candle and dispose of the remains. Place the charm in an automobile or other mode of travel, or carry somewhere when traveling, such as a purse or pocket.

Dark Moon

- **ARCAPH, the Eye of the Lion** (12♋51 to 25♋42) **ruled by RAUBIEL for destroying harvests, hindering travel, and creating discord or infirmities**

This candle calls upon the energy of the stars to ward against the discord energy.

Magical work: star candle to ward discord. Dress a red working candle with sandalwood oil: **Red for power and energy; sandalwood for protection and warding negativity.** Light the working candle from the center altar candle: **This flame burns to ward discord!** Consecrate a black votive spell candle and dress with vetiver oil: **Black to ward negativity and remove discord; vetiver to ward negative energies and exorcise discord.** In the wax, carve around it: **I call upon the energy of** ⚹◇⚹⟨ **Sirius for the favor of the spirits of Earth and Air! I call upon the energy of** ⚹⚹⚹ **Procyon for enhancing magic power!** Charge the candle and set it in a cauldron on top of the pentacle. Light a taper from the working candle and use it to light the spell candle. With the wand or athame, gather energy widdershins: **Through the guidance of the Veiled Goddess and the God; through the hidden Moon and the setting Sun; through the power of the Elementals and the shining stars; this candle exorcises the discord energy of Raubiel in Arcaph!** Direct and release the energy into the candle: **DISCORD PURGED! So Mote It Be!** Let the candle burn for thirty minutes to an hour, then snuff. Scry the melted wax for relevant images. Bury the candle remains outside the home.

New Moon Waning

• **ALGEBH, the Forehead of the Lion** (25♋42 to 8♌34) **ruled by ARDESIEL to destroy enemies, ease childbirth, and banish illness.**

This is a mansion where the diminishing energy has a positive effect, so this candle may be burned in conjunction with medical treatment to banish illness.

Magical work: candle spell to banish illness. Dress a black working candle with patchouli oil: **Black to ward negativity; patchouli for physical strength and well-being.** Light the working candle from the center altar candle: **This flame burns to banish illness!** Consecrate an orange votive spell candle and dress with rosemary oil: **Orange for healing and vitality; rosemary for protection and good health.** In the wax, carve around it: ♃ **Jupiter for health!** ♂ **Mars for dynamic energy!** ⋈⊳⊞(**Sirius for the favor of earth and air spirits in regaining good health!** ⋏⚹⋎ **Procyon for magic power and good health!** Charge the candle and set it in a cauldron on top of the pentacle. Light a taper from the working candle and use it to light the spell candle. With the wand or athame, gather energy deosil: **Through the Goddess and the God; through the Moon and the Sun; through the Elementals, planets, and stars; with the energy of Ardesiel in Algebh; this candle banishes illness!** Direct and release the energy into the candle: **ILLNESS FLEES! So Mote It Be!** Let the candle burn for thirty minutes to an hour, then snuff and look at the wax for images indicating the time frame for the results to manifest. Dispose of candle remains.

Dark Moon

• **ALGEBH, the Forehead of the Lion** (25♋42 to 8♌34) **ruled by ARDESIEL to destroy enemies, ease childbirth, and banish illness**

This tarot reading helps identify enemies or adversaries in any area of life, and offers guidance on how to deal with this in an ethical way.

Magical work: tarot reading on enemies. Dress a purple working candle with bay oil: **Purple for protection and intuitive power; bay for divination and psychic power.** In the wax, carve around it: ♋ **Cancer, the Crab, for intuition and insight;** ☽ **The Moon for psychic energy;** ⚺▷⧗⟨ **Canis Major for the favor of earth and air spirits with grounding and insight;** ⤙⚹⤚ **Canis Minor for magical power; and** ♆ **Neptune for psychic awareness.** Light the working candle from the center altar candle: **This flame burns to reveal adversaries and how to deal with them!** Charge a tarot deck and set it on top of the pentacle. Focus on identifying enemies and how to deal with them: **Through the wisdom of the Veiled Goddess, and with the energy of Ardesiel in Algebh these cards reveal to me what weaknesses I can utilize, or options I have available, to negate or work around the negativity of adversaries!** Shuffle the deck, cut the deck and restack the cards or spread them on a table. Deal or select three cards and lay in a row from left to right, then another three cards beneath that row, and another three cards beneath that one for a total of nine cards forming three rows and three columns. The first row: **This is the recent past.** Interpret the cards as they relate to identifying adversaries. The second row: **This is the current situation.** Interpret the cards as they relate to the actions of adversaries. The third row: **This is the possible near future.** Interpret the cards as they relate to dealing with the adversaries. Look at the center card: **This is the heart of the problem.** Read the card as it relates to the source of the problem or the solution to dealing with the adversaries. Look at the diagonal cards, left top corner to bottom-right corner and right-top corner to bottom-left corner: **These are energies available for my use.** Interpret the cards as they relate to dealing with adversaries. The center card may indicate one thing when read in conjunction with the middle row, and another when read with the diagonals. If the answer seems unclear, deal out another card on the one in question and read the two together for more information. While a solution may not seem apparent, there may be information on what motivates an enemy, which can be used in dealing with the situation. Snuff the candle and dispose of the remains. If still uncertain, at bedtime, ask the universe for clarification. An answer should come through lucid dreaming within a few days, or by sudden insight upon awakening.

LEO

Tonight the Moon is in ♌ Leo, the Lion, ruled by ☉ the Sun, with the energy of success, individuality, power, optimism, vitality, and sociability, and the available energy of one fixed star:

Cor Leonis, the Heart of the Lion (Regulus): Strength, nobility; Jupiter and Mars; Leo; Granite; mugwort

In the Mansion of the Moon called:

New Moon Waning

• **ALGEBH, the Forehead of the Lion** (25♋42 to 8♌34) **ruled by ARDESIEL to destroy enemies, ease childbirth, and banish illness**

Use this amulet in conjunction with medical treatment to get over an illness and restore good health. While sardonyx can be used to absorb any type of negativity, it needs to be periodically cleansed.

Magical work: amulet to banish illness. Dress an orange working candle with rosemary oil: **Orange for healing and successful recovery; rosemary for protection, purification, and good health.** In the wax, carve around it: ♃ **Jupiter for good health;** ♂ **Mars for dynamic energy; and ⚡ Sigel, the Sun Wheel for strength, vitality, and healing.** Light the working candle from the center altar candle: **This flame burns to banish illness!** Consecrate a sardonyx. Hold the stone up over the pentacle: **I call upon you sardonyx for strength, protection, and absorbing of baneful energies!** Using blue marker: **Blue for health!** Draw on the stone: **Cor Leonis for physical strength!** Hold up the stone over the pentacle: **I call upon you sardonyx to take within yourself the energy of illness!** Set the stone on the pentacle and charge. With the wand or athame, gather energy deosil: **Through the Goddess and the God; through the Moon and the Sun; through the Elementals, planets, stars, and stone; with the energy of Ardesiel in Algebh; this sardonyx absorbs the baneful energy of illness!** Direct and release the energy into the stone: **ILLNESS BANISHED! So Mote It Be!** Pass the stone through the natural energy field surrounding your body and feel the sardonyx absorbing your illness. Leave the stone on the pentacle for thirty minutes to an hour. Snuff the candle and dispose of the remains. Carry or place the sardonyx where desired. When the illness passes, cover the stone with sea salt: **I call upon you salt of the sea to cleanse this sardonyx of the baneful energy it has collected!** Rinse the stone in spring water: **Let the purifying water cleanse this sardonyx of all baneful energies.** Set the cleansed stone on the pentacle and charge once more. Dispose of the water outside and put the salt out in the trash.

Dark Moon

• **ALGEBH, the Forehead of the Lion** (25♋42 to 8♌34) **ruled by ARDESIEL to destroy enemies, ease childbirth, and banish illness**

This candle is made in the mansion where the diminishing energy has a positive effect for reducing pain or difficulty in childbirth. The candle may then be stored and lit when the first indications of birthing begin so as to ease the process.

Magical work: candle to ease childbirth. Dress a red working candle with rosemary oil: **Red for strength, energy, health, and vigor; frankincense for protection, power, and blessing.** In the wax, carve around it: ☽ **The Moon for nurture and family;** ᚲ **Ken for strength, physical well-being, and love; and** ᚹ **Wyn for comfort, happiness, success, and joy.** Light the working candle from the center altar candle: **This flame burns to ease childbirth!** Consecrate a light blue votive spell candle and dress with rosemary oil: **Light blue for health and tranquility; rosemary for protection, health, and love.** In the wax, carve around it: ☉ **The Sun for energy, success, and happiness!** 🦁 **Regulus (Cor Leonis), the Heart of the Lion for strength!** ᛋ **Sigel for strength, success, vitality, and life-force!** ᛚ **Lagu for female vitality and life-force!** ᛒ **Beorc for protection, motherhood, and family!** ᚢ **Uruz for strength and physical health! and** ᛃ **Gera for a good outcome to endeavors!** Set the spell candle on top of the pentacle and charge it. With the wand or athame, gather energy deosil: **Through the Goddess and the God; through the Moon, Sun, and stars; through the Elementals and runes; with the energy of Ardesiel in Algebh; this candle eases childbirth!** Wrap the candle in a white cloth and set aside to light when labor begins. Let the candle then burn for thirty minutes to an hour, then snuff it and scry the wax for relevant images. When the candle cools, wrap again in the white cloth and place with the mother's things in the birthing area, such as in a suitcase for hospital care.

New Moon Waning

- **AZOBRA, the Mane of the Lion** (8♌34 to 21♌25) **ruled by NECIEL for attacking, aggression, and inspiring fear**

The mansion's aggressive attack energy is directed into a beneficial use when high energy is needed to banish or overcome the competition or an adversary. Good for those who argue cases before the law, engage in competitive sports, or require drive and strong energy to meet a challenge for success.

Magical work: elixir to overcome an adversary or competitor. Dress an orange working candle with frankincense oil: **Orange for strength, vitality, dominance, and success; frankincense to energize and protect.** In the wax, carve around it: ⟩⟨ **Cor Leonis for strength and nobility of spirit;** ☉ **the Sun for success and vitality;** ♃ **Jupiter for growth, optimism, and justice;** ♂ **Mars for dynamic energy and willpower; and** ♅ **Uranus for originality and handling tensions.** Light the working candle from the center altar candle: **This flame burns to ignite my inner fire for success!** Hold up an agate over the pentacle: **I call upon you agate for energy, self-confidence, and gaining my goals!** Place the stone in a small jar of spring water. Use black marker: **Black to ward negativity!** Draw on the jar: ⟩⟨ **Cor Leonis for strength and power, but also for nobility of spirit!** Set the jar on the pentacle and cup your hands over the top of the water: **This water inspires dynamic energy to ethically achieve success!** Hold up a teaspoon of vodka, brandy, whiskey, or rum over the pentacle, state the intention, and add the alcohol to the jar of water: **This elixir fixed and sealed!** Charge the blend. With the wand or athame, gather energy deosil: **Through the Goddess and the God; through the Moon and the Sun; through the Elementals, planets, and stars; through water and stone; with the energy of Neciel in Azobra; this elixir ethically overcomes adversaries and competitors!** Direct and release the energy into the elixir: **I WIN! So Mote It Be!** Leave the elixir on the pentacle for thirty minutes to an hour. Snuff the candle and dispose of the remains. Remove the agate and cleanse. Store the tightly covered jar of elixir away from light. Sip a tablespoon of the elixir as needed to inspire self-confidence and be energized to achieve the goals desired.

Dark Moon

- **AZOBRA, the Mane of the Lion** (8♌34 to 21♌25) **ruled by NECIEL for attacking, aggression, and inspiring fear**

The energy of this mansion may manifest as generating fear or being fearful, and this divination aids with finding the cause behind either.

Magical work: rune reading to find the cause of fear. Dress a black working candle with frankincense oil: **Black for truth, warding negativity, and protection; frankincense for power, protection, and spirituality.** In the wax, carve around it: ⟨symbol⟩ **Cor Leonis for strength and sincerity.** Light the working candle from the center altar candle: **This flame burns for learning what I fear or why I seek to inspire fear in others!** Charge a bag of runes and set it on top of the pentacle. Focus on a matter that has inspired fear: **Let the wisdom of the Veiled Goddess and the energy of Neciel in Azobra show the source of fear!** Shake the bag and pull out a rune: **This is the foundation of fear.** Examine the symbol and consider how the basis of fear relates to you. Shake the bag and pull out another rune: **This is the current situation.** Meditate on this symbol and consider how you relate to fear. Shake the bag and pull out a third rune: **This is a choice for overcoming the situation.** Examine the symbol and interpret it in relation to the prior rune. If you cannot understand the solution given, meditate on the rune, or draw another for guidance. Snuff the candle and dispose of the remains. If still uncertain, at bedtime, ask the universe for clarification. An answer should come through lucid dreaming within a few days, or by sudden insight upon awakening.

New Moon Waning

• **ALZARPHA, the Tail of the Lion** (21♌25 to 4♍17) **ruled by ABDIZUEL for hindering sailing, loss of investment, and separation**

Burn this incense to secure your investments and finances by banishing the threat of loss.

Magical work: incense to banish loss of investment. Dress an orange working candle with vetiver oil: **Orange for business matters, property, career, and general success; vetiver for protecting finances, warding negativity, and exorcising hindrances or losses.** In the wax, carve around it: ♃ **Jupiter for finances and business success; ♄ Saturn for self-preservation, business, and restricting losses; ᚨ Ethel for protection of possessions, acquisitions, and benefits; | Is for halting negative energies; and** ꕐ **Bethor for preserving wealth.** Light the working candle from the center altar candle: **This flame burns to banish loss of investment!** One at a time, hold up an equal amount of each herb over the pentacle, state the intention, and drop into a mortar with pestle: **I call upon you basil for protection of wealth and repelling negativity! I call upon you bergamot for breaking hindrances to wealth and success! I call upon you burdock root for protection and warding negativity! I call upon you cinnamon for protection of business and success! I call upon you cumin for protection of investments; I call upon you clove for warding negativity toward finances and investments! And I call upon you fennel for deflecting negative energies!** Grind the herbs together into a powder: **Seven herbs of power, blend together to protect my investments and banish loss!** Bottle the incense and set it on the pentacle. Charge the powder. With the wand or athame, gather energy deosil: **Through the Goddess and the God; through the Moon and the Sun; through the Elementals, planets, runes, and herbs; with the power of Bethor; this incense banishes the loss of investment energy of Abdizuel in Alzarpha!** Direct and release the energy into the powder: **LOSS BANISHED! So Mote It Be!** Leave the incense on the pentacle for thirty minutes to an hour. Snuff the candle and dispose of the remains. Burn the incense on a charcoal diskette.

Dark Moon

• **ALZARPHA, the Tail of the Lion** (21♌25 to 4♍17) **ruled by ABDIZUEL for hindering sailing, loss of investment, and separation**

This meditation uses the separation energy to assess which is functional and reveal what is not so you may release the useless much as winnowing separates the wheat from the chaff.

Magical work: meditation to separate from the functional that which is worthless and release it. Dress a violet working candle with lavender oil: **Violet for self-improvement; lavender for cleansing and balance.** In the wax, carve around it: ⊣ **Och for wisdom; ♓ Phul for transformation; ♄ Saturn for realistic assessment and removing restrictions; ♇ Pluto for transformation and evolution; ⏁ and Cor Leonis, the Heart of the Lion for strength and courage to accomplish what needs to be done.** Light the working candle from the center altar candle: **This flame burns to reveal and release what is useless in my life!** (*Go to MEDITATION BEGINNING.*)

Through the guidance of the Veiled Goddess, let Abdizuel in Alzarpha reveal to me what has no value in my life and how to let it go for personal change and evolution. You are comfortable in your safe place, and this is a good time to look at your surroundings. Are there objects in your haven? Look and see how you have decorated your safe place to make it a refuge. Is there something you want to add? If there is, then now is the time to form in your thoughts what you desire to add, and let it materialize in your safe place. Is there something you want to remove? If there is, simply look at it and will it away. It is gone. If you change your mind, you can always bring it back simply by visualizing it.

Sit comfortably in your safe place, perhaps on a large, soft cushion, or a chair, or any other object that is appropriate for you. Look at the colors and feel the textures of your comfortable place. The sunlight brightens your haven, and there is a gentle, cool breeze drifting through. You think about the fresh energy of early autumn and the cleansing influence coming into your sanctuary. Now consider, is there some influence or thing in your life that has become useless to you? Has it become burdensome? Are you tying yourself to routines and practices that offer no fulfillment or purpose to you? Have you let yourself become attached to things that only serve to drain your energy?

A fluffy white cloud slowly passes and obscures the sunlight in your retreat. Take this time of shadow to release into it that which you have discovered is useless in your life. The shadow starts to lighten as the cloud continues to move across the Sun. Do you feel regret? A pang of worry that you are letting go of something familiar? A touch of fear of change? The spring breeze plays upon your face and gently reminds you that holding on to that which is useless because it is familiar is a choice that you make, just as separating it out and letting it go is a choice only you can make.

As the cool breeze refreshes and encourages you, it also moves the cloud further across the Sun, and more light is returning to your haven. Now is the time to decide. Do you release what is useless? If so, see it separate from you and enter into the shadow of your sanctuary. See the Sun returning, shining brightly, and see the shadow retreating, shrinking, and finally vanquishing as the light fills your sanctuary. New energy inspires you for a new beginning in which you embrace change and growth. The sunlight washes away your fears or indecision. You have cast away the chaff to retain the wheat, and having made your choice, you take a deep breath, drawing into yourself the strength and power of the Sun and the energy of change. Release the breath as a sigh of relief, and know that you are able to release what is worthless so there may be change and growth in your life. (*Go to MEDITATION ENDING.*) Snuff the candle and dispose of the remains.

VIRGO

Tonight the Moon is in ♍ Virgo, the Virgin, ruled by ☿ Mercury, with the skillful and agile energy of analysis, service, modesty, and perfectionism, in the Mansion of the Moon called:

New Moon Waning

- **ALZARPHA, the Tail of the Lion** (21♌25 to 4♍17) **ruled by ABDIZUEL for hindering sailing, loss of investment, and separation**

Burning this candle when the waning New Moon is in Virgo will draw upon that analytical energy to temper emotions and help ease the pain that comes with an inevitable separation, such as with moving, business travel, children growing up and leaving the home, military service, divorce, a passing over, and so on.

Magical work: candle spell to ease separation. Dress a red working candle with dragon's blood oil: **Red for strength and energy; dragon's blood for protection, power, changes, and life cycles.** In the wax, carve around it: ᚲ **Ken for transformation, strength, healing, and a fresh start;** ᚻ **Haegl for security, protection, and positive change;** ᛇ **Eoh for removal of obstacles and dynamic action;** ᛞ **Daeg for change, breakthrough, and a fresh start; and** ᚢ **Uruz for strength, health, courage, passage, and drawing new situations.** Light the working candle from the center altar candle: **This flame burns for easing separations and transitions!** Consecrate a yellow votive spell candle and dress with rosemary oil: **Yellow for changes, health, and harmony; rosemary for protection, courage, love, and health.** In the wax, carve around it: ♍ **Virgo for analytical thinking!** ☿ **Mercury for skill with self-expression and communication!** ☽ **The Moon for sensitivity and cycles!** ♇ **Pluto for change and evolution!** ♃ **Och for wisdom and healing!** ♅ **Phul for transformation!** ♄ **Phaleg for courage and triumph over adversity!** Charge the candle and set it in a cauldron on top of the pentacle. Light a taper from the working candle and use it to light the spell candle: **There are many types of separation such as those that come in the course of a career, a life transition, moving into a new phase, physical distance, or endings. This flame burns for easing separation of any kind.** One at a time, hold up a pinch of each herb over the pentacle, state the intention, and add it to the flame: **Into this flame I cast nine power herbs of protection, courage, a healthy mind, and healing: I call** upon you burdock for protection, purification, and warding negativity! I call upon you basil for courage, protection, and repelling negativity!

I call upon you clove for memory and cleansing!

I call upon you mullein for purification, courage, and healing!

I call upon you carnation for strength and healing!

I call upon you cinquefoil for healing and well-being!

I call upon you comfrey for healing and safe passage!

I call upon you nettle for protection, life cycles, and restoring balance!

I call upon you chamomile for purification, calm, and peace of mind!

With the wand or athame, gather energy deosil: **Through the Goddess and the God; through the Moon and the Sun; through the Elementals and planets; through runes and herbs; with the powers of Och, Phul, and Phaleg; this candle eases the separation energy of Abdizuel in Alzarpha!** Direct and release the energy into the candle: **SEPARATION EASED! So Mote It Be!** Let the candle burn for thirty minutes to an hour, then snuff and look at the wax for relevant images. Dispose of candle remains.

Dark Moon

• **ALZARPHA, the Tail of the Lion** (21♌25 to 4♍17) **ruled by ABDIZUEL for hindering sailing, loss of investment, and separation**

Doing this meditation when the Dark Moon is in Virgo draws upon analytical energy for dealing with and easing a separation of any kind, such as with moving, business travel, children growing up and leaving the home, military service, divorce, a passing over, etcetera.

Magical work: meditation to ease separation. Dress a white working candle with lavender oil: **White for protection, peace, and warding doubts and fears; lavender for cleansing, calm, balance, and peace.** Light the working candle from the center altar candle: **This flame burns for easing separation!** (*Go to MEDITATION BEGINNING.*)

Through the wisdom of the Veiled Goddess, and with the energy of Virgo, the way is opened to understanding separation and accepting the changes brought by Abdizuel in Alzarpha. In your safe place you may be yourself without any restrictions imposed by others. Here you may look into your heart, mind, and spirit and see if separations bring you pain or relief; anxiety or peace of mind; fear or new hope.

You hear the splashing sound of a fountain outside your haven, and you step out to see a beautiful fountain with crystalline waters cascading into a deep cool pool.

See the fountain and hear the waters. Smell the cleansing waters and feel the gentle spray drifting to you on a soothing breeze. You watch the sparkling waters, listening to the musical sound of the flow. Now, you sit by the fountain and look into the waters, letting your hand dabble in the cool refreshing liquid. Consider now the flow of the waters and the flow of life. As much as the water changes, it is still part of the whole. This is also true of life. As much as there are changes, separations, and transitions, this is all part of the whole. The water moves on, and so does life. The water fills the space that contains it, yet it flows with ease and brings contentment and peace of mind. Now is the time to consider your feelings, for coming to terms with changes, and for releasing your anxieties, fears, and pain. Take a deep breath and draw into yourself the strength and power of the cool waters. Release the breath as a sigh, letting the waters soothe and cleanse you emotionally, physically, and mentally. You know that you are strong and able to cope with separations, changes, and transitions, for these are but moments in the wholeness of life. (*Go to MEDITATION ENDING.*) Snuff the candle and dispose of the remains.

New Moon Waning

- **ALHAIRE, the Wings of Virgo** (4♍17 to 17♍8) **ruled by JAZERIEL for diminishing gains or the status quo, and for clever financial dealings**

Use this candle to draw on the attention to the detail energy of Virgo to ward against the threat of losing what has previously been gained while the Moon is in this mansion.

Magical work: candle to ward against diminishing gains. Dress a red working candle with dragon's blood oil: **Red for dynamic energy; dragon's blood for power and protection.** In the wax, carve around it: ᛖ **Eh for security of gains;** ᛇ **Eoh to banish threats to gains;** ᚾ **Nyd to halt negative energies and unwanted forces;** ᛉ **Eolh for protection from loss of gains; and** ᚦ **Thorn for protection and neutralizing foes.** Light the working candle from the center altar candle: **This flame burns to ward against diminishment of gains!** Consecrate a black votive spell candle and dress with sandalwood oil: **Black for protection and warding negativity; sandalwood for protection and warding negativity.** In the wax, carve around it: ᛗ **Mannaz to restrict excesses that may diminish gains!** ᛝ **Ing to hold the benefits of completed labor!** ᛟ **Ethel for protection of acquisitions and possessions!** ♄ **Saturn for self-preservation and restricting loss of gains! and Phul to defeat negativity!** Set the spell candle in a cauldron on top of the pentacle. Light a taper from the working candle and use it to light the spell candle. Charge a piece of red jasper, then drop it into the candle flame: **With red jasper to deflect negative energy and defend gains!** Charge the candle. With the wand or athame, gather energy deosil: **Through the Goddess and the God; through the Moon and the Sun; through the Elementals, planets, runes, and stone; with the power of Phul; this candle wards against the energy of Jazeriel in Alhaire for diminishing gains!** Direct and release the energy into the candle: **GAINS REMAIN! So Mote It Be!** Let the candle burn for thirty minutes to an hour, then snuff it and look at the wax for relevant images. Remove the red jasper and clean it to place, carry, or wear as desired. Dispose of candle remains.

Dark Moon

- ALHAIRE, the Wings of Virgo (4♍17 to 17♍8) **ruled by JAZERIEL for diminishing gains or the status quo, and for clever financial dealings**

This candle meditation helps with warding against the diminishment of the status quo. By maintaining the current conditions stable during the dark phase of the Moon, you can then seek improvements during the waxing phase.

Magical work: candle meditation to ward against diminishing status quo. Dress a red working candle with sandalwood oil: **Red for energy and strength; sandalwood for protection and warding negativity.** In the wax, carve around it: 🜨 **Bethor for preserving honors and wealth; ♀ Venus for preserving comfort and sociability.** Light the working candle from the center altar candle: **This flame burns to preserve current conditions against threats of diminishment!** Consecrate a black votive spell candle and dress with myrrh oil: **Black for protection, warding negativity, and removing discord that the status quo be retained; myrrh for protection and warding negativity in the time of the Dark Moon that the status quo be maintained.** In the wax, carve around it: **With the energies of** (your sun sign symbol) **and** (the ruling planet) **to represent me! ♄ Saturn for self-preservation and restricting negativity to maintaining the status quo!** Set the spell candle in a cauldron on top of the pentacle. Light a taper from the working candle and use it to light the spell candle. Charge the candle. With the wand or athame, gather energy deosil: **Through the Goddess and the God; through the Moon and the Sun; through the Elementals, planets, and herbs; with the power of Bethor; this candle wards the diminishment energy of Jazeriel in Alhaire and preserves the status quo!** Direct and release the energy into the candle: **STATUS QUO MAINTAINED! So Mote It Be!** (*Go to MEDITATION BEGINNING.*)

You see a mirror outside your secure space, and you walk out to look into it and see it is filled with swirling clouds. What colors are the clouds? What do these colors mean to you? Now, you see that some of the clouds are taking on shapes. These are the shapes of what you seek to preserve in a time of risk and diminishing energies. What shapes do you see? You continue to look at the shapes and begin to understand that these are not solid, but are illusions of the things you seek to maintain and the things you feel might threaten them. Now, you notice an incense burner is nearby as the aromatic smoke drifts to you. You pick up the incense burner and take it to the mirror. You blow the smoke gently across the mirror and all the clouds turn white and glistening. You gently waft the incense around the mirror and you see the threatening clouds disperse, leaving only the clouds shaped like the things you want to preserve and protect. You smile and set the incense burner down in front of the mirror. You know that the status quo will be maintained until you choose to change it. Now, you turn and return to your secure place. Sitting in your space, you are at peace, knowing that you have the power to make changes in your current condition when you feel ready do to so. (*Go to MEDITATION ENDING.*) Snuff the candle and dispose of the remains.

New Moon Waning

- **AZIMETH, the Flying Spike** (17♍8 to 0♎0) **ruled by ERGEDIEL for destroying harvests, destroying desires, hindering land journeys, for divorce, and for separations**

Use this talisman to banish energies that are destructive to reaping a harvest of any kind, be it crops or rewards for labor and efforts in any area.

Magical work: talisman to banish hazards to a harvest. Dress a black working candle with myrrh oil: **Black for warding negativity, binding spell work, and protection; myrrh for protection, warding negativity, and binding destructive energies.** In the wax, carve around it: ᚦ **Thorn for protection, safety from evil, and for neutralizing negativity;** ᛇ **Eoh for defense, dynamic action, protection, and banishing negativity;** ᛞ **Daeg for breakthough in banishing negativity;** ᛃ **Gera for a successful harvest and tangible rewards from effort; and** ᛉ **Osa for a favorable outcome.** Light the working candle from the center altar candle: **This flame burns to protect my harvest and to bind and banish negative energies!** On a piece of parchment or paper no more than 3 inches square, draw in black ink a double ring circle to fill the space: ◯ **I draw this mandala in black for warding negativity and banishing harmful energy!**

In the center of the circle and touching the inner rim, draw: ☆ **The Pentagram for the balance of the Elementals and Spirit!** In the center of the star, draw: 〼 **Phul to defeat malevolence!** In the upper right point, draw: 〤 **Och for success, and power to overcome any threat to my harvest!** In the upper left point, draw: 〣 **Aratron for magical power and binding energy!** In the lower right point, draw: ♇ **Pluto for binding negative energy and for transformation that positive energy prevails!** In the lower left point, draw: ♄ **Saturn for restriction of negativity and for self-preservation against threats to my harvest!** In the space between the lower points, draw: ✳ **Omeliel, the Seal of Saturn, for the restriction of negativity and for the preservation of harvests!** Inside the double ring, write around the circle: **OCH · PHUL · ARATRON · OMELIEL · AGIEL·** On the back of the paper, draw:

4	9	2
3	5	7
8	1	6

15

With the Square of Saturn is destructive energy restricted and bound that it not interfere with my harvest! Over the square, draw: **With** ∿ **Agiel, the Intelligence of Saturn to hold negativity and restrict it that it not interfere with my harvest!** Turn the talisman over so the mandala is face up and set it on the pentacle. Consecrate a piece of jet and set it in the center of the talisman: **Jet to bind this energy so that no hazard or negativity interferes with my harvest!** Wrap the jet in the talisman and tie with black string or thread: **Black to ward negativity and to bind this spell to a satisfactory completion!** Charge the talisman and jet. With wand or athame, gather energy deosil: **Through the Goddess and the God; the Moon and the Sun; through the Elementals and the runes; through the power of Phul, Och, Aratron, Omeliel, and Agiel is the energy of Ergediel in Azimeth to destroy harvests bound and banished that no harm come to my endeavors!** Direct and release the energy into the talisman: **HAZARDS BANISHED! So Mote It Be!** Leave the talisman on the pentacle for thirty minutes to an hour. Snuff the candle and dispose of the remains. Place, carry, or wear the talisman as desired. When the harvest is completed, untie the string, bury the paper in the ground, cleanse the jet and put it away.

Dark Moon

• **AZIMETH, the Flying Spike** (17♍8 to 0♎0) **ruled by ERGEDIEL for destroying harvests, destroying desires, hindering land journeys, for divorce, and for separations**

Use this meditation for internal work to destroy unwanted desires, such as food cravings when dieting, and in this way the destructive energy is directed to a beneficial outcome.

Magical work: meditation for banishing desires for unhealthy foods when dieting. Dress a white candle with frankincense oil: **White for meditation; frankincense for meditation and cleansing energy.** Light the working candle from the center altar candle: **This flame burns to banish unwanted desires!** (*Go to MEDITATION BEGINNING.*)

Through the wisdom of the Veiled Goddess, let Ergediel in Azimeth help destroy the desires that impede my diet, be it for weight reduction, health restrictions, binging, difficulty in rejecting foods or drinks offered, or any other behavior where unhealthy or harmful foods or beverages are consumed.

From your safe place, you hear the sounds of glasses tinkling, plates being moved around, and utensils clinking, and you smell aromas that tantalize you. Step from your haven and all becomes calm and quiet again as you see that outside a buffet is set up. Many foods and beverages are laid out on the buffet. Some of these you believe you like to eat, and others are of little interest to you. Consider now what foods and beverages you need to avoid for a healthy life. Are these on the buffet? You look at the spread and see them. Consider now what foods and beverages you have been advised to consume. Are these on the buffet? You look at the spread and see them as well.

There is a chair in front of the buffet and you sit on it. There is a small table in front of the chair, and each item of the buffet is presented to you. You may only look at the food or beverages being presented to you, but you may not touch, eat, or drink any, for this is the Goblin Market where all is poisonous enchantment. Carefully look at each person presenting an item to you. Each is a goblin, wearing the face and appearance of someone you know. Does the image represent a person who cares about you? Or is this someone who resents you? Is the image of a person grinning with bad intentions or smiling with loving care? The food or beverage being shown to you may be something you are to avoid consuming or something that you should be consuming. Each goblin in the guise of someone you know

presents the item and gives you a message. You might not like what the person has to say, but you listen to the messages of each: Here is something to eat that will make me look better than you! Here is something to drink that will give me the chance to belittle you! Here is something that will make you sick! Here is something that will make you hate yourself! Here is something that will let me mock you! Here is something that will humiliate you! Here is something to eat that will help you to live longer and healthier. Here is something to drink that will make you strong. Here is something that will help you maintain your composure. Here is something that will prevent stress.

Hear the messages that go with the foods and beverages presented. The people vanish, but the buffet remains. On the little table in front of you appears a large crystal point. You take the point and go to the buffet. Looking at all the items, you point to each as you walk past the array. Those that are unhealthy for you vanish. Those that are healthy remain. You look at the foods and beverages that remain, and see them shining and bright. Remember the items that were unhealthy and the message of the goblins who presented them to you. Sweep the crystal point down the length of your body and feel yourself cleansed of any desire for those foods and beverages. Remember the healthy items from the buffet and the message of those who presented them to you. Sweep the crystal point up the length of your body and feel only the desire for these healthy foods and beverages. Now that you know what to eat and drink, you turn away from foods of the Goblin Market. The buffet vanishes, but the crystal point remains in your hands as you return to your safe place. Sitting in your haven, you remember the power of the crystal point. The crystal shines brightly in your hands, radiating compassion and caring. Take a deep breath and draw the crystal into yourself. Release the breath, and know that the shining crystal resides within you to remind you of the healthy choices for food and beverages. (*Go to MEDITATION ENDING.*) Snuff the candle and dispose of the remains.

LIBRA

Tonight the Moon is in ♎ Libra, the Scale, ruled by ♀ Venus, with the energy of affection, harmony, balance, and uncertainty, and the available energy of three fixed stars:

Ala Corvi, the Wing of the Crow (Gienah): strength of will, induce sleep, create hostility, bind another's magic; Saturn and Mars; Libra; onyx; burdock root

Spica, the Ear of Grain: resolve disputes, bind enemies, protect from danger, enhance telepathy, reap abundance; Venus and Mercury; Libra; emerald; sage

Alchameth (Arcturus): good health, heal wounds and fever; Mars and Jupiter; Libra; Jasper; snakeweed (common plantain)

In the Mansion of the Moon called:

New Moon Waning

• **AGRAPHA, Covered or Covered Flying (0♎0 to 12♎51) ruled by ACHALIEL for hindering travelers, promoting divorce, promoting discord, destroying houses, and destroying enemies**

Use this oil to repel the energy for discord, especially in the home.

Magical work: oil to repel domestic discord. Dress a red working candle with sandalwood oil: **Red for power; sandalwood for cleansing, protection, and warding of negativity. In the wax, carve around it:** 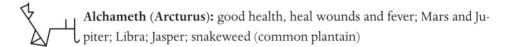 **Ala Corvi for strength of will; Spica to protect from danger and bind enemies; ♎ Libra for balance; and ♀ Venus for harmony.** Light the working candle from the center altar candle: **This flame burns to repel domestic discord!** In a small glass bottle with lid, blend the following essential oils: 1 part lavender: **I call upon you lavender for cleansing, balance, and exorcising negativity!** 4 parts orange: **I call upon you orange for love and restful energy!** 2 parts rose: **I call upon you rose for peace, a tranquil home, and positive energy!** Add 4 parts grapeseed, saffron, or canola oil. Put the lid on the bottle and shake: **All are blended to work together to repel discord!** Place the bottle on the pentacle. Charge the oil. With the wand or athame, gather energy deosil: **Through the Goddess and the God, the Moon and the Sun; through the Elementals, planets, stars and herbs; this oil repels the discord energy of Achaliel in Agrapha!** Direct and release the energy into the bottle: **DISCORD BEGONE! So Mote It Be!** Leave the oil on the pentacle for thirty minutes to an hour. Snuff the candle and dispose of the remains. When desired, use the oil to dress a pink candle: **Pink for a peaceful, nurturing home!** Or to dress a black candle: **Black to remove discord and ward negativity!**

Dark Moon

• **AGRAPHA, Covered or Covered Flying** (0♎ to 12♎51) **ruled by ACHALIEL to hinder travelers, promote divorce and/or discord, destroy houses and enemies**

This divination helps to identify the source of discord and how to overcome it.

Magical work: rune reading to banish discord. Dress a black working candle with sandalwood oil: **Black for truth, protection, banishing discord, and warding negativity; sandalwood for psychic energy, protection, and warding negativity.** Light the working candle from the center altar candle: **This flame burns for warding discord!** Charge a bag of runes and set it on top of the pentacle. Focus on the discord you have recently encountered: **Let the wisdom of the Veiled Goddess and reveal to me how the discord energy of Achaliel in Agrapha is manifesting in my life and how I might overcome this!** Shake the bag and pull out one rune: **This rune shows the source of discord!** Examine the symbol and consider how it relates to the matter, then pull out a second rune: **This rune shows a possible action for overcoming the discord!** Examine the symbol and consider how it relates to the matter. Draw a third rune: **And this rune shows the likely outcome from the action if taken!** Examine the symbol and consider how it relates to the matter. Look at all three runes and interpret them together for dealing with discord. If it appears there is nothing you can do to alleviate the discord, hold the bag and ask: **What is the best way to handle this situation?** Draw a rune and interpret. If no action is indicated, it may mean that the source of the discord will disappear on its own. Snuff the candle and dispose of the remains. If you are still uncertain, at bedtime, ask the universe for clarification. An answer should come through lucid dreaming within a few days, or by sudden insight upon awakening.

New Moon Waning

• **AZUBENE, the Horns of Scorpio** (12♎51 to 25♎42) **ruled by AZERUEL for hindering journeys or trips, hindering wedlock, and hindering harvests or merchandise**

Use this oil to banish hindrance energies for trips, weddings, buying and selling, or harvests of any kind.

Magical work: oil for candle to avert hindrance. Dress a red working candle with vetiver oil: **Red for power; vetiver for warding negativity and exorcising hindrance energies.** Inscribe the candle with the star symbols: **Ala Corvi for strength of will; Spica to protect from danger and bind hindrance energies; Alchameth for good health; ♎ Libra for balance; and ♀ Venus for harmony.** Light the working candle from the center altar candle: **This flame burns to banish hindrance!** In a small glass bottle with lid, blend the following essential oils: 4 parts dragon's blood: **I call upon you dragon's blood for power and strength to exorcise hindrance!** 3 parts bay: **I call upon you bay for success in banishing hindrance!** 3 parts cedar: **I call upon you cedar for strength and cleansing of hindrance energy!** Add 4 parts grapeseed, saffron, or canola oil. Hold up a small black onyx: **I call upon the power in this onyx to bind any malevolent energy from impeding or hindering my plans, my tranquility, or and my work!** Drop the onyx into the oil, put the lid on the bottle, and shake: **All are blended to work together to banish hindrance!** Place the bottle on the pentacle. Charge the oil. With the wand or athame, gather energy deosil: **Through the Goddess and the God, the Moon and the Sun; through the Elementals, planets, and stars; through herbs and stone; this oil banishes the hindrance energy of Azeruel in Azubene!** Direct and release the energy into the bottle: **HINDRANCE BANISHED! So Mote It Be!** Leave the oil on the pentacle for thirty minutes to an hour. Snuff the candle and dispose of the remains. Dab the oil where desired.

Dark Moon

• **AZUBENE, the Horns of Scorpio** (12♎51 to 25♎42) **ruled by AZERUEL for hindering journeys or trips, hindering wedlock, and hindering harvests or merchandise**

The focus of this divination is to reveal the source of hindrances and gain insight on how to overcome this.

Magical work: tarot reading for revealing the source of hindrances. Dress a purple working candle with frankincense oil: **Purple for spirituality; frankincense for protection and psychic energy.** In the wax, carve around it: ♆ **Neptune for psychic awareness; ⚸ Ala Corvi for strength of will; ♃ Spica to protect from danger; ♎ Libra for balance; and ♀ Venus for harmony.** Light the working candle from the center altar candle: **This flame burns for revealing the source of hindrances!** Charge a tarot deck and set it on top of the pentacle. Focus on seeking weaknesses in friendships or alliances. **Through the wisdom of the Veiled Goddess, these cards open my sight to reveal the hindrance energies of Azeruel in Azubene to my activities and relationships, that I may overcome them!** Shuffle the deck, cut the deck and restack the cards or spread them on a table. Deal or select one card: **This is the source of hindrances.** Deal or select a second card: **This is where hindrance is strongest.** Deal or select a third card: **This is the action I may take to banish the hindrance.** Deal or select a fourth card: **This is the likely outcome from taking this action.** Interpret each card as it relates to the question; then read them together for an orderly progression of information. If the answer seems unclear, deal or select a card and place it next to the one in question, then read the two together for more information. While a solution may not be given, understanding the possible source of hindrances may be enough to determine how to avoid it. Snuff the candle and dispose of the remains. If still uncertain, at bedtime, ask the universe for clarification. An answer should come through lucid dreaming within a few days, or by sudden awareness upon awakening. Snuff the candle and dispose of the remains.

New Moon Waning

- **ALCHIL, the Crown of Scorpio** (25♎42 to 8♏34) **ruled by ADRIEL to drive away thieves and robbers, seek redress**

This incense uses the mansion and lunar phase energies to drive away thieves and robbers, bringing a positive result from a banishing energy.

Magical work: incense to banish thieves and robbers. Dress a red working candle with myrrh oil: **Red for power; myrrh to ward and bind danger and negativity.** In the wax ,carve around it: **Ala Corvi to strengthen the energy of Alchil in the Waning Moon; Eoh to banish thieves and robbers; Ken to protect valuables; Spica to bind enemies and banish thieves and robbers.** Light the working candle from the center altar candle: **This flame burns to banish thieves and robbers!** With red marker or ink: **Red for power!** On a small piece of parchment or white paper write ADRIEL IN ALCHIL: **With the power of Adriel in Alchil do I drive away thieves and robbers and protect my valuables, my property, and my person.** Place the paper inside a cauldron or ceramic bowl and set on top of the pentacle. One at a time, hold up an equal amount of each herb over the pentacle, state the intention, and drop into a mortar with pestle: **I call upon you thyme for warding negativity! I call upon you fennel for protection and deflecting negativity! I call upon you yarrow for defense, protection, and warding negativity! I call upon you basil for protection and the repelling of negativity! I call upon you rosemary for protection and consecration of these blended energies!** Grind the herbs together into a powder. Add the powder to the bowl or cauldron containing the paper on top of the pentacle. Stir with the athame, feeling positive energy entering through the blade: **I stir these herbs once, twice, thrice, that by the power of 3 these energies blend to banish robbers and thieves!** Charge the powder. With the wand or athame, gather energy deosil: **Through the Goddess and the God; through the Moon and the Sun; through the Elementals, stars, runes, and herbs; with the energy of Adriel in Alchil, this powdered incense drives away thieves and robbers!** Direct and release the energy into the powder: **ROBBERS AND THIEVES FLEE! So Mote It Be!** Remove the paper and shake it saying: **With blessings given and received, good Adriel in Alchil drives harm away from me!** Package the powdered incense to be used as desired. Leave it on the pentacle for thirty minutes to an hour. Snuff the candle and dispose of the remains. Bury the paper in the soil.

Sprinkle the incense around entry points, burn the incense on a charcoal diskette, or add to the flame of a black candle.

Dark Moon

• **ALCHIL, the Crown of Scorpio** (25♎42 to 8♏34) **ruled by ADRIEL to drive away thieves and robbers, seek redress**

Use this divination to find a remedy to a negative situation and means of seeking redress.

Magical work: rune divination for seeking redress. Dress a black working candle with lavender oil: **Black for gaining the truth and for justice; lavender for cleansing, clearing away obstacles to balance, and peace.** In the wax, carve around it: **Ala Corvi to strengthen the energy of Alchil in the Dark Moon; and Spica to bind opposition to redress and protect against danger.** Light the working candle from the center altar candle: **This flame burns for seeking redress!** Charge a bag of runes and set it on top of the pentacle. Focus on the matter for which you seek redress: **Through the Veiled Goddess and the God; through the Hidden Moon and the Setting Sun; through the Elementals and stars; with the energy of Adriel in Alchil let these runes reveal to me how I may gain redress and justice!** Shake the bag and pull out one rune: **This rune shows the background of the matter for which I seek redress!** Examine the symbol and consider how it relates to the situation, then pull out a second rune: **This rune shows a possible action for gaining redress and justice in this matter!** Examine the symbol and consider how it relates to the situation. Draw a third rune: **And this rune shows the likely outcome from the action if taken!** Examine the symbol and consider how it relates to the situation. Look at all three runes and interpret them together for gaining redress. If it appears there is nothing you can do to gain justice, hold the bag and ask: **What is the best way for me to handle this situation?** Draw a rune and interpret. If no action is indicated, it may mean that the matter will be resolved through outside influences. Snuff the candle and dispose of the remains. If you are still uncertain, at bedtime, ask the universe for clarification. An answer should come through lucid dreaming within a few days, or by sudden insight upon awakening. Snuff the candle and dispose of the remains.

SCORPIO

Tonight the Moon is in ♏ Scorpio, the Scorpion, ruled by ♇ Pluto, with the guarded energy of order, transformation, passion, and the available energy of one fixed star:

Alphecca Lucida Corone (Elpheia): love and honor, restoration of purity; Venus and Mars; Scorpio; topaz; rosemary

In the Mansion of the Moon called:

New Moon Waning

• **ALCHIL, the Crown of Scorpio** (25♎42 to 8♏34) **ruled by ADRIEL to drive away thieves and robbers, seek redress**

This oil uses the energy of the mansion and the Waning Moon combine to banish obstacles when seeking redress, which opens the way for positive influences to take hold with the Waxing Moon.

Magical work: oil seeking redress. Dress a red working candle with vetiver oil: **Red for energy; vetiver for exorcism of injustice.** In the wax, carve around it: **Elpheia for honor and rectification;** ♃ **Jupiter for justice and opportunity;** ᛗ **Mannaz for cooperation and help from others in achieving redress;** ᛞ **Daeg for a breakthrough in gaining redress; and** ᛟ **Osa for a favorable outcome in seeking redress.** Light the working candle from the center altar candle: **This flame burns to remove obstacles to my seeking redress!** In a small glass bottle with lid, blend the following essential oils: 3 parts sandalwood: **I call upon you sandalwood to remove obstacles, ward negativity, and bring purification through the cleansing of past wrongs!** 2 parts bergamot: **I call upon you bergamot to banish opposition to justice as I seek redress!** 1 part myrrh: **I call upon you myrrh to ward negativity and bind negative energies that would interfere with my seeking redress!** Add 2 parts grapeseed, saffron, or canola oil. Put the lid on the bottle, shake: **All are blended to banish obstacles to seeking redress!** Use red marker or ink: **Red for energy and power!** Draw on the bottle: **Phaleg for victory in banishing obstacles to my seeking redress!** Place the bottle on the pentacle. Charge the oil. With the wand or athame, gather energy deosil: **Through the Goddess and the God, the Moon and the Sun; through the Elementals, planets, and star; through runes and herbs; with the power of Phaleg and the energy of**

Adriel in Alchil; this oil removes obstacles to my seeking redress! Direct and release the energy into the bottle: **REDRESS IS MINE! So Mote It Be!** Leave the oil on the pentacle for thirty minutes to an hour. Snuff the candle and dispose of the remains. Dab the oil where desired.

Dark Moon

• **ALCHIL, the Crown of Scorpio** (25♎42 to 8♏34) **ruled by ADRIEL to drive away thieves and robbers, seek redress**

Use this divination to reveal a means of removing obstructions to seeking redress and gaining justice in a matter.

Magical work: rune reading on removing obstacles to seeking redress. Dress a white working candle with frankincense oil: **White for protection, purity, truth, and justice; frankincense for power, energy, and cleansing.** In the wax, carve around it: ᚷᚾᛃ **Elpheia for honor and restoration of purity;** ♏ **Scorpio for order;** ♇ **Pluto for transformation;** ♃ **Jupiter for justice and opportunity; and** ♂ **Mars for will power and dynamic energy to succeed.** Light the working candle from the center altar candle: **This flame burns to clear away obstacles to seeking redress!** Charge a bag of runes and set it on top of the pentacle. Focus on a personal matter where the energy for justice seems blocked: **Let the wisdom of the Veiled Goddess and the energy of Adriel in Alchil show me the way to removing obstacles to seeking redress!** Shake the bag and pull out a rune. Examine the symbol and consider how this relates to the matter. It may indicate the nature of the obstacle, or a process or method for removing it, the need for assistance, a matter of timing, and so on. While a solution may not be directly given, understanding the energy around this issue may be enough to determine how to handle it. Meditate on the rune, or draw another for further guidance. Snuff the candle and dispose of the remains. If still uncertain, at bedtime, ask the universe for clarification. An answer should come through lucid dreaming within a few days, or by sudden insight upon awakening.

New Moon Waning

- **ALCAB, the Heart of Scorpio** (8♏34 to 21♏25) **ruled by EGRIBIEL for discord, sedition, conspiracy, and destroying friendships**

Use this elixir to restrict the energies that lead to destruction of friendships during this time by exercising control over emotions and behavior.

Magical work: elixir to ward against destroying friendships through control of emotions and negative behavior. Rub a red working candle with sandalwood oil: **Red for energy; sandalwood for cleansing and warding negativity.** In the wax, carve around it: ⎍ **Aratron for magical power and restriction of negative energy;** ♄ **Saturn for self-preservation and restriction of negativity;** ⚴ **Phul for controlling the emotions against negative energy;** ♇ **Pluto for controlling extremes; and** ⎍ **Och for healing discord and anger.** Light the working candle from the center altar candle: **This flame burns to ward against destroying friendships by controlling emotions and restricting negative behavior!** Hold up a piece of snowflake obsidian over the pentacle: **I call upon you snowflake obsidian to restrain destructive emotions that self-control prevail!** Place the stone in a small jar of spring water. Set the jar on the pentacle and cup your hands over the top of the water: **This water restricts behavior that destroys friendships and aids with self-control!** Hold up a teaspoon of vodka, brandy, whiskey, or rum over the pentacle, state the intention, and add the alcohol to the jar of water: **This elixir fixed and sealed!** Charge the blend. With the wand or athame, gather energy deosil: **Through the guidance of the Veiled Goddess and the God; through the Moon and the Sun; through the Elementals, planets, and stone; with the powers of Phul, Och, and Aratron; this elixir wards against the energy of Egribiel in Alcab that destroys friendships!** Direct and release the energy into the elixir: **WARDED ENERGY! So Mote It Be!** Leave the elixir on the pentacle for thirty minutes to an hour. Snuff the candle and dispose of the remains. Remove the stone from the water and cleanse. Store the tightly covered jar of elixir away from light. Sip a tablespoon of the elixir as needed for curbing rage and negative behavior, or sprinkle where there is anger, discord, and negativity.

Dark Moon

• **ALCAB, the Heart of Scorpio** (8♏34 to 21♏25) **ruled by EGRIBIEL for discord, sedition, conspiracy, and destroying friendships**

Use this divination energy of the Dark Moon to identify the source of disputes in a friendship, so it can be dealt with and the friendship restored to balance and peace with the Waxing Moon.

Magical work: tarot reading to expose what is destroying a friendship. Dress a purple working candle with frankincense oil: **Purple for divination and for spirituality; frankincense for protection and psychic energy.** In the wax, carve around it: ♒︎ Elpheia **for love, honor, and restoring friendship; ♀ Venus for friendship and sociability; ♂ Mars for energy and will power; Hagith for friendship and stability; ♆ Neptune for psychic awareness.** Light the working candle from the center altar candle: **This flame burns to reveal what destroys a friendship!** Charge a tTarot deck and set it on top of the pentacle. Focus on the damaged friendship and seeking a remedy to the situation. **Through the wisdom of the Veiled Goddess these cards reveal how the energy of Egribiel in Alcab endangers a friendship and how this may be overcome!** Shuffle the deck, cut the deck, and restack the cards or spread them on a table. Deal or select one card: **This is what destroys the friendship.** Deal or select a second card: **This is the possible action to repair the friendship.** Deal or select a third card: **This is the possible outcome of taking that action.** Interpret the cards as they relate to the matter. If the answer seems unclear, deal or select another card on the one in question and read the two together for more information. While a solution may not be given, understanding what might be creating a problem in the friendship may be enough to determine how to handle the situation. Snuff the candle and dispose of the remains. If still uncertain, at bedtime, ask the universe for clarification. An answer should come through lucid dreaming within a few days, or by sudden awareness upon awakening.

New Moon Waning

• **AXAULAH, the Tail of Scorpio** (21 ♏ 25 to 4 ♐ 17) **ruled by ANUCIEL for destroying ships, and for the ruination of captives**

Use this charm when in a difficult position with employment, finances, or relationships to bind the ruination energy and thereby maintain the status quo until liberation becomes available with a waxing lunar phase.

Magical work: charm bag to bind ruination energy. Dress a red working candle with rosemary oil: **Red for power and energy; rosemary for strength to bind negative energy.** In the wax, carve around it: | **Is to halt negative energies;** ᚦ **Thorn for protection;** ᛗ **Eh for safety;** ᚢ **Uruz for passage through a difficult time;** ᛉ **Osa for a favorable outcome.** Light the working candle from the center altar candle: **This flame burns to bind ruination energies!** Lay out a six-inch square of black cloth: **Black to bind negative energies!** Set out a six-inch long narrow red ribbon to tie the charm bundle (or thread if sewing it): **Red for power!** One at a time, hold up over the pentacle some of each of the following herbs, state the intention, then place on the cloth: **I call upon you yarrow for defense, protection, and warding negativity! I call upon you vetiver for exorcism of ruination energy and warding negativity! I call upon you fennel to deflect negative energies! I call upon you paprika to deflect negative energy! I call upon you peppercorn for protection and binding ruination energy!** Tie the bundle with the ribbon (or sew shut) and set it on the pentacle. Charge the charm. With the wand or athame, raise energy moving deosil: **Through the Goddess and the God; through the Moon and the Sun; through the Elementals, runes, and herbs; with this charm is the ruination energy of Anuciel in Axaulah restricted!** Direct and release the energy into the charm: **RUINATION CONSTRAINED! So Mote It Be!** Leave the charm on the pentacle for thirty minutes to an hour. Snuff the candle and dispose of the remains. Carry or place the charm where desired. When liberation is to be achieved, bury the charm in the ground.

Dark Moon

• **AXAULAH, the Tail of Scorpio** (21 ♏ 25 to 4 ♐ 17) **ruled by ANUCIEL for destroying ships, and for the ruination of captives**

Use this meditation to determine if energy from a past-life experience is intruding in this life leading to current captivity by choice or circumstance and threat of a downfall. By confronting the past-life episode, release may be initiated in a waxing lunar phase.

Magical work: meditation to reveal the source of current captivity and ruination energies emanating from a past life. Dress a purple working candle with bay oil: **Purple for spiritual communication and healing; bay for clear vision and success.** In the wax, carve around it: ♒⏜♌ **Elpheia for love and restoration of purity;** ♇ **Pluto for evolution and transformation;** ♆ **Neptune for psychic awareness;** ♄ **Saturn for removing restrictions that interfere with this life;** ☉ **the Sun for power and success in gaining independence from the negativity of the past.** Light the working candle from the center altar candle: **This flame burns to reveal past-life negativity that holds me captive and in fear of ruination in this life!** Dress a grey votive spell candle with clove oil: **Grey for vision into the past; clove for psychic vision, cleansing, and warding negativity.** Set the candle in front of a propped up black mirror. Light a taper from the working candle and use it to light the spell candle: **This candle lights the way into the past to show what holds me captive in this life!** (*Go to MEDITATION BEGINNING.*)

Sit comfortably before the mirror and gaze through the flickering candle flame at your reflection. Focus on discovering what issue from a past life holds you captive and threatens you with ruination in this life. This issue could be manifesting as an inability, pain, discomfort, allergy, bad habit, difficult work or relationships, and so on. Ask the Veiled Goddess if the current situation is a dark reflection of a past problem. Ask her to shine her torches upon the matter so a solution may be found.

The image in the mirror may be changing now. Ask the mirror to show you the matter from your past life that holds you captive and in threat of ruination in this current life. See the mirror as a dark pool, black as ink and deep as a well. Gaze into this dark pool, for it is still a black mirror and reflects the images from other worlds and other times. Look into the water and see the issue from a past life that is manifesting negatively in this one. Remember what you see.

Ask now what it is that you need to understand or do to release this matter so that you are no longer held captive in this life and threatened with a downfall. Look again into the water and see the solution rise to the surface. What do you see? Do you need simply to understand the past experience? Is it a matter of releasing an anger or resentment that has haunted you with restricting energy? Is there a need to forgive? Let the answer enter into your subconscious mind. Remember what you have seen, and know that as you gaze into the black mirror, you see an image from a past-life and now understand how to heal an injury or issue that has intruded into this life.

The pool returns to being a black mirror. Remember the problem you discovered in your past life. Remember the solution that frees you from the captivity of that past life difficulty. Take a deep breath and see your own face in the mirror. Release the breath and release the pain from the past. (*Go to MEDITATION ENDING.*)

Snuff the grey candle: **Through the Goddess and the God, through the Moon and the Sun, through the Elementals, planets, and star; this meditation reveals the past so that the ruination energy of Anuciel in Axaulah no longer holds me captive nor threatens me with ruination!** Cover the black mirror, snuff the working candle, and dispose of the remains. Sometimes just knowing what happened in a past life is sufficient to release the hold it has on this life. You may gain a new perspective or understanding for your current situation and to work from this to restore balance.

SAGITTARIUS

Tonight the Moon is in ♐ Sagittarius, the Centaur, ruled by ♃ Jupiter, with the jovial energy of idealism, independence, education, opportunity, and expansion, and the available energy of one fixed star:

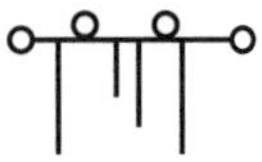

Cor Scorpii, the Heart of The Scorpion (Antares): aid memory, restore good health, defense, protection; Venus and Jupiter; Sagittarius; sardonyx; birthwort (snakeroot or aristolochia)

In the Mansion of the Moon called:

New Moon Waning

- **AXAULAH, the Tail of Scorpio** (21♏25 to 4♐17) **ruled by ANUCIEL for destroying ships, and for the ruination of captives**

Use this amulet to ward against the energies that threaten to destroy a ship, be it a cruise liner, military vessel, merchant ship, or personal boat.

Magical work: amulet to ward against the destruction of ships. Dress a black working candle with dragon's blood oil: **Black for protection and binding destructive energies; dragon's blood for power and strength.** In the wax, carve around it: **Cor Scorpii for defense and protection; ᚱ Rad for safe journey and ease of travel; ᛖ Eh for safe journey and progress; ᚦ Thorn for defense, protection, and neutralizing destruction energy; and ᚩ Osa for a favorable outcome to travels.** Light the working candle from the center altar candle: **This flame burns to ward against the destruction of ships!** Cleanse and consecrate a piece of sardonyx. Hold the stone up over the pentacle: **I call upon you sardonyx to bind energy that threatens the destruction of ships, that this negativity be absorbed into you until cleansed anew!** Set the sardonyx on the pentacle and charge it. With the wand or athame, gather energy deosil: **Through the Goddess and the God; through the Moon and the Sun; through the Elementals and star; through runes and stone; this amulet wards against the destruction of ships energy of Anuciel in Axaulah!** Direct and release the energy into the stone: **DESTRUCTION WARDED! So Mote It Be!** Leave the sardonyx on the pentacle for thirty minutes to an hour. Snuff the candle and dispose of the remains. Carry or place the stone as needed.

Dark Moon

• **AXAULAH, the Tail of Scorpio** (21♏25 to 4♐17) **ruled by ANUCIEL for destroying ships, and for the ruination of captives**.

Use this divination to find the source of enmity fueling the ruination of one who seems constantly impeded and confined in aspirations and relationships.

Magical work: tarot reading to reveal enmity behind the ruination of captive's energy. Dress a purple working candle with frankincense oil: **Purple for spirituality; frankincense for protection and psychic energy.** In the wax, carve around it: ⛤ **Phul to defeat malevolence;** ♆ **Neptune for psychic awareness;** ⊞ **Aratron for knowledge and information;** ♅ **Uranus for divination and understanding; and** ♄ **Saturn for self-preservation and restricting negativity.** Light the working candle from the center altar candle: **This flame burns to reveal the source of enmity and ruination energy!** Charge a tarot deck and set it on top of the pentacle. Focus on seeking hidden hostility. **May the torchlight of the Veiled Goddess reveal any enmity harbored for ruination through the energy of Anuciel in Axaulah!** Shuffle the deck, cut the deck and restack the cards or spread them on a table. Deal or select 3 cards each in 3 rows so they also form 3 columns. The first row: **This is the recent past.** Interpret the cards as they relate to the matter. The second row: **This is the present.** Interpret the cards as they relate to the matter. The third row: **This is the evolving situation.** Interpret the cards as they relate to the matter. Look at the center card: **This is the heart of the problem.** Read the card as it relates to the matter. Look at the diagonal cards left to right and right to left: **These are energies available for use against ruination.** Interpret the cards as they relate to the matter. If the answer seems unclear, deal out another card on the one in question and read the two together for more information. While a solution may not seem apparent, there may be information on what motivates an adversary, which can be used in dealing with the situation. Snuff the candle and dispose of the remains. If still uncertain, at bedtime, ask the universe for clarification. An answer should come through lucid dreaming within a few days, or by sudden insight upon awakening.

New Moon Waning

- **ABNAHAYA, the Beam** (4♐17 to 17♐8) **ruled by KYHIEL for destroying social wealth, and creating arguments among friends**

   Use this elixir to restrict the source of arguments among friends and thereby retain peace.

Magical work: elixir to restrict arguments among friends. Dress a black working candle with lavender oil: **Black to remove discord and for binding; dragon's blood for protection and power.** In the wax, carve around it: 𖤓 **Phul for defusing arguments;** ⸶𝍫° **Cor Scopii for defense and protection;** ⊔ **Och for healing emotions;** ☿ **Mercury for communication skills; and** ♀ **Venus for sociability.** Light the working candle from the center altar candle: **This flame burns to restrict arguments among friends!** Hold up a piece of iolite or smoky quartz over the pentacle: **I call upon you iolite to end discord in relationships!** (or: **I call upon you smoky quartz to disperse negative energies!**) Place the stone in a small jar of spring water. Set the jar on the pentacle and cup your hands over the top of the water: **With this water is the argumentative energy of Kyhiel in Abnahaya restricted so that peace may prevail!** Hold up a teaspoon of vodka, brandy, whiskey, or rum over the pentacle, state the intention, and add the alcohol to the jar of water: **Through the spirit of the alcohol is this elixir fixed and sealed!** Charge the blend. With the wand or athame, gather energy deosil: **Through the guidance of the Veiled Goddess and the God; through the Hidden Moon and the Setting Sun; through the Elementals, planets, star, and stone; with the power of Phul and Och; this elixir restricts the argumentative energy of Kyhiel in Abnahaya!** Direct and release the energy into the elixir: **ARGUMENTS STOP! So Mote It Be!** Leave the elixir on the pentacle for thirty minutes to an hour. Snuff the candle and dispose of the remains. Remove the stone and cleanse. Store the tightly covered jar of elixir away from light. Sprinkle where there are likely to be arguments among friends or sip a tablespoon of the elixir as needed for maintaining peace and goodwill.

Dark Moon

• **ABNAHAYA, the Beam** (4♐17 to 17♐8) **ruled by KYHIEL to destroy social wealth; create arguments among friends**

Use this meditation to counteract the argumentative energy of this mansion so that peace is maintained during the dark season.

Magical work: meditation to banish argumentative energy. Dress a purple working candle with vetiver oil: **Purple for wisdom and protection; vetiver to exorcise argumentative energy and ward negativity.** Light the working candle from the center altar candle: **This flame burns for wisdom and exorcism of argumentative energy!** (*Go to MEDITATION BEGINNING.*)

Through the wisdom of the Veiled Goddess, let the energy of Kyhiel in Abnahaya be exorcised that it not affect friendships. This is the season of hunting, thinning the herds, putting up food in storage, and making the last preparations for survival before the onslaught of winter. As the time of confining weather approaches, it is easy for people to be curt or short-tempered with one another. Now is the time to end disharmony between friends so there can be a joyful anticipation for the rebirth of the Sun and an appreciation for the comfort of home, family, and community. This is the time to halt the disruptive energies of Kyhiel in Abnahaya, and to instead renew the bonds of friendship and strengthen relationships. Here is also the opportunity to honor the creatures who give their lives for food, seeing them not as symbols of social wealth, but as part of the great cycle of life, for life feeds on life. This, too, is a time for honoring the creatures who give their comfort and companionship with total devotion as pets and workers.

In your heart, let your friendships, stability, and the abundance of the Earth be reaffirmed. Remember to honor friendship and be attuned with the cycle of life. Remember to honor partners and companions so that comfort and harmony come into all relationships. Now is the time to honor the companions of life, to mend broken friendships, and to humbly accept the gift of nurturing life meekly given by that which becomes sustenance. As this candle burns, so is the energy of Kyhiel in Abnahaya diminished and restricted so that only nurturing love, peace, and respect abide in this Dark Season. Through the guidance of the Veiled Goddess there is peace. The light of wisdom touches the heart, vision, and understanding of all. Through the power of the Goddess and the God is protection granted. (*Go to MEDITATION ENDING.*) Let the candle burn down completely, then bury the candle remains.

New Moon Waning

• **ALBELDA, Defeat** (17♐8 to 0♑0) **ruled by BETHNAEL for causing divorce and destroying a person**

This charm is used for self-preservation and warding of the mansion energy for destroying a person.

Magical work: charm bag to ward against the energy for destroying a person. Dress a red working candle with dragon's blood oil: **Red for energy and strength; dragon's blood for power.** In the wax, carve around it: ♏ **Cor Scorpii for protection and defense;** ♃ **Jupiter for justice;** ᚦ **Thorn for protection and defense;** ᛇ **Eoh for defense, banishing negativity, and protection; and** ♇ **Phul for defeating evil.** Light the working candle from the center altar candle: **This flame burns for self-defense!** Lay out a six-inch square of black cloth: **Black for protection and warding negativity!** Set out a six-inch long narrow red ribbon to tie the charm bundle (or thread if sewing it): **Red for strength, energy, and power!** One at a time, hold up over the pentacle some of each of the following herbs, state the intention, then place on the cloth: **I call upon you snakeroot, herb of Cor Scorpii, for protection and defense! I call upon you yarrow for defense, protection, and warding negativity! I call upon you peppercorn for protection and warding negativity! I call upon you burdock for protection and warding negativity!** Hold up over the pentacle a piece of sardonyx: **I call upon you sardonyx, stone of Cor Scorpii, to draw away negativity in defense of me!** Put the stone on top of the herbs, tie the bundle with the ribbon (or sew shut), and set it on the pentacle. Charge the charm. With the wand or athame, raise energy moving deosil: **Through the Goddess and the God; through the Moon and the Sun; through the Elementals, planets, and star; through runes, herbs, and stone; with the power of Phul; this charm wards against the destruction energy of Bethnael in Albelda!** Direct and release the energy into the charm: **DESTRUCTION WARDED AGAINST! So Mote It Be!** Leave the charm on the pentacle for thirty minutes to an hour. Snuff the candle and dispose of the remains. Carry or place the charm where desired.

Dark Moon

• **ALBELDA, Defeat** (17♐8 to 0♑0) **ruled by BETHNAEL for causing divorce and destroying a person**

This is an old-fashioned charm for deflecting destructive energies deliberately sent out of malice, jealousy, resentment, or any other type of ill will.

Magical work: mirror charm to deflect destructive energy. Dress a red working candle with dragon's blood oil: **Red for energy and strength; dragon's blood for power.** In the wax, carve around it: ᛚ **Thorn for protection and defense;** ᛇ **Eoh for defense, banishing negativity, and protection; and** ᛁ **Is to halt negative energies and unwanted forces.** Light the working candle from the center altar candle: **This flame burns for deflect destructive energies!** Set out a small mirror: **All destructive energies sent against at me, will back to the sender reflected be!** Use a black marker: **Black for protection and warding negativity!** Draw on the mirror surface: ꜛꟷꜛ° **Cor Scorpii for protection and defense!** Under this, draw: ꝃ **Phul to defeat evil sent and reflect it back to the sender!** Set the mirror face down on the pentacle. Charge the charm. With the wand or athame, raise energy moving deosil: **Through the Goddess and the God;, through the Moon and the Sun; through the Elementals, stars, and runes; with the power of Phul; this mirror deflects destructive energy sent to me, reflecting it back to the sender that the negative energy of Bethnael in Albelda be warded!** Direct and release the energy into the mirror: **DESTRUCTION REFLECTED BACK TO SENDER! So Mote It Be!** Leave the charm face down on the pentacle for thirty minutes to an hour. Snuff the candle and dispose of the remains. Place the mirror facing outward to protect an area or residence, in a window, facing the door, or facing any direction from where ill will is likely to approach. When not in use, wrap in a black cloth and keep it face down on a surface.

CAPRICORN

Tonight the Moon is in ♑ Capricorn, the Sea Goat, ruled by ♄ Saturn, with the energy of materialism, industry, discipline, and solitude, and the available energy of one fixed star:

 Vega, the Vulture Falling: avert fears, talk with animals, avert/end nightmares; Mercury and Venus; Capricorn; chrysolite (golden peridot); winter savory

In the Mansion of the Moon called:

New Moon Waning

- **ZODEBOLUCH, a Pastor** (0♑0 to 12♑51) **ruled by GELIEL for creating discord between two people, breaking an engagement or enduring constant marital conflicts**

  Light this candle to banish conflicts and emotional discord in relationships, especially if generated by other people.

Magical work: candle to banish discord between two people. Dress a red working candle with clove oil: **Red for strength, power, and energy; clove for cleansing and warding negativity.** In the wax, carve around it: ᚦ **Thorn for protection, defense, safety from negativity, and neutralizing foes;** ᛉ **Eolh for protection from enemies and ill will; and** ᛟ **Osa for a favorable outcome.** Light the working candle from the center altar candle: **This flame burns to banish discord in relationships!** Consecrate a black votive spell candle and dress with vetiver oil: **Black to avert discord and ward negativity in relationships; vetiver for alignment, unified energies, and warding negativity.** In the wax, carve around it: ⊗ **Vega, to avert fears!** ☿ **Mercury for communication skill and agility!** ♀ **Venus for sociability and camaraderie!** ⊞ **Hagith for friendships!** ♅ **Phul to defeat negativity!** ᛁ **Is to halt negative energies and unwanted forces!** ᛇ **Eoh for dynamic action in protection, banishing discord, and removing obstacles to peaceful relationships!** Set the spell candle in a cauldron on top of the pentacle. Light a taper from the working candle and use it to light the spell candle. Charge the candle. With the wand or athame, gather energy deosil: **Through the Goddess and the God; through the Moon and the Sun; through the Elementals, star, and runes; with the power of Hagith and Phul; this candle banishes the discord energy of Geliel in Zodeboluch!** Direct and release the energy into the candle: **DIS-**

CORD FLEE! So Mote It Be! Let the candle burn for thirty minutes to an hour, then snuff it and look at the wax for images indicating the time frame for the results to manifest. Dispose of candle remains.

Dark Moon

• **ZODEBOLUCH, a Pastor** (0♑0 to 12♑51) **ruled by GELIEL for creating discord between two people, breaking an engagement or enduring constant marital conflicts**

Use this divination to reveal the source of discord in a relationship and possible solutions for restoring peace.

Magical work: rune divination to uncover the source of discord in a relationship. Dress a purple working candle with frankincense oil: **Purple for occult wisdom, power, and protection; frankincense for psychic awareness, energy, power, and protection.** In the wax, carve around it: ♆ **Neptune for psychic readings and the occult;** ♅ **Uranus for divination and knowledge;** ⚹ **Vega for averting fears;** ⊞ **Hagith for friendships and relationships; and** ♊ **Phul to defeat ill will and discord.** Light the working candle from the center altar candle: **This flame burns to reveal the source of discord in a relationship!** Charge a bag of runes and set it on top of the pentacle. Focus on the problem areas in a relationship: **With the light of the torches held by the Veiled Goddess, may her wisdom reveal the source of discord giving access to the negative energy of Geliel in Zodeboluch!** Shake the bag and pull out one rune: **This is the current situation!** Pull out a second rune: **This is a possible course of action to take!** Pull out a third rune: **This is the likely outcome of taking this action!** Examine the symbols and interpret the runes as relating to the matter. For example, the relationship could be affected by financial issues, the strain of travel and absences, a sense of insecurity, illness, or the interference of other people. While a solution may not be given, understanding what might be causing the problem may be enough to determine how to handle the situation. Consider how to best utilize the action rune, and if the outcome will be to your benefit. No matter what the runes indicate, the choices remain our own to make. Meditate on the runes, or draw another for guidance. Snuff the candle and dispose of the remains. If still uncertain, at bedtime, ask the universe for clarification. An answer should come through lucid dreaming within a few days, or by sudden insight upon awakening.

New Moon Waning

• **ZABADOLA, Swallowing** (12 ♑ 51 to 25 ♑ 42) **ruled by ZEQUIEL for destruction, laying waste, and divorce**

Use this powder to repel the destructive mansion energy in any area, be it material, financial, physical, or emotional.

Magical work: powder to repel destructive energy. Dress a black working candle with vetiver oil: **Black to remove discord and bind negativity; vetiver for exorcising destructive energy and warding negativity.** In the wax, carve around it: 𝍏 **Phul to defeat evil and negativity;** ⚔ **Vega for averting fears and terrors;** ☿ **Mercury for communication skill and agility;** ♀ **Venus for love, sociability and camaraderie;** 𝍖 **Phaleg for valor and victory.** Light the working candle from the center altar candle: **This flame burns to bind and repel the destructive energies that threaten material, financial, physical, or emotional matters!** One at a time, hold up an equal amount of each herb over the pentacle, state the intention, and drop into a mortar with pestle: **I call upon you savory, herb of Vega, for averting terror and fears! I call upon you fennel for protection and deflecting negative energies! I call upon you basil for protection and to repel negativity! I call upon you thyme for swift action in warding negativity! I call upon you St. John's Wort to banish destructive energies!** Grind the herbs together into a powder, bottle it and set the powder on the pentacle. Charge the powder. With the wand or athame, gather energy deosil: **Through the Goddess and the God; through the Moon and the Sun; through the Elementals, planets, star, and herbs; with the power of Phaleg and Phul; this powder repels the destructive energy of Zequiel in Zabadola!** Direct and release the energy into the powder: **DESTRUCTION REPELLED! So Mote It Be!** Leave the powder on the pentacle for thirty minutes to an hour. Snuff the candle and dispose of the remains. Sprinkle the powder where desired or add to charms or oils.

Dark Moon

- **ZABADOLA, Swallowing** (12 ♑ 51 to 25 ♑ 42) **ruled by ZEQUIEL for destruction, laying waste, divorce**

    Use this divination to reveal the hidden threats to security in material, financial, or emotional areas, and possible actions to ward against the destructive energy.

Magical work: rune divination on hidden threats to security in any area. Dress a purple working candle with frankincense oil: **Purple for power, wisdom, insight, and protection; frankincense for power, protection, cleansing, and opening psychic awareness.** In the wax, carve around it: ⚹ **Vega to avert fears;** ☿ **Mercury for communication;** ♄ **Saturn for the preservation of material and personal matters; and** ♀ **Venus for compassion, love, and sociability.** Light the working candle from the center altar candle: **This flame burns for revealing what threatens my security in any area!** Charge a bag of runes and set it on top of the pentacle. Focus on a personal matter where energy seems blocked: **May the torchlight of the Veiled Goddess reveal where security is threatened by the destructive energy of Zequiel in Zabadola and how I might contravene this threat!** Shake the bag and pull out one rune: **This is what threatens my security!** Pull out a second rune: **This is a course of action to take!** Pull out a third rune: **This is the likely outcome of taking this action!** Examine the symbols and interpret the runes as relating to threats of destruction in any matter of security. There may not be any actual threat, in which case awareness of the negative mansion energy is sufficient to rebuff it. But if there is a threat, the runes may indicate in what area of security there is a weakness, such as in structures, in relationships, in work, and the like. Understanding what might be an underlying concern in an area relating to security may be enough to determine how to handle the situation. Consider how to overcome this or work around it to regain a sense of security by meditating on the runes or drawing another for guidance. Snuff the candle and dispose of the remains. If still uncertain, at bedtime, ask the universe for clarification. An answer should come through lucid dreaming within a few days, or by sudden insight upon awakening.

New Moon Waning

- **SADABATH, the Star of Fortune** (25♑42 to 8♒34) **ruled by ABRINIEL for gaining power over enemies, and hindering governance or rule**

While the energy of gaining power over enemies could be initiated or received, this oil is used for self-defense and protection from adversaries who seek, and have the means, to gain power over you.

Magical work: oil to banish the power of foes. Dress a grey working candle with vetiver oil: **Grey to veil and neutralize the power of foes; vetiver to unify energies for exorcising negativity and breaking the hexes of adversaries.** In the wax, carve around it: **♄ Saturn for restriction of negativity and self-preservation;** ⚔ **Vega to avert fears instigated by others; ☿ Mercury for agility and skill; þ Thorn for protection, defense, safety from evil, and neutralizing foes; and ᛇ Eoh for defense, protection, and dynamic action to banish the power of foes.** Light the working candle from the center altar candle: **This flame burns to neutralize the power of my foes!** In a small glass bottle with lid, blend the following essential oils: 4 parts vetiver: **I call upon you vetiver to ward negativity, and to banish and break the hexes of foes!** 1 part pine: **I call upon you pine for energy, protection, courage, and clear action to neutralize the power of my foes!** Consecrate a piece of chrysolite and add to the bottle: **Chrysolite, stone of Vega, I call upon you to add your energy to this oil for protection and clearing away the negativity sent out by enemies!** Add 4 parts grapeseed, saffron, or canola oil. Put the lid on the bottle, shake: **All are blended in this oil to banish the power of my foes!** With a red marker or ink: **Red for power, strength, force, and energy!** draw on a label on the bottle: ⌐†⌐ **Phaleg for victory in banishing the power of my foes!** Place the bottle on the pentacle. Charge the oil. With the wand or athame, gather energy deosil: **Through the Goddess and the God; through the Moon and the Sun; through the Elementals, planets, and star; through runes, herbs, and stone; with the power of Phaleg; this oil banishes the power of my foes through the energy of Abriniel in Sadabath!** Direct and release the energy into the bottle: **ENEMY POWER BANISHED! So Mote It Be!** Leave the oil on the pentacle for thirty minutes to an hour. Snuff the candle and dispose of the remains. Use a dab of oil as needed.

Dark Moon

- **SADABATH, the Star of Fortune** (25♑42 to 8♒34) **ruled by ABRINIEL for gaining power over enemies, and hindering governance or rule**

Use this divination to reveal those who seek to have power over you, and for possible ways to restrict this energy in order to retain independence.

Magical work: tarot reading to reveal those who seek power over another. Dress a purple working candle with frankincense oil: **Purple for power, insight, self-assurance, and protection; frankincense for psychic awareness, protection, power, and energy.** In the wax, carve around it: ⊞ **Aratron for gaining knowledge, psychic communication, and magical power;** ♄ **Saturn for structure, restricting the power of others, self-preservation, and ambition;** ☿ **Mercury for agility, skill, and communication;** ♅ **Uranus for divination and revealing power struggles; and** ♆ **Neptune for psychic awareness.** Light the working candle from the center altar candle: **This flame burns to reveal those who seek power over me!** Charge a tarot deck and set it on top of the pentacle. Focus on seeking how to retain personal independence and hinder the attempts of others to have power over you. **Through these cards, with the influence of planets, the power of Aratron, and the energy of Abriniel in Sadabath, I seek the wisdom of the Veiled Goddess, that her torches reveal the source of threats to my autonomy and how to deal with these!** Shuffle the deck, cut the deck, and restack the cards or spread them on a table. Deal or select three cards and place in a row: **This is where I am now.** Interpret the cards as they relate to the matter. Deal or select three cards and place in a second row under the first row: **This is what threatens my independence.** Interpret the cards as they relate to the matter. Deal or select three cards and place in a third row under the second row: **This shows the actions needed to maintain my autonomy.** Interpret the cards as they relate to the matter. Look at the center card: **This is the heart of the situation.** Read the card as it relates to the matter. Look at the diagonal cards left to right and right to left: **These are energies available for maintaining my autonomy.** Interpret the cards as they relate to the situation. The choice of taking action or not rests with the individual, and if unsure, lay three more cards on top of the cards in the top row: **This shows how things are likely to progress if I do nothing.** Then another three on the middle row: **This shows how my autonomy will be affected.** And three more cards on the bottom row: **This is how things may change.** Look at the center card: **This shows how I feel about the evolving situation.** While a solution may not seem apparent, there may be sufficient information to consider how to work with the energies to alleviate threats to your autonomy. Snuff the candle and dispose of the remains. If still uncertain, at bedtime, ask the universe for clarification. An answer should come through lucid dreaming within a few days, or by sudden insight upon awakening.

AQUARIUS

Tonight the Moon is in ♒ Aquarius, the Water Bearer, ruled by ♅ Uranus, with the energy of originality, individuality, idealism, and unpredictability, in the Mansion of the Moon called:

New Moon Waning

• **SADABATH, the Star of Fortune** (25♑42 to 8♒34) **ruled by ABRINIEL for gaining power over enemies, and hindering governance or rule**

Use this elixir to restrict the ability of others, especially those who have malevolent intent, from gaining power over you, so that you retain your individuality or independence.

Magical work: elixir to restrict others from gaining power over you. Dress a red working candle with dragon's blood oil: **Red for strength, energy, and power; dragon's blood for power and protection.** In the wax, carve around it: ⊙ **The Sun for individuality, success and vitality;** ⼔ **Thorn for defense, protection, and neutralizing foes;** ⼣ **As for creativity and communication skill;** ⼦ **Eolh for protection from enemies; and** ⼧ **Sigel for achievement, self-confidence, and power.** Light the working candle from the center altar candle: **This flame burns to restrict others from gaining power over me!** Hold up a piece of red jasper over the pentacle: **I call upon you red jasper for self-defense and banishing the negative energy directed toward me by my foes so that I retain my individuality or independence!** Place the stone in a small lidded jar of spring water. Use red marker: **Red for power!** Draw on the jar or label for it: ⼨ **Ing for independence and the power to retain the benefits of my labors!** Set the jar on the pentacle and cup your hands over the top of the water: **This water brings me power to overcome any attempt at restricting my autonomy!** Hold up a teaspoon of vodka, brandy, whiskey, or rum over the pentacle, state the intention, and add the alcohol to the jar of water: **This elixir fixed and sealed!** Charge the blend. With the wand or athame, gather energy deosil: **Through the Goddess and the God; through the Moon and the Sun; through the Elementals, runes, water, and stone; this elixir restricts the energy of Abriniel in Sadabath that no one may gain power over me!** Direct and release the energy into the elixir: **EMPOWERED ME! So Mote It Be!** Leave the elixir on the pentacle for thirty minutes to an hour. Snuff the candle and dispose of the remains. Remove the red jasper and cleanse. Store the tightly covered jar of elixir away from light. Sprinkle the elixir where desired or sip a tablespoon of the elixir when needing to bolster self-confidence and energy to achieve the goals.

Dark Moon

• **SADABATH, the Star of Fortune** (25 ♑ 42 to 8 ♒ 34) **ruled by ABRINIEL for gaining power over enemies, and hindering governance or rule**

The hindrance energy can apply to various types of governance or rule such as to those who run corporate offices, schools, classrooms, local, county, state, or national agencies or commissions, or any type of organization, as well as to personal sovereignty, being able to retain your independence and lead a satisfying life. This meditation aids with identifying the source of such hindrances and how to overcome this opposition.

Magical work: meditation for overcoming hindrances to governance or rule. Dress a purple working candle with frankincense oil: **Purple for spirituality; frankincense for protection and psychic energy.** Light the working candle from the center altar candle: **This flame burns for discovering the source of hindrance to governance or rule!** (*Go to MEDITATION BEGINNING.*)

Through the wisdom of the Veiled Goddess, let Abriniel in Sadabath open the way to understanding how to overcome opposition. From your safe place you see a bright star in the sky. This is the Star of Fortune, but there are dark clouds drawing near to cover it. You wonder to yourself how the star will overcome the clouds. Now a shining but stern-looking figure appears outside your safe place. You look at the person and know that this is Abriniel, the ruler who dwells in the mansion of Sadabath, and the Star of Fortune is his abode. Abriniel beckons to you and you leave your safe place, for you sense that although the mansion has both positive and negative aspects, the ruler is kindly disposed to you. You take hold of the offered hand, and in an instant you are transported beyond the clouds, and into the brightly lit mansion of Abriniel.

You feel that the powerful energy of Abriniel in Sadabath, and know this is a safe place. The ruler is willing to show you that even the energies of his mansion that offer hindrance may be turned aside by the worthy and deserving. Abriniel motions you to a beautiful table in the center of the great hall, and on it you see a large, round mirror in a decorative frame. At the behest of this ruler, you focus on an area in your life which you govern and where you feel there is hindrance from others creating a blockage. You gaze into the mirror and see swirling dark clouds flit across the mirror. You realize that these dark clouds represent the forces that oppose you, that seek to hinder you in those areas in which you rule. As you look

at the clouds, they begin to take form. Is there a face or a figure? Is this someone you know? Or is there a symbol or design indicating some other message? Remember what you see in the mirror.

Now, you look up from the mirror and see the bright room, feel the invigorating and protective energy of the mansion, and realize that clouds may be swept aside with a gentle breeze. With a smile, you look back at the mirror and the swirling dark clouds. You know what to do. You hold your hand out to the mirror and blow across your palm. You become the breeze, and the clouds part and scatter. Will you use gentle speech to turn aside the opposition? Or will you see through the opposition? You know that the power of thought is strong, and that when you see the opposition as a passing cloud, it will melt away.

You gaze into the mirror again, and the way is clear for you. The power of Abriniel in Sadabath surrounds you, and you understand now how to deal with opposition. Remember the mirror. Remember what you saw and felt about those who hinder you. Abriniel touches your shoulder and in an instant, you are back in front of your safe haven. Enter your safe place and take a deep breath and draw into yourself the strength and power of the Star of Fortune. Remember all that you have discovered on your journey. Release the breath, knowing that you are able to overcome opposition and retain your individuality. (*Go to MEDITATION END-ING.*) Snuff the candle and dispose of the remains.

New Moon Waning

- **SADALAHBIA, a Butterfly** (8♒34 to 21♒25) **ruled by AZIEL for divorce, revenge, besieging, and binding someone against their duty**

A person may feel besieged when being overwhelmed by the hostility of another. This can happen anywhere, but is more common in the workplace or schools. Light this candle to banish the hostile energies of others that besiege you so that you are not affected.

Magical work: candle to banish besieging energies. Dress a red working candle with bay oil: **Red for power and energy; bay for clear vision and wisdom to attain success in banishing hostile energy.** In the wax, carve around it: **Ƅ Daeg for a breakthrough and transformation; Ƿ Gera for reaping good rewards; Ƿ Osa for a favorable outcome; ↓ Eoh for protection and banishing obstacles; and ⊔ Och for wisdom and healing.** Light the working candle from the center altar candle: **This flame burns to banish the hostility that besieges me!** Consecrate an orange votive spell candle and dress with vetiver oil:

Orange for justice, dominance, vitality, and success; vetiver for warding negativity and banishing hindrance and besieging energy. In the wax, carve around it: ⚏ **Phul for transformation and defeating evil!** ☉ **the Sun for energy and success!** ↑ **Tyr for victory in banishing hostility!** ▷ **Thorn for defense and neutralizing foes!** ⚡ **Sigel for power, self-confidence, victory, and success in banishing hostility!** Set the spell candle in a cauldron on top of the pentacle. Light a taper from the working candle and use it to light the spell candle. Consecrate a piece of smoky quartz and drop it into the candle flame: **With smoky quartz for protection and dispersing negative energies!** Charge the candle. With the wand or athame, gather energy deosil: **Through the Goddess and the God; through the Moon and the Sun; through the Elementals and planets; through runes and stone; with the power of Och and Phul; this candle banishes the besieging energy of Aziel in Sadalahbia!** Direct and release the energy into the candle: **HOSTIL-ITY FLEES! So Mote It Be!** Let the candle burn for thirty minutes to an hour, then snuff and look at the wax for images indicating the time frame for the results to manifest. Remove the smoky quartz and clean it to place, carry, or wear as desired. Dispose of candle remains.

Dark Moon

- **SADALAHBIA, a Butterfly (8♒34 to 21♒25) ruled by AZIEL for divorce, revenge, besieging, and binding someone against their duty**

There are times when a person feels a need for revenge over some wrong, but this is a negative energy that can diminish the light of one's spirit. Use this meditation to release your need for revenge, so that the matter which caused this emotion can be addressed with a calmer heart and mind.

Magical work: meditation to release revenge energy. Dress a black working candle with frankincense oil: **Black for protection and warding negativity; frankincense for protection, power, and meditation.** Light the working candle from the center altar candle: **This flame burns to release vengeful energy!** (*Go to MEDITATION BEGINNING.*)

Let the torchlight of the Veiled Goddess show the way to release from your life the energy of Aziel in Sadalahbia for revenge. You step out from your safe place into an open meadow in the bright sunlight. In the distance you see a dark forest, and you walk toward it. Just within the shadow at the edge of the forest your guide is awaits you. Together you enter into the cool woods, walking along a familiar trail. This time you are shown a new path and turn aside to follow it. The sounds

of the forest are cheerful, but you realize that you have not heard water flowing as has been usual. You wonder why the little stream is so quiet, but then you enter a small clearing where you see that the mouth of the stream is closed by a jumble of stones.

Your guide tells you that water represents the emotions, and that the stones impede the healthy flow of water that keeps the forest alive, just as feelings of anger and revenge block the flow of the positive emotions that keep the body and mind healthy. You look at the stones and see there are words carved into them. What are these words? You sigh, and you know what to do. With determination, you start to remove the stones that block the stream, one by one, and you discover that most are easy to move, but some are heavier than others. The heavier stones are the strongest burdens that anchor you in negative energy. Your guide touches your shoulder and you feel new energy and strength flow into your muscles, and you realize that with the aid of love, the heaviest stones move easily. As you remove the stones, you know that you are removing the anger that had bottled up your emotions, just as the stones bottled up the stream. The stream begins to trickle through where the stones are being removed and set aside to be covered by the power of nature. You remove more stones, and finally the stream flows unhindered and animals venture from the woods to come drink at the waters. Like them, you feel refreshed and relieved that your emotional drought is over. Now, your guide beckons you to return to the meadow, and together you leave the woods. At the edge of the meadow, your guide bids you farewell, and you return into your safe place. Remember the words on the rocks. Remember the aid of love in relieving you of the burdens. Remember the refreshment of casting aside the rocks and letting nature cover them once more.

Take a deep breath and draw into yourself the power to release anger and revenge. Release the breath and feel the need for revenge evaporate.

(*Go to MEDITATION ENDING.*) Snuff the candle and dispose of the remains.

New Moon Waning

• **ALPHARG, the Spout of the Urn** (21♒25 to 4♓17) **ruled by TAGRIEL for breaking barriers, and destroying buildings and prisons**

Draw on the mansion energy to remove barriers in areas of importance to you, such as with studies, work, relationships, or finances, thus turning waning energy to a positive result.

Magical work: candle spell to remove barriers. Dress a red working candle with rosemary oil: **Red for power; rosemary for protection.** In the wax, carve around it: ᛞ **Daeg for a breakthrough and change;** ᛗ **Eh for movement and growth;** ᛝ **Ing for energy and the power to achieve goals.** Light the working candle from the center altar candle: **This flame burns to remove barriers!** Consecrate a black votive spell candle and dress with bay oil: **Orange for ambition achieved and attracting what is sought; bay for success in attaining what is desired.** In the wax, carve around it: ᚠ **Feoh for energy and fulfillment!** ᛇ **Eoh for dynamic action and the removal of obstacles!** ♃ **Jupiter for opportunity and growth!** ♅ **Uranus for change!** ↻ **Gera for tangible results and a good outcome from endeavors!** Charge the candle and set it in a cauldron on top of the pentacle. Light a taper from the working candle and use it to light the spell candle. One at a time, hold up a pinch of each herb over the pentacle, state the intention, and add it to the flame: **I call upon you hyssop for protection and warding negativity! I call upon you vetiver to ward negativity and exorcise barriers! I call upon you St. John's Wort to banish negativity and enhance willpower! I call upon you woodruff for protection, removing barriers, and successful change! I call upon you fir for manifestation of my goals!** With the wand or athame, gather energy deosil: **Through the Goddess and the God; through the Moon and the Sun; through the Elementals and planets; through runes and herbs; with the energy of Tagriel in Alpharg; this spell breaks barriers to achieving my goals!** Direct and release the energy into the candle: **BREAKTHROUGH! So Mote It Be!** Let the candle burn for thirty minutes to an hour, then snuff and look at the wax for images indicating the time frame for the results to manifest. Dispose of candle remains.

Dark Moon

• **ALPHARG, the Spout of the Urn** (21♒25 to 4♓17) **ruled by TAGRIEL for breaking barriers, and destroying buildings and prisons**

This rune divination helps reveal obstructions to desired changes by addressing the material or physical, the mental or inventive, the drive or ambition, and the emotional or intuitive aspects of the matter through their ruling Elementals. By identifying the barriers to your goals, you may be able to find a way to break through them.

Magical work: rune divination for breaking the barriers to gaining goals. Dress a purple working candle with bay oil: **Purple for intuition, occultism, and removing discord or confusion; bay for clear vision, divination, and success in attaining what is desired.** In the wax, carve around it: ♆ **Neptune for psychic awareness and the occult;** ♅ **Uranus for divination, news, knowledge, and change;** ☿ **Mercury for skill and communication;** ♄ **Saturn to learn of restrictions and how to overcome them;** ☉ **the Sun for success and power.** Light the working candle from the center altar candle: **This flame burns for revealing the barriers to my goals and how to overcome these!** Charge a bag of runes and set it on top of the pentacle. Focus on a desired change that seems to be impeded or blocked: **Let the wisdom of the Veiled Goddess and the energy of Tagriel in Alpharg show what barriers impede my goals and how I may overcome these!** Shake the bag and pull out one rune: **Elemental earth shows the barrier that needs to be overcome!** Pull out a second rune: **Elemental air shows the change that needs to occur!** Pull out a third rune: **Elemental fire shows the action that is advised!** Pull out a fourth rune: **And Elemental water shows the outcome projected from that action!** Examine the symbols and read them in relation to the Elemental and the matter being addressed. While a solution may not be given, understanding what might be impeding you in gaining your goals, may be sufficient for finding a way to handle the situation. Meditate on the runes, or draw another round of four runes, pairing in the same order with the prior runes for each Elemental. Read both sets together for guidance. Snuff the candle and dispose of the remains. If still uncertain, at bedtime, ask the universe for clarification. An answer should come through lucid dreaming within a few days, or by sudden insight upon awakening.

PISCES

Tonight the Moon is in ♓ Pisces, the Fishes, ruled by ♆ Neptune, with the energy of mysticism, sensitivity, imagination, and intuition, and the available energy of one fixed star:

Cauda Capricorni, the Tail of the Sea-Goat (Deneb Algedi): Aid a just cause, bring peace, protect from harm; Saturn and Mercury; Pisces; Chalcedony; marjoram

In the Mansion of the Moon called:

New Moon Waning

• **ALPHARG, the Spout of the Urn** (21♒25 to 4♓17) **ruled by TAGRIEL for breaking barriers, and destroying buildings and prisons**

This candle draws upon the energy for breaking barriers to the psychic, mystical, and intuitive energy of Pisces, so it is best to create the candle during the seven hours forty minutes that the Moon is in this mansion in Pisces.

Magical work: candle to break psychic barriers. Dress a red working candle with bergamot oil: **Red for power and energy; bergamot for success in breaking barriers and hindrances. In the wax, carve around it: ᛒ Beorc for the blessing of the Goddess; and ᚩ Osa for the blessing of the God.** Light the working candle from the center altar candle: **This flame burns to break barriers to intuition and psychic insight!** Consecrate a black votive spell candle and dress with bay oil: **Black for protection, warding negativity, and removing confusion; bay for psychic power and divination. In the wax, carve around it: Cauda Capricorni for aid and protection! With Aratron for magic, spirits, and knowledge! ♆ Neptune for psychic awareness, the subconscious, and spirit communication! ᛗ Daeg for a breakthrough in working between the worlds! ᛇ Eoh to remove obstacles, increase power, and communication with other worlds! ᛚ Lagu for psychic power and to let intuition to flow! and ᚦ Thorn for protection and safety at the psychic gateway.** Charge the candle and set it in a cauldron on top of the pentacle. Light a taper from the working candle and use it to light the spell candle. One at a time, hold up a pinch of each herb over the pentacle, state the intention, and add it to the flame: **I call upon you burdock root to ward negativity! I call upon you woodruff for protection and removing barriers to psychic** awareness! I call upon you cinnamon for protection, spirit communication, and psychic power! I call upon you bay for psychic power and wisdom! I call upon you mace for alertness and psychic power! With the wand or athame, gather energy deosil: **Through the Goddess and the God; through the Moon and the Sun; through the Elementals, planets, stars, runes and herbs; with the power of Aratron; this candle uses the energy of Tagriel in Alpharg to break the barriers to psychic insight and communication!** Direct and release the energy into the candle: **PSYCHIC OPENING! So Mote It Be!** Let the candle burn for thirty minutes to an hour, then snuff and look at the wax for images indicating the time frame for the results to manifest. Dispose of candle remains.

Dark Moon

- ALPHARG, the Spout of the Urn (21♒25 to 4♓17) **ruled by TAGRIEL for breaking barriers, and destroying buildings and prisons**

Create this tea during the seven hours forty minutes that the Moon is in this mansion in Pisces to draw upon the mystical and psychic energy of the sign. Drink a cup of this tea for aid in breaking through the barriers to your psychic ability. It may also be used for receptivity when doing psychic readings.

Magical work: tea to remove barriers to psychic ability. Dress a purple working candle with frankincense oil: **Purple for spirituality and spirit communication; frankincense to energize psychic power and spirit communication.** In the wax, carve around it: ⚸ **Cauda Capricorni for aid and protection! With ⊞ Aratron for magic, spirits, and knowledge! And ♆ Neptune for psychic awareness, the subconscious, and spirit communication.** Light the working candle from the center altar candle: **This flame burns to remove barriers to psychic ability!** Set on the pentacle a clean nonplastic or metal bowl in which to blend herbs. Add to the bowl ½ cup of loose black tea leaves. **Black tea for vigor and strength!** Break up one cinnamon stick into small pieces, then, one at a time, hold up over the pentacle the cinnamon sticks and ⅛ cup of each herb, state the intention, and add it to the bowl: **I call upon you cinnamon for protection and psychic power! I call upon you dandelion root for psychic power and good fortune! I call upon you mugwort for the blessing of the Veiled Goddess to open the way to psychic ability!** Blend the herbs and black tea with a wooden spoon. Charge the blend. With the wand or athame, gather energy deosil: **Through the Veiled Goddess and the God; through the hidden Moon and the setting Sun;**

through the Elementals, planets, stars, and herbs; with the power of Aratron; this tea uses the energy of Tagriel in Alpharg to break barriers to psychic ability! Direct and release the energy into the tea: **PSYCHIC TEA! So Mote It Be!** Leave the tea blend on the pentacle for thirty minutes to an hour. Snuff the candle and dispose of the remains. Put the tea blend in a tightly covered jar and store away from light. Brew a cup of tea when desired.

New Moon Waning

• **ALCHARYA, the Lip of the Urn** (4♓17 to 17♓8) **ruled by ABLEMIEL for obstructing the construction of buildings, endangering sailors, destroying springs and wells, destroying baths and medicinal waters, and sending mischief as desired**

Use this charm bag for general protection to ward against all kinds of mischief and disruptive energies.

Magical work: charm bag for protection and warding against mischief. Dress a red working candle with frankincense oil: **Red for energy; frankincense to cleanse, energize, and protect.** In the wax, carve around it: ⚹⚐ **Cauda Capricorni for protection and aid in a just cause;** ᚦ **Thorn for protection;** ᛗ **Eh for safety;** ᛁ **Is to halt negative energies and unwanted forces; and** ᛇ **Eoh for dynamic action to banish mischief.** Light the working candle from the center altar candle: **This flame burns for protection and warding against mischief!** Lay out a six-inch square of black cloth: **Black for protection and warding negativity, discord, and confusion!** Set out a six-inch long narrow white ribbon to tie the charm bundle (or thread if sewing it): **White for protection and peace!** One at a time, hold up over the pentacle some of each of the following herbs, state the intention, then place on the cloth: **I call upon you marjoram for protection from mischief! I call upon you burdock for protection and warding negativity! I call upon you fennel for protection and deflecting mischief from me! I call upon you vetiver to ward negativity and to exorcise and banish any mischief directed at me! I call upon you St. John's Wort to banish negativity and mischief!** Consecrate a piece of amethyst and hold over the pentacle: **I call upon you amethyst to relieve the tensions of mischief and energize this charm!** Set the stone on top of the bundle. Tie the bundle with the ribbon (or sew shut) and set it on the pentacle. Charge the charm. With the wand or athame, raise energy moving deosil: **Through the Goddess and the God; through the Moon and the Sun; through the Elementals and runes; through herbs, stone, and star; this charm wards against the mischief energy of Ablemiel in Alcharya!** Direct and release the energy into the charm: **MISCHIEF FLEES! So**

Mote It Be! Leave the charm on the pentacle for thirty minutes to an hour. Snuff the candle and dispose of the remains. Carry or place the charm where desired.

Dark Moon

- **ALCHARYA, the Lip of the Urn** (4♓17 to 17♓8) **ruled by ABLEMIEL for obstructing the construction of buildings, endangering sailors, destroying springs and wells, destroying baths and medicinal waters, and sending mischief as desired**

    This divination is used to identify the source of mischief interfering in some area of your life and offer options on handling the situation.

Magical work: tarot reading to reveal mischief. Dress a purple working candle with frankincense oil: **Purple for spirituality, intuition, and the occult; frankincense for protection, power, and psychic energy.** In the wax, carve around it: ⚹⟞⟝ **Cauda Capricorni for aid and protection!** ⊞ **Aratron for magic and knowledge;** ♆ **Neptune for psychic awareness;** ♅ **Uranus for divination and knowledge; and** ☿ **Mercury for communication skill and intellectual agility.** Light the working candle from the center altar candle: **This flame burns to reveal mischief directed at me!** Charge a tarot deck and set it on top of the pentacle. Focus on seeking hidden mischief and disruptions directed at you: **Through the wisdom of the Veiled Goddess, and with the energy of the star, Cauda Capricorni, these cards open my sight to reveal what mischief or disruptions are directed at me and how I might deal with the situation!** Shuffle the deck, cut the deck and restack the cards or spread them on a table. Deal or select one card: **This is where I am now.** Deal or select a second card: **This is how others see me.** Deal or select a third card: **This is what mischief is directed at me.** Interpret the cards as they relate to the question. There may not be mischief directed at you, but if it is indicated that there is, then deal or select one more card: **This is how I can overcome the situation.** Interpret the card, adding another if needed to help clarify the answer. If the tarot has indicated that no one is directing mischief to you, then deal or select one card: **Why do I feel a sense of unease?** If the answer seems unclear, deal or select another card and read these two together for more information. While a solution may not seem apparent, there may be information on what motivates an adversary, which can be used in dealing with the situation. Snuff the candle and dispose of the remains. If still uncertain, at bedtime, ask the universe for clarification. An answer should come through lucid dreaming within a few days, or by sudden insight upon awakening.

New Moon Waning

• **ALBOTHAM, the Belly of the Fish** (17♓8 to 0♈0) **ruled by ANUXIEL for strengthening captivity, and instigating loss of wealth and/or treasures**

   Use this amulet to protect your finances by warding against the energy for loss of wealth.

Magical work: amulet to ward against loss of wealth. Dress a black working candle with almond oil: **Black for protection; almond for prosperity and money.** In the wax, carve around it: ᛏ **Nyd to constrain against losses and to overcome distress; ᛁ Is to halt negative energies and unwanted forces; and ᛇ Eoh to banish obstacles and protect finances.** Light the working candle from the center altar candle: **This flame burns to ward against loss of wealth and finances!** Hold up over the pentacle a whole clove: **I call upon you clove to ward negativity toward my wealth!** Hold up over the pentacle a whole star anise: **I call upon you star anise for good fortune in my finances!** Glue the clove to the star anise, set them on the pentacle and charge. With the wand or athame, gather energy deosil: **Through the Goddess and the God; through the Moon and the Sun; through the Elementals, runes, and herbs; this amulet wards against the financial loss energy of Selhiel in Alarzach!** Direct and release the energy into the star anise: **LOSS WARDED AGAINST! So Mote It Be!** Leave the amulet on the pentacle for thirty minutes to an hour. Snuff the candle and dispose of the remains. Wrap the amulet in a black cloth or place in a pouch or envelope. Carry or place the amulet in your wallet, purse, safe-deposit box, or other area where you keep money until the waxing Moon appears to protect finances. Afterwards, take out the amulet and bury in the ground.

Dark Moon

• **ALBOTHAM, the Belly of the Fish** (17♓8 to 0♈0) **ruled by ANUXIEL for strengthening captivity, and instigating loss of wealth and/or treasures**

This rune divination shows the source of trouble threatening you with loss of wealth and offers options for dealing with the situation.

Magical work: rune divination on threatened loss of wealth. Dress a green working candle with patchouli oil: **Green for prosperity and balance; patchouli for money and protection.** In the wax, carve around it: ✂⚏ **Cauda Capricorni for protection;** ⊔ **Bethor for wealth and honors;** ♆ **Neptune for psychic communication;** ♄ **Saturn for business and self-preservation of prosperity;** ☽ **and the Moon for psychic insight.** Light the working candle from the center altar candle: **This flame burns for advice on protecting prosperity against loss!** Charge a bag of runes and set it on top of the pentacle. Focus on a personal matter where energy seems blocked: **Let the wisdom of the Veiled Goddess and the energy of the star, Cauda Capricorni, advise me on what is instigating loss of wealth for me!** Shake the bag and pull out one rune: **This rune shows my current situation.** Examine the symbol and consider how it relates to the matter. Pull out a second rune: **This rune shows dangers to my prosperity.** Examine the symbol and consider how it relates to the matter. Pull out a third rune: **And this rune shows what I can do to avoid a loss of finances.** Examine the symbol and consider how it relates to the matter. Look at all three runes and see if there is a progression of events indicated or if all is well. If there is a threat of loss, pull out a fourth rune: **This rune shows the likely outcome of doing what is suggested for avoiding loss of finances.** If the runes have indicated that there is no threat to your finances, then pull another rune: **This rune shows why I feel a threat to my wealth.** While a solution may not seem apparent, sometimes simply understanding what is instigating a threat of loss of wealth may be sufficient to handle the matter. Snuff the candle and dispose of the remains. If still uncertain, at bedtime, ask the universe for clarification. An answer should come through lucid dreaming within a few days, or by sudden insight upon awakening.

APPENDIX OF CORRESPONDENCES

Runes for Magical Symbolism

Osa: the God, good fortune, favorable outcome

As: ancestor, signs, gain ancient wisdom, psychic power, creativity, communication skill, success in tests

Beorc: the Goddess, Great Mother, female representation, fertility, family, growth, new beginnings, protection, ideas brought to fruition

Daeg: daybreak, breakthrough, fresh start, financial increase, change in perspective, ambition, working between the worlds, transformation, growth, time for change, course of action concluded

Eh: movement, safe journey, progress, swift changes, growth, gaining security in position, empathic or telepathic communication

Feoh: prosperity, material wealth, send energy, fulfillment, ambition satisfied

Gefu: partnership, union, gifts, love, individuality, self-confidence, equality, love/sex magic, increase magical powers, mental and physical equilibrium

Eoh: a channel, defense, dynamic action, banishing and protection, increase power, removal of obstacles, communication with other worlds

Haegl: hail, limits, disruptions, awakening, security, protection, luck, get positive results in a fixed time frame, brings positive change, constrictive ideas

Is: ice, standstill, rest period, halt negative energies, pause in activity, immobility, time not right for action, stop slander, inertia, freeze a situation, halt unwanted forces, development of will, entropy

Gera: year, harvest, rewards, tangible results from outlay of money, time, or effort, cycles, good outcome from endeavors, gains come in due time

Ken: transforming fire, opening energy, strength, healing, physical well-being, fresh start, free to receive, love and stability, protect valuables

Lagu: fluidity, water, psychic power, intuition, imagination, strength, movement, vitality in life-force (especially female), gather energies for use by the will, revise for success

Mannaz: self, humanity, gain help from others, increase mental power, self-improvement, cooperation, language skill, meditation, no excesses

Nyd: constraint, patience, self-control, overcome obstacles, goals achieved, overcoming distress, need, distress, protection, find a lover, impetus to a new relationship

Ing: Horned God, Consort of the Earth Mother, fertility, family, completion, power to achieve goals, new life or path, sudden burst of energy, good conclusion, hold the benefits of completed labor, independence

Ethel: possessions, home, social status, acquisitions, benefits, heritage, new Path, ancestral lands and characteristics, health of the elderly, protection of possessions, monetary gains when used with Feoh

Perth: time and change, destiny, opportunity, unexpected luck, initiation, secrets (revealed), hidden forces, gain from investments and speculations, find lost things, promote good mental health in healing

Rad: safe journey, travel, quest, find what is sought, justice, communication, attunement, order, right

Sigel: Sun wheel, victory, success, strength, wholeness, healing, vitality, power, achievement, honor, self-confidence, life-force, willpower

Tyr: victory, success, courage, favorable outcome, ardent male

Thorn: thorn, protection, defense, gateway, neutralize foes, safe from evil, luck, release the past to open a new beginning

Uruz: strength, physical health, courage, promotion, draw new situations, initiate changes, passage

Wyn: success, happiness, joy, comfort, harmony, love, fulfillment in love and career, material gain, well-being, gainful travel

Eolh: protection, promote friendship, protect from enemies or evil, assistance, strengthen luck and life-force, gain aspirations, go unnoticed, optimism, control emotions

Wyrd: (blank rune; not used by everyone) unknowable fate, destiny, cosmic power, total trust, self-change, endings and new beginnings, shaping own destiny

Color Correspondences

Black: protection, ward negativity, remove hexes, spirit contact, night, the universe, truth, remove discord or confusion, binding for spell work

Blue [Dark]: the Goddess [ritual candle], Water Elemental, truth, dreams, protection, change, meditation, impulse

Blue [Light]: psychic awareness, intuition, opportunity, understanding, quests, safe journey, patience, tranquility, ward depression, health.

Brown: earth riches, endurance, animal health, steadiness, houses/homes, physical objects, uncertainties, special favors, influence friendships.

Green: Lord and Lady of the Wild Wood, Earth Elemental, herbs, plants, nature, luck, fertility, healing, balance, courage, employment, prosperity, agriculture, changing direction or attitudes.

Grey: Otherworld travel, vision quests, veiling, neutralize.

Indigo: meditation, spirit communication, Karma workings, learn ancient wisdom, neutralize baneful magic, ward against slander.

Lavender: spiritual development, psychic growth, divination, Otherworld.

Orange: the God [ritual candle], strength, healing, attracting things, vitality, adaptability, luck, encouragement, clearing the mind, dominance, justice, career goals, legal matters, selling, action, property deals, ambition, general success.

Pink: honor, morality, friendships, emotional love, social ability, goodwill, caring, healing emotions, peace, affection, nurturing, romance, partnership.

Purple: power, spirit, spiritual development, intuition, ambition, healing, wisdom, progress, business, spirit communication, protection, occultism, self-assurance, influence superiors.

Rainbow: variegate colors, inner development by relaxation and introspection.

Red: Fire Elemental, strength, power, energy, health, vigor, enthusiasm, courage, passion, sexuality, vibrancy, survival, driving force.

Violet: self-improvement, intuition, success in searches.

White: the Lady and the Lord together [ritual candle], Full Moon magic, purity, protection, truth, meditation, peace, sincerity, justice, ward doubt/fear.

Yellow: the Goddess and the God [ritual candle], Air Elemental, divination, clairvoyance, mental alertness, intellect, memory, prosperity, learning, changes, harmony, creativity, self-promotion, health, gain employment.

Correspondences for Essential Oils

Almond: prosperous harvest

Bay: psychic powers, purification, wishes, divination, justice, wisdom, promotion

Bergamot: success, wealth, justice, break hexes/hindrances

Cinnamon: spiritual/psychic powers, protection, success, business, healing

Clove: attract wealth, purification, ward negativity, cleansing, memory, vision

Dragon's Blood: consecration, power, strength, life cycle, changes, protection

Frankincense: protection, blessing, spirituality, meditation, power, sacredness

Ginger: love, goodwill, success, money, power

Jasmine: love, health, dream visions, meditation, spirituality

Lavender: Elves, purification, peace, psychicness, creativity, cleansing, love

Lilac: protection, banishing, Summerland, beauty, clairvoyance, past life

Myrrh: protection, ward negativity, purification/consecration, Underworld, binding

Orange (or Neroli): love, good fortune, divination, money

Patchouli: money, fertility, protection, Earth, Underworld

Pine: purification, cleansing, money, courage

Rose: love, attraction, divination, psychic power

Rosemary: purification, blessing, protection, love, health, Elves, courage, mind

Sandalwood: protection, ward negativity, spirit offering, third eye, past lives

Spikenard: luck, health, faithfulness, anoint sacred objects, Egyptian deities

Vetiver: love, money, ward negativity, exorcism, break hexes/hindrances

Correspondences for Herbs, Plants, and Resins

Acacia: altar offering/consecration, psychic powers, meditation, protection

Agrimony: protection, returns spells to their sender, promotes sleep

Allspice: prosperity, energy, money, luck, healing

Almond: prosperous harvest

Angelica: protection, divination, visions, consecration, exorcism

Anise: purify/consecrate, protection, spirit aid in spells, divination, aids creativity

Ash: wands, protection, prosperity, prophetic dreams, death passage

Basil: protection, courage, wealth, love, divination, creativity, repels negativity

Bay: psychic powers, purification, wishes, divination, justice, wisdom, promotion

Bayberry: peace, harmony, health, draw good fortune

Benzoin: purification, prosperity, meditation

Bergamot: success, wealth, justice, break hexes/hindrances

Betony: purification, protection, psychic awareness, banish despair/nightmares

Birch: wands, protection, purification, ward negativity, cleansing, the Goddess

Blackberry: protection, health, prosperity, Underworld, rebirth, the God

Blackthorn: return evil to the sender, thwart negative energies, barrier, Hecate

Borage: psychic power, protection, courage

Burdock: ward negativity, purification, protection

Cardamom: love, romance

Carnation [Dianthus]: protection, strength, healing, Goddess offering

Catnip: love, creativity, cat magic, familiars, restfulness

Chamomile: meditation, rest, purification, calmness, prosperity

Cinnamon: spiritual/psychic powers, protection, success, business, healing

Cinquefoil: prosperity, protection, purification, divination, healing, good fortune

Citron: psychic ability, clarity

Clove: attract wealth, purification, ward negativity, cleansing, memory, vision

Clover: divination, consecrations, money, luck, love, Otherworld

Coltsfoot: faithfulness, love, goodwill, visions, political power, tranquility

Comfrey: healing, safe travel, money

Coriander: health, money, love

Cumin: protection of belongings, harmony in home, unity

Damiana: divination, protection of property, the Goddess, love, sexuality

Dill: money, protection, love

Dragon's blood: consecration, add power, life cycle, changes, protection

Elderflower: Fairies, blessings (never burn the wood), magic power

Elm: Elves, love

Eyebright: aiding mental powers, divination

Fennel: protection, the God, deflect negative energies

Feverfew: ward sickness, ward accidents in travel

Fir: manifestation

Frankincense: protection, blessing, spirituality, meditation, power, sacredness

Garlic: protection, power

Geranium: health, fertility, love

Ginger: love, goodwill, success, money, power

Hawthorn: wands, fertility, protection, creativity, witchery skills, attract Fairies

Hazel: Fairies, healing, protection, luck, communication, wands, witchery skills

Heather: [red] love, [white] protection, [purple] spiritual development, beauty

High John the Conqueror: money, love, happiness, protection, breaking hexes

Honeysuckle: divination, dreams, psychic awareness, mental agility, prosperity

Hops: health, sleep, relaxation, divination

Hyssop: purification, wards negativity, protection, increase income

Jasmine: love, health, dream visions, meditation, spirituality

Juniper: aid psychic power, protection, health

Lavender: Elves, purification, peace, psychic ability, creativity, cleansing, love

Lemon balm: success, health, love, unity, justice, good luck

Lemon grass: psychic power

Lilac: protection, banishing, Summerland, beauty, clairvoyance, past life

Linden [Tila]: protection, immortality, good fortune, sleep, love

Lotus: blessing, spirituality, happiness, luck, health and healing, meditation

Mace: psychic power, alertness

Marigold: marriage, clairvoyant dreams, Fairies, protection, psychic powers

Marjoram: love, protection, wealth

Mint: protection, prosperity, offering to helpful spirits, business growth

Mugwort: divination, consecration, strength, protection

Mullein: protection, purification, divination, health, courage

Mustard: good luck, health, protection, fertility

Myrrh: protection, ward negativity, purification/consecration, Underworld, binding

Nettle: Elves, Fairies, consecration, restore balance, protection, life cycles

Nutmeg: prosperity, comfort, fertility, luck, meditation, induce sleep, protection

Nuts and cones: fertility, drawing wealth

Oak: wands; purification, money, health, fertility, the God

Oats: wealth, security, offering

Orange peel: love, good fortune, divination, money

Orris root: good companions, spirit communication, protection, divination

Parsley: purification, protection

Patchouli: money, fertility, protection, Earth, Underworld

Pepper: protection, ward negativity

Pine: purification, cleansing, money, courage

Rose: love, goodwill, attraction, cooperation, divination, psychic power

Rose geranium: protection, fertility, love, health, anoint censers

Rosemary: purification, blessing, protection, love, health, Elves, courage, mind

Rue: bless, consecration, protection, health, ward negative energy

Sage: protection, totem guides, wisdom, health, purification, artistic ability

St. John's Wort: good health, willpower, enhanced creativity, banish negativity

Sandalwood: protection, ward negativity, spirit offering, third eye, past lives

Spikenard: luck, health, faithfulness, anoint sacred objects, Egyptian deities

Star anise: psychic power, good fortune

Sunflower: Elves, purification, consecrations, changes, bright prospects

Tansy: health, happiness

Thistle: protection, purification, breaking hexes

Thyme: ward negativity, courage, purification, healing, psychicness, swift action

Trefoil: Faerie, protection, luck

Vervain: love, wealth, creativity, purification, psychicness, ward psychic attack

Vetiver: love, money, ward negativity, exorcism, break hexes/hindrances

Willow: wands, divination, love, protection, the Goddess

Woodruff: remove barriers, protection, success, change, psychic ability, the God

Wormwood: evocation, psychic power, scrying, protection

Yarrow: divination, love, happy marriage, ward negativity, defense, protection

Correspondences for Stones

Agate: gain goals, health, energy, self-confidence, calm, strength, promote trust

Amber: manifestation, success, healing, love, strengthen/break a spell

Amethyst: cleansing, energizing, spirituality, intuition, relieve tension, psychic protection, meditation

Aquamarine: inspire thought process, good luck in tests and interviews

Aventurine: creativity, courage, calm, luck in physical activities, leadership, decision-making, curb pride or aloofness

Azurite: psychic development; healing, meditation; facing fears

Bloodstone: remove obstacles, enhance talent/courage/strength/integrity/vitality, purify the blood

Calcite: energy, remove blockages, clarity, cheer, healing, calm, manifest goals

Carnelian: career success, fast action, protection, motivation, self-confidence

Chalcedony: optimism, spiritual and artistic creativity

Charoite: cleansing aura, spiritual insight, transformative energy

Chrysocolla: balance, cleanse negativity, contentment, healing, prosperity

Chrysoprase: peace, meditation, clairvoyance, gain incentive

Citrine: success, clear thinking, protection, self-image / confidence, prosperity

Coral: calm, protect from illness, focus on positive thinking

Diamond: protection, avert unseen danger, heal emotions, strength, purity

Fluorite: intuition, meditation, gateway to Otherworld, dreams, past lives, aid intellect, heal energy drains in the aura, discernment, concentration

Garnet: swift action, self-esteem, energy, confidence, courage, love, devotion

Green garnet (grossular): health, prosperity / abundance, speed physical healing

Orange garnet (spessartine): creativity, optimism, manifest ideas, weight loss

Hematite: communication skills, balance / focus energy, reasoning, relationships

Herkimer diamond: relieve stress, power boost for crystals, psychic attunement

Howlite: meditation, tranquility, calms fear / anger, honesty

Iolite: psychic vision, break bad habits / addictions, relationships, end discord / debt

Iron pyrite: draw success / health / wealth / joy, intellect, creativity, psychic ability

Jade: harmony, friendship, good luck, protection, safe travel, longevity, money

Jasper: energy, protection, stress relief, safe astral travel, balance

Brown jasper: grounding, stability, soothes the nerves

Green jasper: healing, fertility

Red jasper: defense, deflect negative energy

Ocean jasper: counter depression, relaxation, calm, enjoyment of life

Jet: bind energy to a goal, balance, calm fears, protection

Kyanite: meditation, communication, visualization, altered states, serenity

Labradorite: magic, divination, psychic ability, protection, gateway to Underworld

Lapis lazuli: authority, power booster, aura cleanser, psychic development, mental balance, self-awareness, inner truth / wisdom, access universal knowledge

Lodestone: attraction, draw love / money, binding

Malachite: business success, remove obstacles, transformation, protection, joy

Moonstone: psychic ability, sensitivity, empathy, divination, love, comfort, peace

Obsidian: creativity, energy, protection, self-control, prophecy

Black obsidian: psychic protection, scrying stone, Underworld and Otherworld, spirit communication, healing, kindness, banish grief

Green obsidian: protect income, open financial opportunities

Snowflake obsidian: grounding, insight, purification, change, growth, deflect negative energy, perseverance

Rainbow obsidian: heal trauma, cleanse and align chakras

Onyx: strength, vigor, overcome fears/worries, balance, concentration, devotion, guidance through dreams/meditation

Black onyx: deal with emotions/frustration

Opal: self-confidence, communication, personal power, protection, psychic vision, meditation

Pearl: astral projection, focus, integrity, sincerity, protection, allay fears

Peridot: awareness, clairvoyance, cleansing, progress, protection, prosperity, ease stress, ward negative energy

Pumice: power, manifestation

Purpurite: remove barriers, recognize self-worth, increase spirituality, aid assets

Quartz crystal: store/focus/direct/transmit energy, psychic power, protection, divination, attain goals, cleanse aura, meditation, insight

Rose quartz: peace, love, comfort, companionship

Smoky quartz: disperse negative/draw positive energy, protection, purification, communicate with other worlds

Snowy quartz: meditation, serenity, peace, contemplation

Rhodonite: self-esteem, physical energy, self-actualization, service

Ruby: protect health/wealth, increase energy/creativity, self-confidence, intuition

Sapphire: wisdom, material gains, attract good influences, peace of mind, hope

Sardonyx: absorb negativity, purification, protection, strength, integrity

Seraphinite: astral travel, enlightenment, meditation, spirituality, weight loss

Sodalite: self-control, relief of stress, aid memory/sleep, blend intuition with logic

Sugilite: logic, business expertise, astral travel, manifestation, self-healing

Sunstone: energy, healing, success

Tiger eye: luck, motivation, protection, healing, self-confidence, stability, objectivity, harmony, grounding, instinctive/psychic ability, wisdom

Topaz: mental clarity, psychic ability, spirituality

Blue topaz: concentration, calming, clear communication, insight, leadership

Yellow topaz: manifest intentions, vitality, prosperity

Tourmaline: joy, love, balance, cleansing, divination, friendship, healing, beauty, grounding, protection, self-confidence, discernment, inspiration

Black tourmaline: direct restlessness into productivity, ground/absorb negativity

Blue tourmaline: clear speech, remove mental blocks, open the emotions

Green/black tourmaline: prosperity, deflect negative energies

Green tourmaline: set reasonable goals

Pink tourmaline: encourage creativity, free the personality

Watermelon tourmaline: encourage practical approach to manifesting ideas

Watermelon/pink Tourmaline: self-understanding

Turquoise: actualization, balance, communication, intuition, protection, meditation, purification, spirituality, strength, love, joy, health, sociability

Unakite: calm, healing, grounding, balance, stability, psychic vision

BIBLIOGRAPHY

Agrippa, Henry Cornelius Agrippa. *Three Books of Occult Philosophy*. Edited and annotated by Donald Tyson. St. Paul, Minnesota: Llewellyn Publications, 2000.

Barrett, Francis. *The Magus, or Celestial Intelligencer*. Boston, Massachusetts / York Beach, Maine: Weiser Books, 2000.

Dee, John. *John Dee's Five Books of Mystery*. Edited by Joseph Peterson. San Francisco, California / Newburyport, Massachussetts: Weiser Books, 2003.

Gonzáles-Wippler, Migene. *The Complete Book of Spells, Ceremonies & Magic*. St. Paul, Minnesota: Llewellyn Publications, 1988.

Hulse, David Allen. *The Western Mysteries*. St. Paul, Minnesota: Llewellyn Publications, 2000.

Michelsen, Neil F. *The American Ephemeris for the 21st Century 2000 to 2050 at Midnight*. El Cajon, California: ACS Publications, 1997.

Moura, Ann. *Green Magic: The Sacred Connection to Nature*. St. Paul, Minnesota: Llewellyn Publications, 2002.

_____. *Green Witchcraft: Folk Magic, Fairy Lore, & Herb Craft*. St. Paul, Minnesota: Llewellyn Publications, 1996.

_____. *Grimoire for the Green Witch: A Complete Book of Shadows*. St. Paul, Minnesota: Llewellyn Publications, 2003.

Pennick, Nigel. *The Complete Illustrated Guide to Runes*. Boston, Massachusetts: Element, 1999.

Skinner, Stephen, editor. *The Fourth Book of Occult Philosophy*. Translated by Robert Turner. Berwick, Maine: Ibis Press, 2005.

Thorsson, Edred. *Northern Magic: Mysteries of the Norse, Germans & English*. St. Paul, Minnesota: Llewellyn Publications, 1992.

Von Worms, Abraham. *The Book of Abramelin*. Translated by Steven Guth, compiled and edited by Georg Dehn. Lake Worth, Florida: Ibis Press, 2006.

Whitcomb, Bill. *The Magician's Companion*. St. Paul, Minnesota: Llewellyn Publications, 1998.

INDEX